# DEATHS IN VENICE

LEONARD HASTINGS SCHOFF LECTURES

# UNIVERSITY SEMINARS
# LEONARD HASTINGS SCHOFF MEMORIAL LECTURES

The University Seminars at Columbia University sponsor an annual series of lectures, with the support of the Leonard Hastings Schoff and Suzanne Levick Schoff Memorial Fund. A member of the Columbia faculty is invited to deliver before a general audience three lectures on a topic of his or her choosing. Columbia University Press publishes the lectures.

David Cannadine, *The Rise and Fall of Class in Britain*, 1993
Charles Larmore, *The Romantic Legacy*, 1994
Saskia Sassen, *Sovereignty Transformed: States and the New Transnational Actors*, 1995
Robert Pollack, *The Faith of Biology and the Biology of Faith: Order, Meaning, and Free Will in Modern Medical Science*, 2000
Ira Katznelson, *Desolation and Enlightenment: Political Knowledge After the Holocaust, Totalitarianism, and Total War*, 2003
Lisa Anderson, *Pursuing Truth, Exercising Power: Social Science and Public Policy in the Twenty-First Century*, 2003
Partha Chatterjee, *The Politics of the Governed: Reflections on Popular Politics in Most of the World*, 2004
David Rosand, *The Invention of Painting in America*, 2004
George Rupp, *Globalization Challenged: Conviction, Conflict, Community*, 2007
Lesley A. Sharp, *Bodies, Commodities, and Technologies*, 2007
Robert Hanning, *Serious Play: Desire and Authority in the Poetry of Ovid, Chaucer, and Ariosto*, 2010
Douglas A. Chalmers, *Reforming Democracies: Six Facts About Politics That Demand a New Agenda*, 2013

# Deaths in Venice
## THE CASES OF
## GUSTAV VON ASCHENBACH

Philip Kitcher

Columbia University Press
New York

Columbia University Press
*Publishers Since 1893*
New York   Chichester, West Sussex
cup.columbia.edu
Copyright © 2013 Columbia University Press
All rights reserved

Library of Congress Cataloging-in-Publication Data
Kitcher, Philip, 1947–
    Deaths in Venice : the cases of Gustav von Aschenbach / Philip Kitcher
      pages cm. — (Leonard Hastings Schoff Memorial Lectures)
      ISBN 978-0-231-16264-7 (cloth : acid-free paper) —
      ISBN 978-0-231-53603-5 (e-book)
 1. Mann, Thomas, 1875–1955. Tod in Venedig. 2. Philosophy in literature.
I. Title.

PT2625.A44T6438      2013
833'.912—dc23                                                            2013007247

Columbia University Press books are printed on permanent and durable acid-free paper.
This book is printed on paper with recycled content.
Printed in the United States of America

c 10 9 8 7 6 5 4 3 2 1

*Jacket design by Julia Kushnirsky*

References to websites (URLs) were accurate at the time of writing. Neither the author nor Columbia University Press is responsible for URLs that may have expired or changed since the manuscript was prepared.

*For Isaac, and in memory of Sidney*

# CONTENTS

List of Illustrations
xi

Preface
xi

List of Abbreviations
xv

A Note on Translations
xix

1. Discipline   1

2. Beauty   61

3. Shadows   125

Notes
193

Index
247

# ILLUSTRATIONS

2.1. *Kinderkarneval*, Friedrich August Kaulbach, 1888 (the five Pringsheim children)   91
2.2. Three declamations (Vere, Claggart, Aschenbach)   108
3.1 The newspaper photograph of Mahler from which Mann worked   133
3.2. *Kindertotenlieder* 1: close   145
3.3. Mahler, Adagietto, opening theme   147
3.4. *Kindertotenlieder 2, Rückertlied*: openings   148
3.5. *Kindertotenlieder* 2: two extracts   151
3.6. *Das Lied von der Erde*: extract from movement 5   159
3.7. *Das Lied von der Erde*: extract from movement 6   161
3.8. *Das Lied von der Erde*: extract from movement 6   164
3.9. *Das Lied von der Erde*: closing measures   165
3.10. *Das Lied von der Erde*: close of movement 1   168
3.11. Tadzio on the sandbar (from Visconti's film)   173

# PREFACE

During the 1990s, when I was teaching at the University of California at San Diego, I had several conversations with Carol Plantamura—music teacher, colleague, and good friend—about the possibility of a course that would focus on operas and their literary or dramatic sources. We planned to explore the ways in which central ideas, including philosophical ideas, were treated differently in the opera or in the story or play. I no longer remember all the possible pairings we discussed, but I recall the examples we definitely planned to use: *Otello* and *Othello*, *Wozzeck* and *Woyzeck*—and *Death in Venice* and *Death in Venice*.

The course was never taught, but, after my move to Columbia, I continued to think about the guiding idea and, as I read and reread Thomas Mann, about the example of *Death in Venice* in particular. Along the way, I became convinced that Luchino Visconti's film also belonged in the mix, although more for its use of Mahler's music than as an artistic work in its own right.

When Robert Belknap honored and delighted me with an invitation to deliver the Schoff Lectures, I saw it as a wonderful occasion for working out something I had pondered for a while. The Schoff Lectures offer Columbia faculty an opportunity to go in new directions, to cut across disciplinary lines with assistance from an audience of wide-ranging experts. I have tried to take advantage of that opportunity, and, although I cannot possibly claim to be a specialist about any, let alone all, of Mann, Britten, and Mahler, I hope readers will welcome an approach that seeks connections not only among them but also to philosophy, and that experts will not feel I have abused the license.

I began working out those connections during a sabbatical in Berlin, when I was a visitor at the Max Planck Institut für Wissenschaftsgeschichte. There, Michael Gordin, Tania Munz, and I formed a collective, die Tod-in-Venedig Gruppe, in which we discussed Mann's novella, and our conversations were immensely illuminating for me. I was also extremely fortunate to be able to participate in an informal discussion group at the Wissenschaftskolleg, with Moira Gatens and Candace Vogler, from both of whom I have learned much about philosophy in/ and/of literature.

My time in Berlin prepared me to write the original lectures, and I am most grateful for the fortitude of those who came out in frigid winter weather to hear them. I learned from many good questions, and I was encouraged by the interest expressed. I owe a particular debt to three friends and colleagues who provided wonderful introductions: many thanks to Edward Mendelson, Wayne Proudfoot, and, especially, Fred Neuhouser.

The lectures were extended to a full book manuscript during the spring and summer of 2011. Columbia University Press obtained the services of two extremely careful and constructive readers, Mark Anderson and Bence Nanay, whose many comments and suggestions have enabled me to make significant improvements. I have also benefited from the insightful suggestions of Moira Gatens, Lydia Goehr, Michael Gordin, Marilyn McCoy, Fred Neuhouser, Chris Peacocke, and Candace Vogler. Although I did not work on rewriting during a second period in Berlin, when I was a fellow at the Wissenschaftskolleg during the academic year 2011–2012, that time was full of valuable conversations about philosophy in literature and music. I am especially indebted to Jeremy Adler, Alfred Brendel, Ayse Bugra, Klaus Reichert, and Mauricio Sotelo. Their insights have helped me in composing the final version.

I feel deeply fortunate to have been able to spend the later years of my career at Columbia. Its combination of intellectual tough-mindedness, openness to new ideas, and readiness to foster connections across many different disciplines makes it, in my experience, a uniquely stimulating environment. I have learned much from colleagues and friends not only across the full range of the arts and sciences, but beyond.

My dedication is intended to acknowledge the ways in which discussions at Columbia have changed my thinking. Two senior colleagues (and—again—friends), my immediate predecessors as John Dewey Professor of Philosophy, have had more influence than they might have suspected. So this book is for Isaac Levi and in memory of Sidney Morgenbesser.

# LIST OF ABBREVIATIONS

AMML  Alma Mahler-Werfel, *Gustav Mahler: Memories and Letters* (Seattle: University of Washington Press, 1968)
*Briefe*  Thomas Mann, *Briefe*, 3 vol. (Frankfurt: Fischer, 1995–1996)
BU  Thomas Mann, *Betrachtungen eines Unpolitischen* (Frankfurt: Fischer, 2004)
DF  Thomas Mann, *Doktor Faustus* (Frankfurt: Fischer, 2005)
dMM  Peter de Mendelssohn, *Der Zauberer: Das Leben des deutschen Schriftstellers Thomas Mann*, 3 vols. (Frankfurt: Fischer, 1975–1992)
*Essays*  Thomas Mann, *Essays*, 6 vols. (Frankfurt: Fischer, 1993–2002)
FGM  Stuart Feder, *Gustav Mahler: A Life in Crisis* (New Haven, Conn.: Yale University Press, 2004)
GKFA  Thomas Mann *Werke, Briefe, Tagebücher; Grosse Kommentierte Frankfurter Ausgabe*, many vols. (Frankfurt: Fischer, 2002–). The volumes come in pairs, the first of each pair consisting of Mann's texts and the second comprising commentary; thus GKFA 8.1 contains the early stories (including

*Death in Venice*), and *GKFA* 8.2 consists of notes, commentary, and so on.

GMB  Gustav Mahler, *Briefe* (Vienna: Zsolnay, 1996)
H  Thomas Mann, *Death in Venice*, trans. Michael Henry Heim (New York: Harper Collins, 2004)
HarpM  Klaus Harpprecht, *Thomas Mann, Eine Biographie*, 2 vols. (Hamburg: Roholt, 1995)
HDL  Stephen Hefling, *Das Lied von der Erde* (Cambridge: Cambridge University Press, 2000)
HLM  Henry-Louis de La Grange, *Mahler*, 4 vols. (New York: Doubleday, 1973 [vol. 1]; New York: Oxford University Press, 1979–1985 [vols. 2–4])
JSB  Thomas Mann, *Joseph und seine Brüder*, 1 vol. ed. (Frankfurt: Fischer, 2007)
K  Thomas Mann, *Death in Venice*, trans. and ed. Clayton Koelb (New York: Norton, 1994). Norton Critical Edition.
KMM  Katia Mann, *Meine ungeschriebenen Memoiren* (Frankfurt: Fischer, 2004)
L  Thomas Mann, *Death in Venice and Other Stories*, trans. David Luke (New York: Bantam, 1988)
LIW  Thomas Mann, *Lotte in Weimar* (Frankfurt: Fischer, 2004)
LP  Thomas Mann, *Death in Venice and Seven Other Stories*, trans. H. T. Lowe-Porter (New York: Vintage, 1936)
MC  Donald Mitchell and Andrew Nicholson, eds., *The Mahler Companion* (Oxford: Oxford University Press, 2002)
NW  Friedrich Nietzsche, *Werke*, 15 vols., ed. G. Colli and M. Montinari (Munich: Deutsche Taschenbuch Verlag, 1999)
PL  August von Platen, *Wer die Schönheit angeschaut mit Augen, Ein Lesebuch* (Munich: Deutsche Taschenbuch, 1996)
PT  August von Platen, *Tagebücher*, 2 vols. (Hildesheim: Olms, 1969). Reproduction of the original edition (Stuttgart: Cotta, 1896, 1900).
PTM  August von Platen, *Memorandum meines Lebens* (selections from *PT*) (Frankfurt: Insel, 1996)
PW  Plato, *Complete Works*, ed. John Cooper (Indianapolis, Ind.: Hackett, 1997)

| | |
|---|---|
| *Reed* | T. J. Reed, *Thomas Mann: The Uses of Tradition* (Oxford: Oxford University Press, 2002) |
| *TB* | Thomas Mann, *Tagebücher*, 10 vols. (Frankfurt: Fischer, 2003) |
| *THBW* | Thomas Mann and Heinrich Mann, *Briefwechsel 1900–49* (Frankfurt: Fischer, 1984) |
| *UMS* | Thomas Mann, *Über mich selbst* (Frankfurt: Fischer, 2002) |
| *WWV* | Arthur Schopenhauer, *Die Welt als Wille und Vorstellung*, vols. 1–4 of *Werke*, 10 vols. (Zurich: Diogenes, 1977) |

# A NOTE ON TRANSLATIONS

Translations from German and French sources are my own. I have not attempted literary elegance but have focused on conveying the sense of the texts I quote or allude to, as I understand them.

As noted in the list of abbreviations, four translations of Thomas Mann's novella *Death in Venice* are frequently cited. The original translation by Mrs. H. T. Lowe-Porter (cited as *LP*) was valuable in introducing Thomas Mann's story to an English audience, but, as Mann eventually came to understand, her renderings of his works were not always distinguished by their accuracy. Although the Lowe-Porter translations continue to be widespread, they have been surpassed in recent years by some truly excellent alternatives. For *Death in Venice*, David Luke's version (cited as *L*) set new and higher standards: Luke's book is also valuable in containing other stories (including "Little Herr Friedemann") that are not often included in collections of Mann's early short fiction. Two other translations meet the demanding precedent set by Luke. Clayton Koelb's Norton Critical Edition (cited as *K*) is, like Luke's version, careful and sensitive to the nuances of Mann's thoughts;

Koelb also reprints some of the best commentary on *Death in Venice* and provides extracts from Mann's letters and the full working notes for the novella. Finally, Michael Henry Heim's translation (cited as *H*) has rightly won acclaim for its literary qualities.

English readers owe much to all these translators. As with so many (all?) major writers, however, there is no substitute for reading Thomas Mann in the original.

# DEATHS IN VENICE

# ONE
# Discipline

## 1

It is a very simple story. A writer of some note has encountered, at least temporarily, obstacles in his current projects. Deciding that he needs release from the pressures of his daily routine, he journeys to Venice. There, on the lido, he becomes fascinated by the beauty of an adolescent boy. Returning to his home in Munich, he is inspired to write a novella about the experience, a work that gains an enthusiastic reception and is retrospectively viewed as an advance in his literary development.

That story describes events in Thomas Mann's life in 1911–1912 and beyond. After the enormous early success of *Buddenbrooks*—among other things it had won him a bride, one of the great catches of early twentieth-century Munich—he had written a sequence of shorter fictions, most notably the novella *Tonio Kröger*, which had been rapturously received by young literati. His attempt at a drama, *Fiorenza*, was, however, almost universally regarded as wooden, and the second novel—the fairy tale (*Märchen*) *Royal Highness* (*Königliche Hoheit*)—despite excellent initial sales, attained only measured success: the critical praise it received was muted and restrained in comparison with the accolades showered upon *Buddenbrooks*.[1] Mann had sketched other projects: a work on the life of Frederick the Great, a novella or novel tentatively entitled "Maia," an essay on *"Geist und Kunst"* ("Intellect and Art").[2] He had also begun the book (or book fragment?) that would eventually—decades later—be published as *The Confessions of Felix Krull*. But in the spring of 1911, progress on this had been halted (Mann had problems sustaining the voice and the humor),[3] and he determined to leave Munich for a holiday, accompanied by his wife, Katia, and his brother Heinrich. On his return, he set the *Krull* manuscript aside and, in a period of about a year, not without struggle, completed *Der Tod in Venedig* (*Death in Venice*).

That long novella, the object of enormous critical scrutiny and discussion—even in 1975, Peter de Mendelssohn could write of the impossibility of examining all the individual studies[4]—is rightly seen as a watershed in Mann's development as a writer (as *Schriftsteller* or, as he hoped, *Dichter*).[5] To record the experiences of his author-protagonist Aschenbach, Mann crafted a new prose style, increasing the length and syntactic complexity of his sentences, the richness of his vocabulary. Aschenbach's voice, the dominant but not the only voice of the novella, expresses ideas and feelings of such intricacy, nuance, ambiguity, and irony that the plainer narrative language common to the earlier stories (even *Tonio Kröger*) and the two novels would be inadequate to them.[6] Through creating Aschenbach's voice and that of his narrator, Mann made Hans Castorp and his successors possible.[7]

Reflecting on *Death in Venice*, Mann explains that "nothing was invented."[8] As in the case of his protagonist, his own journey began with an encounter at the north cemetery in Munich and continued with a false start and a sea voyage to Venice; "the old dandy, the suspicious gondolier, Tadzio and his family, the unsuccessful departure due to a mix-up with the luggage, the cholera, the honest clerk in the travel agency, the malicious itinerant singer, or whatever else is mentioned—everything was given."[9] There are small exaggerations in this claim: although there were rumors of cholera in Venice during the Manns' time there, the actual outbreak was in Palermo; the mix-up with the luggage happened to Heinrich and didn't actually prevent a (temporary) departure. Larger differences between story and experience are also apparent: Mann replaced his thirty-five-year-old self with a significantly older figure: Aschenbach is fifty-three, has completed the works Mann had been sketching, and is recently ennobled (he is now *von* Aschenbach). Mann was traveling with his wife whereas Aschenbach has long been a widower and, as the novella progresses, is often characterized by the narrator as a solitary figure (*"der Einsame"*). And, most decisively, although Mann returns from Venice to write, Aschenbach dies there.

Yet, according to the later judgment of the author, the material "really only needed to be introduced and thereby showed in the most surprising fashion its compositional power of interpretive significance."[10] Mann's murky phrase (*"kompositionelle Deutungsfähigkeit"*) tells us that he found the sequence of experiences pregnant with literary possibilities, which we surely knew already from his decision, on his return, to suspend the writing of *Krull* and undertake the novella. An early polemical essay reveals his sense of the importance of experience—*transformed* experience—to literature. The immediate stimulus for that essay, "Bilse und ich," was a charge made in a Lübeck courtroom, when the prosecutor assimilated *Buddenbrooks* to the novel whose libelous status was being tried and took both to be instances of a genre he dubbed "Bilse novels."[11] Mann responded by downplaying the role of imagination, especially in the construction of plot and character: "It is not the gift of invention, but that of animating experience (*Beseelung*) that makes the serious writer (*Dichter*)."[12] The process of literary creation can be thought of as one of deepening a portrait of reality, and Mann allies himself with what he sees as a school of writers, inspired by Nietzsche, who blur the distinction between literature and discovery, between art and criticism.[13] Writers of this school examine their world with a vision both cool and passionate; their probing is painful, even agonizing, for themselves; they place themselves on trial and must expose themselves if they are to be of real service.[14] The starting point for the painful struggle is the recognition of something capable of valuable transformation in the writer's experience, and this recognition, we can assume, is what prompted Mann to refashion the material of his visit to Venice.

Yet why did he choose to transform it in precisely this way—why do we have *Death in Venice* and not *Rebirth of a Writer*? Part of the answer may lie in frustration at the critical reaction to *Königliche Hoheit*. In a sketch of his life, composed in 1930, Mann aired the thought that

German readers pay respectful attention only to something "serious and weighty," so that, for all its apparently questionable material, the "tragedy" of his novella might testify to the "moral rehabilitation of the author of *Königliche Hoheit*."[15] Happy endings were to be avoided.[16] Perhaps he was convinced that his proper topic was decline:[17] *Buddenbrooks* had charted the decline of a family, and, in *Der Tod in Venedig*, Mann focuses, in shorter compass, on the decline of an individual, the falling apart of an eminent writer. In both instances he can be viewed as experimenting with possibilities for himself. Just as his early experiences in Lübeck had prompted the possibility of the brief, unhappy life of Hanno Buddenbrook, a life that could have been his own, so the flight to the south and the charming vision on the lido inspired him to explore his potential future. Is that how we should understand the power of experience to yield literary significance?

Perhaps—but it is only part of the explanation. As many commentators have recognized, important thematic relationships run through Mann's early work, from the stories that precede *Buddenbrooks* to the first novel itself and the subsequent short fiction. In an early essay, written in response to a question posed to German literati, Mann drew on material for the projected work on *Geist und Kunst* to explore the distinction (for him, a significant but vexed distinction) between the "writer" (*Schriftsteller*) and the "man of letters" (*Dichter*). The latter, he proposes, starts with the idea, to which he gives concrete form; the writer—or, at least, the pure (*absolute*) writer—derives the idea from life, from experience, and converts it into ideas: he "'transforms everything into light and flame,' as Nietzsche says."[18] Much of the fictional work that culminates in *Der Tod in Venedig* can be conceived from a perspective that incorporates and refines the proposal. Rather than thinking of Mann as beginning either from an idea detached from all connection with his experience or from an experience he undergoes in some hypothetical idea-free state, he can be interpreted as working between the two poles toward which he gestures, sometimes as *Dichter* and at others as *Schriftsteller*— a transcendence of the dichotomy that would surely satisfy the essayist who, after giving his proposed account of the distinction, asks (rhetorically) whether it marks any difference in value.[19] A theme emerges from early experiences to generate a relatively simple idea, one that gives rise to embodiment in first attempts at concrete form and is thereby clarified and articulated so that subsequent experience can refine it further, until, to use the Nietzschean metaphor, the light is brilliant and the flame has burned away all impurities—the process leads from the early stories ("Der Wille zum Glück," for example) to culminate in *Death in Venice.*

Not *a* theme, however, but two related complexes of ideas emerge. From early in his career, Mann was preoccupied with the role of the artist and with the relations between artist and citizen (*Künstler* and *Bürger*).[20] He was equally concerned with the struggles and pains of those who feel themselves outside a society in which others are happy.[21] Plainly, these categories overlap—one great achievement of *Tonio Kröger* is the creation of a central figure whose experiences and reflections enable the exploration of both complexes simultaneously—but there are outsiders who have no pretensions to artistic talent (Tobias Mindernickel, Lobgott Piepsam) as well as figures who fit more or less well into bourgeois society and who are in various degrees attracted to or proficient in the arts (from Paolo Hofmann, Thomas Buddenbrook, and little Friedemann through Christian Buddenbrook, Detlef Spinell, and Hanno Buddenbrook to Schiller in his "heavy hour").[22]

The fortunes of the Buddenbrooks lapse for many reasons: unfortunate marriages, religious enthusiasms, distractions of public service, lack of appreciation for technological change, the clear-headed determination of the "new men" (personified by Tony's bête noire, Hermann Hagenström), and, most evidently, the mixture of excessive caution and occasional rashness that constitutes the policy of the family firm under Tom and his father. Interwoven with these causes, however, is the introduction of the artistic life into the household, first in the seduction of Christian (from his childhood penchant for mimicry to the songs and sketches with which he entertains the "club"), later in the arrival of Gerda, reserved and even uncanny, who replaces the blithe, and probably clumsy, flute playing of the old consul with music that must be taken seriously, music whose demands are urgent enough, in the end, to take the widowed Frau Senator back to Amsterdam to a life of duos with her father. With fascination and a sense of his own exclusion, Tom is initially captured, committed to a marriage in which Gerda addresses him as *"lieber Freund"* (dear friend), left to listen at the door as his wife and the visiting officer-pianist achieve a (nonphysical) intimacy that will always be denied to him,[23] brought to ultimate resignation (and perhaps lassitude) by a reading of Schopenhauer (including, presumably, the passages in book 3 of *Die Welt als Wille und Vorstellung* that celebrate music as not only the highest art but also the deepest probing of reality of which we are capable).[24] Tom's son, Hanno, after whom there will be no more Buddenbrooks,[25] fragile, timid, and sickly, in his father's estimation unmanly, and certainly unsuited to the commercial world of the late nineteenth century, inherits the love of and aptitude for music—the bacillus brought by Gerda reproduces itself in him. Just as an infection ends the Buddenbrook line, so too this bacillus of high art is part of the decline of the family.

*Tonio Kröger* adds to the image of the artist's diseased or deformed state other comparisons that divide the *Künstler* from the honorable citizens. In his long declaration to the sympathetic Lisaweta Iwanowna (a good listener if ever there were one), Tonio denies that any "rightly formed, healthy, and decent" person ever writes, acts, or composes. Artists, he asserts, share the fate of those "prepared singers for the papal choir"—they have been deprived of normal functioning. Separated from humanity by an "abyss of irony, disbelief, opposition, recognition, and feeling," they must understand that they are separate, outside, people who do not belong.[26] The banker whose fiction is genuinely good turns out to be a criminal—perhaps every serious artist is a confidence trickster.[27] Lisaweta shrewdly taxes Tonio's declaration by characterizing him as a bourgeois gone astray (*ein Bürger auf Irrwegen*). Her diagnosis brings him to silence, broken only at the end of the novella in his confession that he stands between two worlds, in neither of which he can be at home, and in his expression of loving admiration for the world of the happy and stupid ones, "the blond and blue-eyed" who live lightly and uncaringly, whose unreflective accomplishments are the material to be celebrated in his art.[28]

*Tonio Kröger* might have written a book akin to *Buddenbrooks*: a nostalgic celebration of the world of the decent, upstanding, commercial men, the patriarchs who brought order to small, prosperous towns until their fortunes were undermined by accidents of history, keener rivals, and the bacillus of high culture.[29] Tonio stands for a clear possibility, the writer—even the *Dichter*—who honors or mourns bourgeois life *from the outside*. Can there be a deeper identification, of the sort implied in Lisaweta's characterization of Tonio, a writer who crosses the abyss to incorporate in his life the virtues praised in his prose? Or must any attempt to write (seriously) and simultaneously to live as an insider, a proper member of the bourgeoisie, rest upon a trick, an illusion that will be unmasked if anyone is allowed to go behind the scenes?[30] *Death in Venice* can be understood as developing even further the two thematic complexes—one centered on the relationship between artist and bourgeois society, the other on the plight of outsiders—by leading its readers into the life of a protagonist who promises, to himself as much as to the world, Lisaweta Iwanowna's deeper identification.

Aschenbach is a serious and subtle writer, one whose style is a model for others (and whose style is represented for the reader through Mann's heightening of his own prose), one who has rejected the "Bohemian stereotype," even in the relatively tame versions represented by Tonio and Lisaweta. He has striven for, and apparently achieved, respectability and decency not only in his books but in his life as well. Conscious of the tradition and potential judgment of his ancestors—"officers, judges, and government functionaries, men who had led upright lives of austere decency, devoted to the service of king and country"[31]—he writes to honor and preserve that tradition, to earn the approval of the forefathers. His success in doing so is measured in several ways, perhaps most notably in his recent ennoblement: as the first sentence of the novella informs us, he is now *von* Aschenbach.[32] *Death in Venice* takes us behind the scenes, to the lido where Aschenbach is unmasked, where he is confronted with what he is, and where he dies. He becomes yet another of Mann's unfortunate outsiders, cut off from those around him—his connections and conversations with others are restricted entirely to the practical details of his life—and he is finally deprived of what had sustained him in solitude, a life of thought, feeling, and expression he could endorse as virtuous and honorable.[33]

Yet there is more to Mann's reworking of his experiences for the novella. As the many commentators recognize, *Death in Venice* is remarkable for the wealth of philosophical references and allusions that pervade it. At two critical moments, Aschenbach's ruminations invoke the figure of Socrates, in whose voice he speaks to himself.[34] Equally evident are the ways in which the protagonist's thoughts and the narrator's attitudes are inflected by the two German thinkers, Schopenhauer and Nietzsche, who had most shaped the self-education of intellectuals growing up at the end of the nineteenth century. The influence of Schopenhauer and Nietzsche is not only apparent in the essays Mann devoted to each of them but also explicit in his autobiographical writings.[35] A letter written late in his life to his old friend Ferdinand Lion expresses poignantly Mann's admiration for Schopenhauer:

> You are reading Schopenhauer—that has made the most impression [*am meisten Eindruck*] on me. How I wish I could find time, to read at least the principal work [*The World as Will and Representation*] through one more time, word by word, with love ("*con amore*"). In a nutshell, reading him was the most intense reading experience of my youth. And isn't he also in the *first* rank of European essayists (leaving aside his metaphysical views!), of equal stature with the best of all outside Germany? I hardly need to return to him, for I have never really left or lost him.[36]

As might be anticipated, in the long essay on Schopenhauer Mann emphasizes the deep impression made on him by his reading of *Die Welt als Wille und Vorstellung*. It occupied him for a long time, and what he read during the same period or even shortly thereafter seemed to him "strange, untutored, askew, arbitrary, unconstrained by the truth."[37] The 1930 sketch of his own life recalls his encounter with Schopenhauer (which followed an earlier reading of Nietzsche) as a "spiritual experience of the highest order," comparable to that attributed to Thomas Buddenbrook, an immersion in which he read day and night ("as one only reads once"), more of a "passionate-mystical" than of a "properly philosophical" type.[38] Years earlier, in his contorted wartime defense of "*Deutschtum*," Mann had explained how Schopenhauer, Nietzsche, and Wagner formed for him a trinity of deeply influential figures, and he had provided a vivid description of the occasion of his first reading of Schopenhauer:

> There hovers before my eyes the small upper-storey suburban room, in which, sixteen years ago [in the late 1890s], stretched out the entire day on an oddly shaped chaise-longue or sofa, I read *The World as Will and Representation*. Lonely and impulsive, seeking the world and yet fascinated with death, how my young

self devoured the magic potion of this metaphysics, whose deepest essence is eroticism, and in which I recognized the spiritual source of the music of *Tristan*! One only reads that way once. It does not happen again.[39]

Later, in the long essay on Schopenhauer, Mann asks his readers (hearers) to forgive his similar portrait of Thomas Buddenbrook's reading, inspired as it was by the experience of a "twenty-year-old" who had been intoxicated by a "metaphysical magic potion."[40] Unlike his protagonist, however, the twenty-year-old does not go on to a premature death; instead, imbued with a sympathy with death, he writes with increasing intimacy and precision about it.[41]

I have dwelt at some length on the deep impression Schopenhauer made on Mann and on his enduring interest in and sympathy for the great pessimist, precisely because the role of Nietzsche in his thinking and writing is so much more heavily emphasized—indeed, as we shall see, many commentators on *Death in Venice* write as if a connection to Nietzsche's early work could be taken for granted.[42] Nietzsche lurks behind two of the mature masterpieces—*Der Zauberberg* and *Doktor Faustus*—and references to his writings pervade Mann's essays, letters, and diary entries. Interestingly, almost all of those citations are to Nietzsche's middle and later writings, from *Human, All Too Human* through *Ecce Homo* and beyond to the material collected posthumously.[43] When Mann recalls the early impact of Nietzsche on him—and he tells us that he read Nietzsche before discovering Schopenhauer—he points *first* to a *stylistic* influence, evident in his own earliest prose attempts.[44] Moreover, he is quite explicit about how Nietzsche's ideas influenced him:

> The twenty-year-old understood the relativity [context sensitivity?] of the supposed "immorality" of this great moralist: if I saw the drama of his hate of Christianity, I saw also his fraternal love for Pascal and understood the hate as moralistic throughout, never psychological—a distinction also to be maintained in his battle, culturally of the highest importance, carried through to the death against the figure he loved the most, Richard Wagner. In a word, I saw above all in Nietzsche the man who overcomes himself; I did

not take anything in him literally, I believed hardly anything he wrote, and just this gave my love for him its passionately double-sided character, and gave it its depth.[45]

Mann goes on to ask, pointedly, whether we should take Nietzsche seriously when he praises Bizet over Wagner or when he commends the "blond beasts" for their predatory behavior toward the lambs.[46] Mann's apologia for German militarism had earlier offered a similar assessment of Nietzsche's importance. Nietzsche's attacks on morality are more those of an artist than of a philosopher—indeed, Mann views Nietzsche as an artist *manqué*, someone who would be fortunate to find his great writer (*Dichter*), as Schopenhauer found in Wagner his great composer. That writer would draw from his source "a form of highest irony, erotic in the slyest and most subtle fashion, playing between life and intellect."[47] So far, the writer has failed to appear, but it is not hard to guess the identity of Mann's favorite candidate.

His fascination with philosophy, particularly with Schopenhauer and Nietzsche, is, in my view, important for coming to terms with *Death in Venice*—it is (as almost all commentators recognize) a deeply philosophical novella. Yet it is very easy to make that characterization and not take it with the seriousness it deserves: Mann was no *professional* philosopher, after all—but neither were Schopenhauer or Nietzsche!—so, although he might have *borrowed* from philosophers, we should not see him as *doing* philosophy. Here I demur. It is not enough to think of the evidently philosophical concepts that figure in Mann's writings as counters to be laid out and moved around in discussions of his work but never to be explained, analyzed, or questioned. Nor is it even sufficient to explore the philosophical sources, probing the texts Mann read with the aim of showing how significant ideas are taken over from them and applied or developed in the novella.[48] Mann merits our attention *as a contributor to the philosophical discussions in which his sources were engaged*.

Even if the corpus of studies of *Death in Venice* is unsurveyable, even if four or five generations of responses to the novella already exist, there is—I hope—room for something different. In this book I shall try to treat Mann's original text, together with the Britten opera and Visconti film that it inspired, as philosophical explorations in their own right.

## 2

What exactly does this mean? My answer will begin by distinguishing three grades of philosophical involvement that literary or musical works may manifest.

The first and shallowest grade is that of simply using some philosophical reference or allusion to enrich a literary text. In *Hard Times*, for example, Dickens might have introduced Mr. Gradgrind and the McChoakumchild school without his frequent (heavy-handed) allusions to utilitarianism and political economy—he did not need to call two of the younger Gradgrind children "Adam Smith" and "Malthus," for example. His satires and caricatures are squibs with evanescent effects serving only to enliven the narrative.

The second grade, to which sensitive commentators on Mann assimilate the philosophical references of *Death in Venice*,[49] is exemplified in Dante's *Inferno*, where, as Virgil explicitly points out to the pilgrim, Hell is organized on Aristotelian principles. So, in canto 11, Dante is admonished to study the *Ethics* and the *Physics* to understand why incontinence is less distasteful to God and why usury is an offense.[50] Here, substantive ideas from philosophy are taken over and applied to the literary account of divine justice.

The third grade consists in using a fictional work for the exploration of philosophical questions. Although the issues may descend from philosophical texts (and the writer may adopt the formulations of them that occur in those texts), the author develops answers of his or her own instead of accepting the proposals of others. This deeper grade of philosophical involvement is evident in many novels and plays, particularly when the author or one of his characters launches into a discussion of free will, or justice, or the nature of art (to cite three of the most popular topics). The most obvious examples are the least interesting (at least to my mind)—highlighted for the reader because they are so self-consciously "philosophical," so disconnected from the world of the fiction.

In his review of *Middlemarch*, Henry James offered a mixed verdict on George Eliot's "philosophical" chapters.[51] On the one hand, he appreciated the intellect exhibited in her commentary on the predicaments of her characters: the presence of *"brain"* behind her observations accounts for the superiority of her achievement. James judges, however, that Eliot's qualities bring "corresponding perils" in their train, that her "transcendental flights" are "too clever by half." As I read his critique, the root trouble lies in the interruption of Eliot's depiction of her fictional world by discursive passages more appropriate to a work of critical, intellectual nonfiction. Similarly, in Robert Musil's *Der Mann ohne Eigenschaften*, the chronicle of events in Kakania and the shifting ideas, moods, and intentions of the principal figures is broken by digressions—easily transformable into pages from a standard work of philosophy through eliminating a few references to situations and characters—in which some particular philosophical conundrum is taken up.[52] At first glance, the excursions undertaken by Eliot and Musil do not seem to be organically integrated with the development of plot or character but simply serve as opportunities for the author's expression of views about abstract issues: philosophy is done by *saying*, not by *showing*.[53] Yet in these instances, both authors might be defended by demonstrating how the deliberate insertion of a gap between narrative and philosophical discourse serves novelistic and philosophical purposes: the detachment of the philosophical explorations from the lives of the characters may be important for our understanding of them and the value of what they think and do: Musil can be read as deploying the gap to effect the estrangement so central to his novel.[54] Yet it is easy for works of fiction that oscillate between narrative and abstract exposition and argumentation, between showing and saying, to press too far, to earn the accusation James (wrongly, to my mind) leveled at Eliot, for the "philosophizing" to appear gratuitous and pretentious—as in the novels and plays of Sartre (a far greater philosopher than Musil but a much inferior writer of fiction).[55] Fiction that argues is typically dead.

I want to focus on a different category of philosophical fiction, one that comprises works in which philosophical explorations are organically integrated with the narrative, with the evocation and development of character, and with the literary style. Works of this sort may take over questions descending from canonical philosophical texts—and the author may even adopt the formulations offered by those texts—but the answers proposed, elaborated, and even defended are the author's own. Or the writer may be concerned with issues he or she takes to be unfocused, or even unposed, in any existing genre. Thus Hermann Broch begins his "commentary" on *Die Schlafwandler* with a provocative claim:

A presupposition of this novel is that literature must concern itself with those human problems, which, on the one hand, are banished from the sciences because they are completely untractable and only lead a shadow existence in a degenerating philosophical journalism [*einem absterbenden philosophischen Feuilletonismus*], and, on the other hand, with those problems that the sciences, in their slow and exact progress, are not yet ready to grasp.[56]

Broch aims to break down the barrier between philosophy—*serious* philosophy—and literature, and he focuses both on questions disdainfully discarded by thinkers who pride themselves on their scientific rigor and on new issues as yet unformulated. I shall be more concerned with the former category, with the recurring questions that seem to resist efforts to find convincing answers and are thereby vulnerable to dismissal by those impatient with philosophy's apparent ability to keep talking forever.

Like Broch, I take the supposed barrier between literature and philosophy to be highly permeable. That barrier has been breached again and again in the recent cultural history of the West, perhaps most evidently in the French and German intellectual traditions. From one side, writers labeled "philosophers" produce *literary* works: Mann was right to view Nietzsche as important for the development of German prose and to celebrate Schopenhauer the great essayist. Examples of figures difficult to classify unambiguously are easy to find—Montaigne, Voltaire, Goethe, Schiller, Kleist, and Coleridge are earlier models; Proust, Kafka, and Camus later instances. I suggest, however, that the class includes far more than these striking exemplars. The deepest grade of philosophical involvement is found in many of the most celebrated literary (and musical) works: in the dramas of Sophocles and Shakespeare, in the song cycles of Schubert and the songs and symphonies of Mahler,[57] in Wagner's *Ring*, in Joyce's fiction (particularly in the two great final novels *Ulysses* and *Finnegans Wake*), and in the novels and novellas of Thomas Mann.[58]

Yet the very idea of philosophy by showing can easily appear dubious. It is easy to wonder how this alleged species can exist, especially if you are impressed with the vision of philosophy as exemplified in the precise specification of theses and the defense of theses by argument, a vision particularly prevalent in the Anglophone world. Our paradigms of linguistic precision are at a far remove from the idioms we value in literary works, and, as noted, works of fiction that argue a case usually succumb to rigor mortis.[59] Is it really possible, then, for *serious* philosophy to be done by a novelist, dramatist, poet, or composer? To answer the skeptic who raises that question, we do best, I believe, to examine what occurs when someone ponders a philosophical issue, responding to a written text or a live interlocutor.

The plausible thought, presupposed by the skeptic, is that the reader or discussant undergoes a change in belief brought about through the presentation of theses and arguments, themselves formulated in more or less clear and precise prose. The more lucid the language and the more explicit and cogent the argument, the easier the apprehension and acceptance of new ideas—so emerges an ideal of philosophical discourse, one in which clarity and rigor are to be prized. Although this picture may seem persuasive—and indeed it is standard among most philosophers, especially in the English-speaking world—it rests on two assumptions. First, the psychological movement that occurs in someone who is thinking through a philosophical issue can be exhaustively characterized in terms of changes in belief (or knowledge): the philosophizing subject passes through a sequence of cognitive states, and, if the philosophizing is well done, the relations among the contents of these states conform to canons of good evidence—that is, if the person comes to believe some new proposition on the basis of prior apprehension of other propositions, then the former (the new conclusion) must stand in appropriate logical relations (broadly construed) to the latter (the previously adopted premises). Second, the changes in belief are sparked by the straightforward presentation of new propositions ideally stated in precise declarative sentences and accompanied by the explicit presentation of cogent reasons: the newly believed conclusions are formulated in the work that is read (or by the interlocutor), and, if all goes well, they are backed by lines of reasoning the subject recognizes—the logical relations apprehended by the subject correspond to the logical structure of the text (or conversation). You come to believe that free will is impossible because I present this proposition to you and provide for it a valid argument all of whose premises you already accept.

*Perhaps* a very large number of changes of philosophical mind, from those produced by Socrates to those that occur in the philosophy classroom today, approximate or realize completely this picture. Even were we to take that for granted, is some such process the *only* way in which someone thinking about a philosophical question might be induced to accept an answer? Surely not. On many philosophical issues, people appear to change their minds because they appreciate new possibilities, or because they imagine vividly the consequences of holding a particular view, or because they come to recognize that something they were inclined to believe "just doesn't fit." Our thoughts are often entangled with our emotions, our hopes, our intentions, and our yearnings—perhaps the recruitment of imagination and emotion is essential to decision making, even when we deliberate at our best.[60] If Plato's dialogues are accurate, Socrates was not above telling stories to his conversational partners (victims?), nor above constructing extensive myths to help them see what he had in mind. Should we then assume that all philosophizing—or even *any* of it—involves passing through a sequence of purely ("cold") cognitive states?[61] Or that the only ways to bring about an appropriate sequence of states is to present the philosophizing subject with clearly stated propositions based on cogent arguments?

I propose a broader view of the activity of philosophizing, one in which what goes on in the mind of the subject can involve a range of different psychological processes—including experiments in imagination and emotional reactions to them—and in which the texts and sounds that generate philosophical changes of mind can be far more various than the luminous rows of precise declarative sentences beloved of the popular model. The proposal faces an obvious objection. The skeptic speaks: "To be sure, people's thinking is often accompanied by all sorts of feelings, and they are moved to conclusions in a wide variety of ways, but we are speaking of *philosophizing*, of thinking at its best, of the activity of Reason. Although some are induced to accept conclusions by the pressure of their emotions, or through some flight of imagination, or a sense of 'fit,' it would be more apt to characterize this as *se*duction. If proper philosophy is to be done, the ancillary psychological processes and the media that spark them should be held in firm check. That is why philosophical prose must be sober—even dull."[62]

My reply to the skeptic will start by offering a general point, after which a focus on a specific philosophical issue will lead us back to Mann and *Death in Venice*. The more general response aims to show that the skeptic's demands cut far too deeply. Skeptics dislike the thought that a work of literature (or music) might expand our conceptual repertoire, leading us to approach our experiences with new categories and to react to experience in different ways: perspectives inspired by our imaginative identification with a character or with the significance of a particular emotional response would be *wrongly* acquired—we would have been seduced into new ways of seeing things, not enlarging our horizons through the sober assessment of reasons. Yet is there really a contrast between the status of our novel perspective and the one we brought to bear in our original state (prior to the successful "seduction")? For it is not that we achieved our concepts and categories through some insight into their special worthiness—there was no Cartesian moment at which they were rigorously assessed and found to pass muster. We acquired them, piece by piece, from the culture(s) in which we were initially socialized, modifying and refining them along the way so that they formed a more or less coherent whole. Careful reasoning may have played some role in the genesis of the product, but it would be folly to pretend that it could support the entire corpus. The human predicament is always to start in the middle.[63]

The prejudice against philosophy by showing stems ultimately from the residues of a foundationalist epistemology, one that few people, including few philosophers, would accept if it were to be made explicit. The work of philosophy is confined when it is assumed that the philosopher's task is to enunciate premises and draw conclusions. All such argumentative activity presupposes a language in which the premises are stated. It is entirely evident, however, that our languages evolve over time, that the concepts confidently deployed by our predecessors come to seem entirely inadequate to the questions with which we wrestle— Gibbon's discussions of the chastity of empresses and Hume's praise for the wit and suavity of eighteenth-century gentlemen now appear inappropriate to the moral terrain that they, and we, are attempting to map: their words are not ours. To hypothesize some process through which the correct philosophical idiom could be definitively established would be to undertake a fools' errand: those foundations will always be lacking. In practice, then, focusing on philosophy as arguing from premises takes the language currently in vogue for granted without considering whether there might be a philosophical task—arguably a highly important task—of reflectively criticizing the concepts and idioms we have inherited. Once that task is recognized, it becomes easy to see that the stimulation of the imagination through literature or music might play an essential role in generating a new perspective on what has hitherto been taken for granted.

So far, an abstract possibility—one that can be made concrete through examples. This section began with Dickens and with the harsh judgment that *Hard Times* displays a low grade of philosophical involvement. Yet Dickens sometimes engages the imagination in powerful ways, moving his readers to change their minds about the justice of social institutions they have taken for granted. From 1853 to the present, a reading of *Bleak House* and, in particular, the descriptions of the plight of Jo, the crossing sweeper, has prompted many to revise their antecedent ideas about obligations to the poor. For the skeptic, the shift in ethical perspective can only be an exercise in *Schwärmerei*, the illicit tugging of receptive heartstrings. I propose an alternative account of what happens: rather than viewing the antecedent attitudes (acquiescence in the benign provisions made for the poor—or, at least, the *deserving* poor) as a well-grounded perspective from which Dickens's eloquence seduces us, we can recognize the arousal of the imagination as essential to a process, one involving further reflection and discussion with others, that leads to a real *advance* in ethical judgment.[64]

*Death in Venice* is not focused on some particular question about moral obligation or social justice. Rather, it is concerned with the oldest and deepest question of philosophy, one that subsumes the complexes of themes distinguished in the preceding section: How to live?[65] The search for understanding what would make a life worthwhile brought the privileged young men of the ancient world to the various philosophical schools, but, throughout more than a millennium, the question lapsed in the intellectual culture of the West—for the obvious reason that it seemed to have received a definitive answer. The rise of Christianity focused attention on human prospects in the hereafter: the valuable life is one directed toward God, centered on faith in Him and on efforts to live as He commanded us. How exactly one should spend the prelude to the long-awaited final union with the Almighty was something about which religious teachers could disagree, but the fundamental commitment to seeing life on earth as a preparatory stage made many activities and projects irrelevant to their discussions. Only with the erosion of religious belief, in the Enlightenment and its aftermath, did the issue of what is to be done in the period between birth and death regain its old weight. Secular philosophy revived the ancient question—and some philosophers who interrogated the issue developed further some of the ancient approaches.[66] And the two post-Enlightenment thinkers who did most to restore the centrality of the issue were the philosophers whose writings impressed themselves on Thomas Mann—Schopenhauer and Nietzsche.

Those who ask how to live might proceed by trying to emulate the popular model of philosophy. They might try to identify those aspects of human lives that contribute to their value, probing and analyzing them and explaining, where they can, why these facets of existence are so significant. Aristotle proceeds in this fashion, drawing up, in the *Nicomachean Ethics*, a catalogue of the places one might look for sources of worth. He proposes that mere pleasure, the pursuit of the hedonist, is not enough, and he commends plausible rivals: activity (particularly social activity), the development of talents, the cultivation and exercise of virtue, the commitments of friendship, the search for disinterested knowledge. More than two millennia on, a secular thinker writing in standard discursive mode might expand Aristotle's catalogue by adding ideas derived from later philosophers, conceptions of autonomy and of individuality advanced by Kant and Mill, for example. The project is, then, to take these abstract elements and to find ways of selecting from them and combining them, so as to articulate some range of conceptions of the worthwhile human life.

Schopenhauer and Nietzsche challenge that project, questioning the capacity of anything like the Aristotelian catalogue (at least as ordinarily understood) to undergird genuine value. For each of them, the problem of achieving a genuinely worthwhile life is far deeper than the ancients or their modern followers realize. To bring home the depth of the difficulty, each makes extensive use of literary resources whose effect, at least on the sensitive (possibly callow?) reader, is to foster an appraisal of the post-Aristotelian "solutions" as shallow and inadequate. The young Thomas Mann, his protagonist Thomas Buddenbrook, and large numbers of other readers were and are moved by the brilliant prose to search for a different answer—supposedly deeper—than any the sober Aristotelian tradition can supply. Without making any judgment about the legitimacy of their response, without deciding whether they have seen something the alternative philosophical approach has inevitably missed, one facet of the Schopenhauer-Nietzsche approach seems to me indisputable. The bare provision of abstract categories is at best only the beginning of an answer to the question. Perhaps it could serve as a useful *anatomy*, delineating form without revealing how functions are discharged, but it needs supplementing with a detailed *physiology*. To understand how to live, one must become vividly aware of what it would be like to live in various ways; one must enter into the substance of a potential life and reflectively evaluate its successes and failures. A well-judged answer to the ancient question would extend the catalogue of values of the austere philosopher with a range (preferably a wide range) of fully elaborated exemplars through which the potential contributions of the items in the catalogue can be assessed.

Literature and music play a role, arguably a necessary role, here. From his early fiction on, Thomas Mann undertook that role, perhaps not as *the* artist (specifically: *Dichter*) who would be the fulfillment of Nietzsche, as Wagner was of Schopenhauer, and, indeed, more as a writerly fulfillment of his great trinity (Schopenhauer-Wagner-Nietzsche) than as an artistic evocation of Nietzsche alone.[67] In *Death in Venice*, he explored the value of a particular type of life: Aschenbach's and, potentially, his own: true to the declaration of "Bilse und ich," Mann placed himself on trial. The succeeding sections of this chapter and parts of the next two will scrutinize his painful self-exposure. Before we begin that examination, however, I want to conclude my response to skeptics who doubt the possibility of philosophy in either a literary or musical mode by briefly considering two other examples. In artistically pondering the problem of how to live, Mann was by no means alone. Among his fellow travelers were a respected predecessor (Wagner) and a little-known contemporary (Joyce).[68]

Although there is an important insight in his claim, Mann overstated when he wrote, "the acquaintance with the philosophy of Arthur Schopenhauer is the great event in the life of Richard Wagner."[69] A great event to be sure—and one that, as Mann clearly saw, could be embodied in the drama and music of *Tristan*.[70] In other works, however, particularly in the *Ring*, Wagner took up the challenge he found in Schopenhauer, offering an independent response to it. The drama of the tetralogy grows out of a world of careless, unthinking beauty and grace—just as the music grows from the opening arpeggios to erupt in Woglinde's joyous song. Neither the blind hedonism of the Rhinemaidens—initially as light hearted as the "blond, blue-eyed ones" whom Tonio Kröger so admires—nor the inchoate, dreamy wisdom of Erda can provide anything of real value. Wotan aspires to more, and, in his tangled efforts to fashion a world of enduring worth, inevitably flawed, despite his successive self-mutilations—the losses of Siegmund and Brünnhilde, the resignation of his recasting himself as the Wanderer, the defeat at the hands of Siegfried—his failure mirrors the predicament diagnosed by Schopenhauer.[71] Yet Wotan's failure is not the end of the *Ring*—although Wagner toyed with a "Schopenhauer ending," he replaced it with something different, a close in which Brünnhilde does not simply "see the world end."[72]

The world the *Ring* presents to us is one in which aspirations to construct something permanently valuable are inevitably defeated, in which a reversion to blind hedonism or bleak darkness is always threatened, yet it is one in which single incidents of love and noble sacrifice are nonetheless deeply worthwhile.[73] Brünnhilde's final action, with its compression of love for her father, Wotan, for her dead husband, Siegfried, and for the virtues she has admired and tried to promote, redeems nothing. Valhalla collapses in flames, the waters of the Rhine rise in a destructive flood, and the world returns to its vapid primordial state. A shallow interpretation might stop there, with the recognition that Brünnhilde (perhaps like an overindulged teenager?) has created chaos. Any interpretation of this sort is oblivious to the drama Wagner constructed and deaf to the music he wrote.

For what Brünnhilde has done *matters*—just as Cordelia's acts of love and forgiveness matter, even though they do not prevent the bleak ending ("All's cheerless, dark, and deadly").[74] Like candles in an enormous darkness, the acts in which Brünnhilde and Cordelia express love and compassion for their tortured fathers are transitory—the candles are snuffed out and glimmer no longer, but the fact that they *have* burned brightly is significant. Brünnhilde's benediction to her father ("*Ruhe, ruhe, Du Gott*"), her voice "gentle and low," cannot be forgotten, and it prepares the hearer for the orchestral music that swells when the voices cease, bringing *Götterdämmerung* (and the *Ring*) to its close.[75] The postlude recalls three major motifs associated with possibilities for the world that has just been consumed—one conjuring the blithe joy of the Rhinemaidens, one recalling Wotan's striving for a value beyond hedonism, and one celebrating the promise of the hero, Siegfried, whose funeral pyre Brünnhilde has lit. All these once promising possibilities might be viewed as mere failures, but, in the closing orchestration, they glow with a new vitality and warmth. For they are framed with a theme that has been heard exactly once earlier in the tetralogy, at the moment when Sieglinde, wretched and yearning for death, learns of the child she is carrying and renews her commitment to life: the words she sings—"O höchstes Wunder!"—are charged with uplift by Wagner's setting of them, and now, at the very end, he not only deploys the motif to illuminate the inevitably frustrated efforts to create a world of real worth but extends it to reach a cadence in which sadness mingles with consolation. Interpretive words are inadequate to the thought and feeling expressed—they can only gesture. One has to *listen* to understand how Wagner offers his own original response to Schopenhauer's challenge.[76]

Joyce does not begin from the problems posed by Schopenhauer and Nietzsche; by contrast, he is more sympathetic to the Aristotelian catalogue, although he protests its elitism, its presumption that only the exceptional—the Stephen Dedaluses of the world—can find lives of genuine worth. Young Stephen aims to fly high, and *A Portrait of the Artist as a Young Man* closes with his determination to "forge in the smithy of [his] soul the uncreated conscience of [his] race."[77] Like the son of the mythical father whom he invokes, Stephen misjudges his flight, and when the reader meets him again in the opening chapters of *Ulysses*, he is bruised and dislocated from his fall. His own aimless wanderings through Dublin contrast with those of a very different figure, Mr Leopold Bloom, a man whose life has lost a direction it once had. Anchored in the ordinary exchanges of a Dublin day, his senses open to frequent grime and occasional beauty, his sympathies often aroused by the pains and discontents of others, Bloom the wanderer gropes toward a possible rediscovery of the life—an ordinary life, but one with structure and value—from which he has gone astray. Molly Bloom's famous closing affirmation points to the *possibility* of that return, as do Bloom's own amorphous ruminations on the two occasions when he falls asleep[78]—but there are no guarantees.

The problem of how lives can attain any worth or meaning hangs over Joyce's prose fiction. *Dubliners* scrutinizes the variety of ways in which human lives may fail (although, for the Conroys, as for the Blooms, there may be possibilities of renewal). A *Portrait* considers a life in prospect, when it may appear, especially to a precociously talented young man, that value can only be the result of some exceptional achievement. *Ulysses* replaces that perspective with the view from middle age, when the "straight way" has been lost and the valuable life, grounded in very ordinary successes, joys, and human relationships, needs to be found again. *Finnegans Wake* offers the view from the end, when there is no longer any question of serious change but only a continued examination of what has been, one that recognizes the flaws and the blotches but hopes to find that it has, after all, been worthwhile.[79]

Joyce absorbs part of the Aristotelian perspective, recognizing social activity, virtue, contemplation, and friendship as potential components of the good life. Yet he distances himself from Aristotle's own understanding of these sources of value, most obviously in allowing more scope to physical pleasures and a very different catalogue of primary virtues (although Bloom shares more with Odysseus than readers might initially suspect, his dominant virtue—sensitivity and kindness to others—has no great weight in either Homer or Aristotle). The most fundamental divergence from Aristotle, however, lies in Joyce's repudiation of commitments to *elitism* and *perfectionism*. Stephen errs in thinking he must fly high—as he begins to learn in *Ulysses*, what he principally needs is to feel the emotion named by "the word known to all men":[80] value can be grounded in the ordinary life. To be worthwhile, that ordinary life can even be messy and misshapen. Despite all that has been, including what has been on June 16, 1904, Bloom and Molly may yet live valuable lives, and their marriage, as it is, may be central to the value of those lives.

The possible worth of the ordinary life, even of the flawed ordinary life, is prefigured in a brief scene at the center of *A Portrait*, when Stephen, having confessed to his sins, returning to the family kitchen, observes the food bought for Sunday breakfast ("White puddings and eggs and sausages"), and sees it as embodying the beauty of life.[81] A similar sensuous appreciation of beauty introduces us to the perceptive Mr Bloom, as he appreciates the contrast between the "gelid light and air" of his own kitchen and the gentle warmth of the early summer day outdoors, as he imagines the tang of the breakfast kidney, and discerns phonemes in the cat's mewing.[82] Eighteen hours later, in the same kitchen, ordinary cups of cocoa (albeit with the extraordinary sacrifice to his guest of the cream intended for Molly's breakfast) will begin a movement, not toward any deep friendship (still less the reunion of a spiritual son with his spiritual father), but a few moments of ordinary—but valuable—companionship between Bloom and Stephen.[83]

Is that really enough? I read *Ulysses* as offering a vivid account of the worth of the ordinary and *Finnegans Wake* as a deep interrogation of the theme. Through the swirling dream of Joyce's last work, readers are brought again and again to rejoice in the everyday, to laugh at its comic mistakes and misunderstandings, and, finally, to recognize the possibility that even flawed relationships may center lives of real value. Even though people wander off course, lives that are blotched and sometimes squalid can nevertheless attain genuine worth. We can "see life foully"[84] and still endorse it. After defeat, humiliation, failures of courage and fidelity, there can still be occasions of forgiveness, moments of generosity, and even affirmation.[85]

Wagner and Joyce do not argue. They do not even present precisely articulated theses about the worth and value of human lives. Nevertheless, they do philosophy, *real* philosophy that can lead listeners and readers to improved perspectives on a (if not the) central philosophical question. The philosophy lies in the showing. Instead of a rigorously connected sequence of clear and precise declarative sentences, we are offered a rich delineation of possibilities—accompanied by a tacit injunction: Consider this.

This philosophical method, the method of showing, is not so far from some excellent work by professional philosophers. Some years ago, the eminent philosopher of science Nancy Cartwright told me rather ruefully that her husband, Stuart Hampshire (himself an extremely distinguished philosopher), complained that she never offered arguments for her views. After some reflection, I suggested what I intended as consolation as well as diagnosis: Cartwright's typical strategy is to describe, exactly and in rich detail, some scientific work of a type overlooked by orthodox philosophical accounts; by considering the phenomena she portrays, her readers are expected to recognize the superiority of the precise claims about the sciences she offers as replacements for orthodoxy. Wagner and Joyce show us that works of music and literature can take Cartwright's first step. The further consideration is up to us, as we listen and read.

Mann would not have put it that way, but he was attuned to the possibility of philosophy as showing. In the 1938 essay on Schopenhauer, after asking his readers to excuse his youthful portrait of intoxicated reading, he continues by proposing that an artist can make use of philosophy: "one can think in the overall conception of a philosopher, without in the least thinking along that philosopher's own lines, or, as I would put it: one can make use of his thoughts—and thereby think as he would never have wanted to think."[86] Mann's own early "use" of philosophy depended on his previous encounter with both Schopenhauer and Nietzsche—thus yielding the "strangest mixture"—and, he adds, that this was caused "less by the teaching of morality and wisdom, which is the intellectual flower of their vitality, than by the vitality itself, the essential and personal substance—so by its passion more than by its wisdom."[87] Passionate reading may find its expression in a work of art—a music drama or a piece of fiction—one that captures vividly part of the essence of a philosopher's view or, even more interestingly, a strange brew distilled from several philosophers, and thus embodying philosophical ideas of a completely novel type. Mann does not explicitly claim that his own novels and novellas achieve this. I do.

A concern with the question whether and how lives can be worthwhile pervades Mann's early writings, subsuming his reflections on the apparent conflict between artist and citizen, his examinations of the predicaments of outsiders.[88] Given the influence of Schopenhauer and Nietzsche on the aspiring young writer—as well as his early passion for Wagner—it might appear that his philosophical explorations are likely to be more Wagnerian than Joycean. Lübeck provided a counterweight, preventing a plunge into the realm (the abyss?) of the "epic mythical": insofar as he harnessed myths for expressing his own perspectives, Mann treated them from an ironic distance.[89] Tonio Kröger's long-winded attempt at self-explanation reveals both a Wagnerian and a Joycean side to his creator. Grounding a life of value in the extraordinary, the gigantesque, the cosmically inflated, is the absurd fantasy of sick and deformed outsiders—yet the return to the ordinary is inadequate, a shallow denial of the challenges posed by the passionate philosophers. How, then, to go beyond Plato and Aristotle, Schopenhauer and Nietzsche, Wagner and Joyce?

*Death in Venice* is *one* of Mann's attempts to answer that question, one interrogation of life and of himself, inspired by experiences that seemed ripe for transformation so as to illuminate issues about the worth of human lives, issues barbed into his consciousness. The task of the philosopher-critic is to highlight the contours of the author's efforts—as Cartwright's descriptions foreground phenomena that have been overlooked. Like the skilled art or music critic who teaches us to attend to particular lines or specific themes and modulations, the aim is to render more apparent what has been shown.[90] Taking the philosophical import of the arts seriously constructs a space in which something more conventionally identifiable as philosophy may operate. On the one hand lie the abstract treatments of philosophy, the catalogue of Aristotle's *Ethics*, or the challenge posed by Schopenhauer. On the other is the rich variety of literary, musical, artistic sources. Philosophical criticism consists in bringing them into relation with one another, of showing how the elaborated presentations of a novel or an opera bear on the problems and schematic answers of philosophical treatises.[91] Its task is to prepare the reader or listener to read or listen differently, in a way that will prepare for recognition of what is presented as a potential way to embody value and thus to serve as a basis for judgment, for endorsement or rejection. In Dewey's apt phrase, philosophy serves as "a liaison officer, making reciprocally intelligible voices speaking provincial tongues."[92]

That service might be rendered in the sober style supposedly essential to philosophy, through distillation of the literary source into precise claims and theses, setting them within a preparatory map of the overall interpretation so as to acquaint readers with the contours of the argument, and thus enabling them to know, at each stage, exactly where they are headed. Although my aim in presenting the cases of Aschenbach from different angles is often to clarify and make precise, I have resisted suggestions that I should take on the role of a fussy tour director and guide the reader's footsteps. If, as I have already claimed in this section and will propose further at the end of chapter 3, literature and music build new ways of conceiving the world and our place in it, a skilled liaison officer should not insist in advance on the form of any eventual understanding: philosophical criticism functions best if it allows for the possibility that the reader may use the critic's suggestions to conceive things differently, to build a perspective the critic has not anticipated. If it is not always evident in the following pages just where the interpretive work is pointing, that is not necessarily a bad thing. Although I believe that, in the end, it will be completely clear how my various suggestions hang together, the aim is not to convince readers of particular theses but to provide materials through which they can transcend what I have written.

### 3

*Death in Venice* was described by its author as a "tragedy,"[93] and a natural conclusion is that the tragedy consists in the failure of Aschenbach, both as presumptive good citizen and as writer. Aschenbach's supposed moral degeneration will occupy us later: for the moment, it is enough to emphasize that it should not be immediately and casually identified with the eruption of longing directed at Tadzio.[94] My first concern is with his unmasking as a writer whose reputation exceeds his accomplishment, an exposé commonly supposed to rest on ideas formulated by the young Nietzsche. Many careful readers attribute to Mann the second grade of philosophical involvement and identify Nietzsche's first work, *The Birth of Tragedy*, as a philosophical text lurking behind the novella. Some critics suppose further that Mann derived from that work a fundamental Nietzschean thesis, namely that great art requires a synthesis of two factors, to be labeled the Apollonian[95] and the Dionysian.[96] The first is connected to form and detachment, possibly to formalism. The latter is linked to passion and intoxication, to ecstasy and rapture. *Death in Venice* introduces us to a writer who has resolutely resisted the Dionysian, repressing the passions within him. In Venice, these impulses erupt and cannot be bridled, so that they lead to his moral dissolution and physical collapse. Aschenbach sees that his work was pale and ephemeral; his death is a tragic repudiation of it.[97]

First, it is important to appreciate how far removed from Mann's habitual practice is so definite a moral verdict.[98] Mann is famous for his ambiguity and his irony, both of which reflect his sensitivity to the nuances of circumstances.[99] When his protagonist, feverish and frustrated in the pursuit of Tadzio, collapses at the fountain, the prose is apparently lucid and severe. Referring to Aschenbach as "the master," "the great success," "the author whose greatness had been officially recognized and whose name bore the title of nobility," the narrator draws attention to his ignominy as he sits, slumped, in the rubbish-filled piazza, across which the gusts of wind bear fumes of the carbolic acid that has been used to mask the smells of decay; his eyes are mostly shut, he only occasionally opens his "cosmetically enhanced" lips, and his mumbled words reflect "the strange dream-logic" of his "half-dozing brain." It is as clear a moral judgment as one might wish.[100] Look how far this paragon of decency has fallen!

Too clear, in fact. The language here is exultant, as if the suspicions the narrative voice has been harboring have now been vindicated. For pages, the designations used for Aschenbach have lost their neutrality, tipping toward the condemnation now offered. In this fifth and final chapter of the novella, he becomes the confused one (*"der Verwirrte"*), the solitary (*"der Einsame"*), the lover (*"der Liebhaber"*), the possessed (*"der Heimgesuchte"*), the man who is feverish under his makeup (*"der unter der Schminke Fiebernde"*).[101] The phrases, deliberately chosen to designate Aschenbach in a particular way, as if the property attributed to him identified his essence, distance us from him and contain in embryo the judgment eventually rendered when he collapses at the fountain.[102] The tone of this narrative voice, that of a moralistic commentator who, losing patience with what he sees as an increasingly errant subject, ultimately issues a self-righteous verdict, is too earnest for Mann. Small wonder that more sophisticated critics have referred to the "second narrator" of *Death in Venice* and seen Mann's characteristic irony in the presentation of moral judgment as if it were his own.[103]

A second reason to reject the reading is its overly simple account of Nietzsche's famous dichotomy. Instead of denying the value of Apollonian art, *The Birth of Tragedy* insists on the significance of the works produced by Apollonian artists.[104] Like the sculptor, the epic poet delights in clarity and beauty of form, creating appearances that can express his genius: though these are *mere* appearances, illusions, they are a great achievement.

> Homeric "naïveté" can only be understood as the most complete victory of the Apollonian illusion: it is an illusion of the sort nature

so often uses for the attainment of her ends. The true goal is covered with an illusory picture: we stretch out our hands toward it and reach the goal through the deception.[105]

The dithyrambic chorus, Nietzsche tells us, replaces the "virgins with laurel-wreaths in their hands" who retain their place as citizens (*"behalten ihren bürgerlichen Namen"*), and Greek tragedy, the Apollonian symbolic representation of Dionysian knowledge and effects, is divided by a great gulf from the epic tradition.[106] Even if one accepts Nietzsche's complex metaphysical argument for believing that tragedy probes reality more deeply than epic (an argument based partly on agreement with Schopenhauer, partly on divergence from him), there is no easy inference to the conclusion that the "beautiful illusions" of Apollonian art are without value—represented as they are, by Homer, who paints so vividly because he looks at so much more.[107] Aschenbach's dedication to beauty and to form, his resolute concern to link his art to canons of conventional decency, do not mean his writings are somehow worthless—or even less than great. Those writings have been canonized, included in books for schoolchildren; they have been read enthusiastically by an international public, from which Aschenbach receives a correspondence whose volume taxes his ability to reply. There is no reason to believe that those captivated by Aschenbach are any more benighted than the millions who have thrilled to Homer, or that the "respectfully shocked" world that learns of his death—a world that will, presumably, remain ignorant of the circumstances immediately preceding his death—will ever modify its high opinion of his accomplishment.[108]

The references to "the Apollonian" and "the Dionysian" that are almost *de rigueur* in discussions of *Death in Venice* should attend to the nuances of Nietzsche's discussion. It is inadequate to suppose that what overtakes Aschenbach on the lido is an outbreak of "the Dionysian," one that exposes the inadequacy of his previously "Apollonian" literary contributions.[109] (As we shall see in chapter 3, this problematic idea receives a forceful but crude expression in Visconti's film, in the dramatic scene where the student Alfred berates the older composer, Gustav Aschenbach, for his failure to embody "passion" in his music.) There is, however, a deeper problem with any hypothesis to the effect that Mann was leaning heavily on ideas drawn from *The Birth of Tragedy*. The Thomas Mann

Archiv in Zürich contains copies of many of his books, and one can look at his edition of Nietzsche's works.[110] In contrast to the later revisionary foreword, part of Nietzsche's critical discussion of Wagner, which is annotated, the text Nietzsche originally published in 1872 is completely unmarked. Absence of evidence must always be handled carefully,[111] but the abrupt cessation after the first dozen pages of marginal lines and underlinings—which Mann uses to mark passages that particularly interest him—inclines me to think that he was drawn to the foreword because of his (often avowed) interest in the Nietzschean critique of Wagner and that the later parts had less impact on him.[112] As has already been noted, Mann's attitude to Nietzsche is subtle: the autobiographical sketch of 1930 protests the idea of simply taking over the provocative claims Nietzsche makes—Mann found the "philosophy of power" and the "blond beast" to be "an embarrassment."[113] "As to his idolization of 'life' at the price of intellect, this poetical conceit that has had such disastrous consequences for German thought—there was only one way for me to assimilate it: as irony."[114] Unlike the mature author of provocative paradoxes, the earnest young disciple who viewed Wagner as the great reviver of tragedy would not be of great interest to an author who read him in this way.[115]

A last reason for rejecting the common interpretative idea that Aschenbach is exposed as an inferior writer concerns the ending of the novella. Aschenbach collapses at the fountain, but Mann does not leave him there. After his murmured quasi-Socratic, anti-Socratic reflections[116] on his predicament, the text breaks, offering not a sixth chapter but a coda.[117] That coda finds Aschenbach back at the lido, physically unwell but on his way to his usual morning station at the beach. Departures from Venice have increased in frequency, and he observes luggage in the foyer. Learning from the hotel manager that the Polish family will leave after lunch, he continues his routine, taking his seat on the almost deserted beach. There he observes a fight between Jaschu and Tadzio, culminating in Jaschu's thrusting of Tadzio's face into the sand and the jerks of the defeated boy's body as he struggles for air. Released, Tadzio walks into the sea and, standing on the sandbar, turns to look back at Aschenbach, as if beckoning, and, in response, Aschenbach half rises, before falling back in his chair, dead.[118]

There are two striking features of this coda. One is that it marks a return to an earlier tone in the narrative voice. Instead of the moralizing epithets, the writer is designated with full respect—the noble particle returns: "Einige Tage später verließ Gustav von Aschenbach . . . [A few days later, Gustav von Aschenbach left . . . ]." The second is that, on the usual critical approach to *Death in Venice*, it seems quite unnecessary.

The obvious way in which to exhibit Aschenbach's death as the result of his unsuccessfully bridled passions would be to have him die at the fountain. There, in pursuit of his obsession, he would be surrounded by, and part of, the corruption of Venice, at a place where the plague can be spread and surrounded by the stench of the carbolic acid that the city fathers use to hide its presence. True enough, if Aschenbach's own death were to be ascribed to cholera,[119] then he would have to have eaten the presumably tainted strawberries somewhat earlier: Mann could not have him eat the infected fruit and die in the same paragraph. That, however, would have been easy to arrange, for the fifth chapter offers plenty of opportunities for some similar incident in which the disease could be transmitted. If the point is to unmask Aschenbach as writer and as morally upstanding citizen, what better place to leave him than the littered piazza? Why does the coda exist?

## 4

My aim has been to clear away some ideas about the "philosophical backdrop" of *Death in Venice* as a prelude to approaching it from a different philosophical angle. Plato, Schopenhauer, and Nietzsche—the Nietzsche who wrote the sequence of works from "Schopenhauer as Educator" to *Ecce Homo*—hover over *Death in Venice*. Their fundamental influence on the novella derives from the question central to their major writings: How should one live? Mann's frequently posed problem of reconciling art and bourgeois decency, of fusing *Künstler* and *Bürger*, is a special case of this question. Not all people perceive the problem, for there are those who live comfortably within bourgeois society, accepting its rules and winning its favor, "those who live lightly," "the blond and blue-eyed ones," as Tonio Kröger calls them. Possibly lives of this sort have genuine worth, even though they are unexamined—that remains to be determined. Yet even if we have not attended to Tonio Kröger's lengthy explanation of himself, no reader of *Death in*

*Venice* can avoid the suspicion that the light-hearted life—observed by Aschenbach from the outside as he sits at his "post" on the lido—may be insufficient.[120] An older contemporary of Mann's, a philosopher almost certainly unknown to him at the time he wrote the novella, formulated the suspicion about the lives of the "healthy-minded" in ways of which Mann might well have approved. William James is no subscriber to the metaphysics that moves Schopenhauer and those Schopenhauer "educates," including Nietzsche, Wagner, and Mann, to think there is a deep challenge to the possibility of a valuable life, but James does worry that the "healthy-minded" have overlooked or ignored the real problem, not solved it.[121] James supposes that the advances of the sciences have generated a picture of the human predicament:

> Mankind is in a position similar to that of a set of people living on a frozen lake, surrounded by cliffs over which there is no escape, yet knowing that little by little the ice is melting, and the inevitable day drawing near when the last film of it will disappear, and to be drowned ignominiously will be the human creature's portion. The merrier the skating, the warmer and more sparkling the sun by day, and the ruddier the bonfires at night, the more poignant the sadness with which one must take in the meaning of the total situation.[122]

Those who view humanity in this image see more deeply, feeling a need to take up the issue of how lives can attain genuine worth and to identify sources of value, even if the values should turn out, in the end, to be those to which the untroubled ones independently conform.

Plato, at least as Mann reads him, raises the question of how the rigorously examined life can be worth living and offers a positive answer to it—although whether that answer could be exemplified in the lives of many actual ancient Greeks or early twentieth-century Germans is a separate question. One facet of the ideal society envisaged in the *Republic* is the availability to *all* of a particular type of valuable life, one in which individuals develop their talents, are guided into virtuous conduct, and contribute to a human enterprise larger than themselves: Socrates tells his interlocutors that "in establishing our city, we aren't aiming to make any one group outstandingly happy but to make the whole city so, as far as possible."[123] People who are not suited for the lengthy education that prepares the philosopher-guardians to run the show are still able to fulfill their potential, to live the good life, even if they cannot understand just what they are doing. Like Mann's "blond and blue-eyed ones" or James's "healthy-minded" types, they do not examine their own lives or confront the real philosophical problem. The philosophers undertake that examination for them, probing the conditions of valuable lives and using their appreciation of those conditions to enable their more carefree fellows to flourish. They are the informed sources of value for all, precisely because they have apprehended the Forms,[124] and, in consequence, their lives take on a higher type of value than any available to the less self-conscious citizens.

In the *Phaedrus*, a dialogue Mann read carefully in preparing his novella, Plato elaborates the metaphysical picture offered in the *Republic*, distinguishing kinds of people (or "souls"). Socrates explains to his young interlocutor how the highest kind of soul will be "delighted ... to be seeing what is real and watching what is true" and will "feast" on the vision of "Justice" and "Self-Control" and "Knowledge."[125] In ordinary life, however, "justice and self-control do not shine out through their images down here" but only become visible to us through the perception of beauty.[126] So, Plato explains, there can arise not only wisdom and understanding but an intense erotic love centered on the passion for virtue and accompanied by self-control. One who understands and enjoys this love can live a life of great worth and even guide others, whose comprehension is less, to lead valuable lives. The philosopher-guardian-lovers even achieve a kind of immortality, for their insights, teaching, and above all their exemplary lives inspire those who come after them and are reproduced in the souls of others—as Diotima tells Socrates, "Everyone would rather have such children than human ones."[127]

The Platonic "solution," just sketched in barest outline, is important to *Death in Venice* because, as we shall see later in this chapter and in the next, the novella is partly an extended exploration of tension between two elements linked in Plato's account—self-control and the appreciation of beauty. Mann's own view of that tension is framed by his sense of a challenge, posed by Schopenhauer and developed differently by Nietzsche—a challenge to which I have alluded but have so far left unexplained—according to which not only Plato's own answer to the philosophical question but *any* answer currently available is inadequate.[128] For all his admiration for Plato, Schopenhauer believes that a correct understanding of metaphysics, of the nature of reality, must recognize that the Platonic Forms are not what is ultimately real but rather general ways in which the fundamental reality—the Will—objectifies itself.[129]

Schopenhauer claims to have a cogent philosophical argument for thinking the problem of the valuable life to be insoluble, an argument that runs from what he takes as the correct insight at the heart of Kant's transcendental idealism to the conclusion that reality is "blind Will," apprehended in the world of experience as different individuals, within and between which there is inevitable strife and struggle.[130] It follows that life is essentially suffering, so that the best we can achieve is a condition of abnegation of the will; if we attain that condition, we take on an attitude of compassion, one fundamental to the ethical life. Fully to understand the impossibility proof, he tells us, we must not only start at the beginning of his book with the Kantian insight but also acquaint ourselves with ancillary works in which he has elaborated some aspects of his correction of Kant in more detail: moreover, it is important to read the entire book (both volumes) at least twice, so that study of the preliminary material can be illuminated by thoughts that, of necessity, occur later in the exposition.[131]

Did Mann follow this rigorous program of reading? Almost certainly not. The intoxication induced by Schopenhauer was probably caused by the particular passages he mentions: the chapter (possibly Schopenhauer's "most beautiful" and "deepest") conveying the "sense for death," the discussions of the insights attainable through art (and particularly music), the exploration of human suffering and its unavoidability.[132] Mann's focused praise indicates the parts of Schopenhauer he pored over most carefully: in the long argument of volume 1, we would expect his interest to be aroused in book 2, to become more lively in book 3, and to be most intense in book 4. The marginal markings and underlinings in the copy of *Die Welt als Wille und Vorstellung* in the Zürich archive reveal exactly this pattern. The opening metaphysics and the critique of Kant provoked no scribbling—hardly surprising, given the young Mann's antipathy to Kant (an early entry in a friend's collection of responses to particular questions specifies Kant as his "insuperable aversion" and characterizes the categorical imperative as "bureaucrats' philosophy").[133] In reading Schopenhauer's masterpiece, Mann's passions were more highly aroused as the pessimism became more explicit.

In this, I suspect, he was typical of his many contemporaries who found reading Schopenhauer a life-changing experience. Despite the ingenuity of many of the arguments developed in books 1 and 2 of WWV 1 (and the corresponding chapters of WWV 2, as well as the "Appendix on Kant"),[134] it is highly doubtful that the many young intellectuals who "rediscovered" Schopenhauer in the later decades of the nineteenth century worked through the reasoning, which the proud author viewed as *forcing* his pessimistic conclusions. Schopenhauer's writing is sufficiently eloquent (and learned in unexpected ways), his sallies at his opponents are often witty, and the general vision sufficiently clearly presented to keep his readers moving through the early parts without pondering the details of the inferences.[135] Once they reach book 3 they are rewarded with an elegant aesthetic theory, and book 4 brings a literarily rich and philosophically passionate exposition of a perspective on life that can easily be detached from the metaphysics and related to the reader's experience.

Mann and many others thrilled to the pessimism without worrying overmuch about whether it rested on philosophically irrefutable foundations. In Mann's own case—as in that of Thomas Buddenbrook—there was an immediate connection with his sense of his own life and its uncertain value. The 1938 essay on Schopenhauer expresses his detached skepticism about a priori philosophical arguments and the greater probative force of considerations drawn from experience: apropos of the philosophical defense of common morality, he suggests that it is not our ordinary ethical views (for example, the condemnation of suicide) that need intricate philosophical defense but rather the philosophical system that gains credibility from its ability to deliver conclusions experience can validate.[136]

For Mann, as for Wagner, Schopenhauer's pessimism had attractions quite independently of its official metaphysical basis. Not only would both men have warmed to the celebration of the arts as portals to reality, but both would have applauded the high place assigned to music. Moreover, Mann plainly resonated with Schopenhauer's insistence on the blind and disruptive character of Will, particularly powerful in the sexual urge, never satisfied and permanently at odds with our higher nature. On Schopenhauer's account, sexual desire is a low grade of objectification of Will, one present in all sexually reproducing animals, sharing the usual feature of Will that desire, once satisfied, soon arises again, but also conflicting sharply with the higher modes of Will available to reflective beings who can consider their situation and set their own goals.[137] It is thus particularly painful for those human beings who have been most profoundly touched by civilization. From his youth on, Mann felt sexual desire as a burden—and he would continue to do so until late in his life. As a nineteen-year-old he wrote to his confidant Otto Grautoff: "Recently, I have nearly become an ascetic. I am ardent, at my beautiful moments, for pure aesthetic sensibility, for the sensibility of the intellect, for intellect, soul, character. I say: let us separate the lower part of the body from love!"[138]

Fifty-odd years later, he recorded in his diary his continued sexual potency ("flattering to my vanity"), lamented that some of the medicines he took acted as aphrodisiacs, and complained that his libido did not leave him in peace.[139] The problem of sexuality is twofold: most obviously (as the next chapter will explore), Mann was troubled by the *direction* of his sexual impulses, but more fundamental to his unease was precisely the aspect of sexuality emphasized in Schopenhauer's discussions, the *constant, insatiable,* and *uncontrollable* demands of this form of Will.

Mann and his contemporaries saw Schopenhauer as modifying the problematic of philosophy, replacing Kantian questions about the world and our knowledge of it with issues about the value of human lives that had been neglected since the Greeks but that were live problems for late nineteenth-century Germans. They did not much care whether Schopenhauer had been right in his "correction of Kant," for they could respond to the claims of the fourth book of *The World as Will and Representation* and to some of those articulated in the second and the third in their own right. Schopenhauer was important for his posing of questions, someone who educated Mann as he educated Nietzsche, reintroducing the ideal of philosophy as something by which the philosopher lives— even if thoughtful and passionate readers would choose to aspire to that ideal in different ways (and even if they doubted that Schopenhauer had been able fully to embody his own pessimism).[140]

Unlike Schopenhauer, Nietzsche offered no systematic treatment either of the possibility of achieving value in one's life or any general argument for the impossibility of doing so.[141] In accordance with the approach to Nietzsche elaborated in Mann's writings, the philosopher's mature works can be regarded as a series of penetrating analyses of general features found in different types of human lives.[142] Nietzsche can be read not as operating on the grand Schopenhauerian scale — demonstrating that Human Life has some deep Metaphysical Feature that renders it worthless — nor as focusing on particular lives in detail and exposing their specific limitations, in the way a writer of fiction (for example, the Joyce of *Dubliners*) might do. Nietzsche explores species and genera of human lives arising and taking shape under particular cultural conditions and diagnoses the shared causes of failure within a general type. On this interpretation, Nietzschean scorn for "the herd," the rejection of ovine conformity to tradition, the call for the *Übermensch*, would serve as provocations, opportunities for ironic assimilation. Provoked and inspired, a writer might focus Nietzsche's broad claims on particular characters in a work of fiction, figures on whom alternative perspectives might be taken and about whom a more ambivalent verdict might be reached. An avowed ironist would not be swept up in enthusiasm for the *Übermensch* — surely an inadequately sketched character if ever there was one — but would appreciate Nietzsche's importance as "the greatest and most experienced psychologist of decadence."[143]

Reading him in this way, Mann would have been profoundly interested in Nietzsche's responses to the proposals about the potential worth of human lives offered by the philosopher's great predecessors — by Schopenhauer and Wagner — and thus particularly concerned with "Schopenhauer as Educator" and the polemical writings against Wagner, works we know Mann read with great care. He would also have been drawn to the many-sided explorations of humanity and its prospects, from *Human, All Too Human* (whose title Mann plays on)[144] and *The Gay Science* to *Beyond Good and Evil* and *The Genealogy of Morality* — all works from which he quotes or to which he alludes. In wrestling with Schopenhauer and Nietzsche, Mann is disposed, throughout his fiction, to counter their abstract treatments with an attempt to embed and explore the questions they raise within the concrete circumstances of human life—as if, inspired and at the same time frustrated by the generality of philosophy, he were to be concerned with the issues as they arise within some surveyable context, in which possibilities can be more confidently understood and appraised.[145]

*Death in Venice* is more "philosophical" than Mann's other early works not because it alone wrestles with the questions Mann shares with philosophers—they arise almost everywhere[146]—but because, as in more austere philosophical treatments, the situation is radically simplified. Not, to be sure, in the extreme way of Schopenhauer as metaphysician, where a generic subject confronts the world. Nevertheless, the character is defined in ways that avoid potential complications. Aschenbach is detached from many of the conditions of human life: his wife is long dead and his daughter has married, and there has been little recent contact with her; even in the years before his journey to Venice, years in which he pursues his routine (Mann's own, of course!)—concentrated work in the morning, the nap, the stroll, the reading, the correspondence— he has probably not had many, even any, intimate conversations with others. We are given a vision of a socially isolated subject whose life is centered on the activity of writing, an activity that is always slow and often painful, in which satisfaction is rarely found, despite the rewards that come from the reception of his works. With an eye to the third essay of Nietzsche's *Genealogy of Morality*, we may conceive of *Death in Venice* as, in part, a response to the potential value of a particular type of asceticism.[147] Aschenbach's watchword is "*Durchhalten*," variously translated as "endure," "stay the course," and "persevere,"[148] with clear implications that one must strive to come through difficulties. Central to the life whose final weeks comprise the bulk of the novella is the concept of discipline.

The question whether a life based on discipline could ipso facto be worthwhile was, for Mann, a deeply personal one. At times, he offered a negative answer about himself. On his thirty-third wedding anniversary, he declared to his wife, Katia,[149] that his life failed the Schopenhauer-Nietzsche test: were he to be given the chance to repeat it, he would refuse, since the pains and sufferings outnumbered the ephemeral successes (including, by that stage, the Nobel Prize for literature).[150] That, however, was much later. It is worth considering if *Death in Venice* allows a different verdict.

## 5

The novella tells of the breakdown of discipline. A writer who has aimed at purity in his art and at a corresponding defense of conventional morality falls prey to an obsessive passion that leads him to physical and moral collapse.[151] The mature Aschenbach had repudiated bohemianism, rejecting the idea of compassion for human follies and lapses, decrying any "sympathy with the abyss."[152] Nevertheless, his overwhelming desire to remain in the presence of Tadzio prompts him to reject what he recognizes as his duty: namely to warn the boy's mother, the "lady of the pearls,"[153] of the presence of cholera in Venice. He explicitly considers the "purifying and proper course of action" and sketches in advance the words he would employ: "Allow a stranger, Madame, to be of service to you with a warning about something which self-interest is keeping from you. Depart at once with Tadzio and your daughters! Venice is infected with plague."[154] It takes only a moment for him decisively to reject offering any counsel of this kind—and, in deciding to remain silent, Aschenbach is completely aware of what he is doing: seduced into dishonesty, intoxicated by the consciousness of his complicity in guilt ("as a tired brain would become intoxicated by a small amount of wine"),[155] he aligns himself with the corrupt city fathers and with their strenuous efforts to conceal the plague.[156]

His decision is followed immediately by the vivid and horrifying dream—or perhaps a state of possession more intense than any dream—in which monstrous and obscene Bacchic rites are enacted around him.[157] In the wake of the dream, he feels compelled to play more completely and more conspicuously the role of lover, driven by an urge to please the beloved and thus to allow himself a cosmetic concealment of his age. Aschenbach transforms himself, recapitulating the elderly fop who, on the voyage to Venice, had so disgusted him. Feverish under his makeup, he pursues Tadzio, as he has done so often before, this time losing the boy in the labyrinth of Venetian alleyways. With burning head, sweating body, shaking neck, and unbearable thirst, he recklessly buys fresh strawberries, soft, musty, and overripe, and collapses at the fountain. There, in his Socratic ruminations, he offers reasons—or rationalizations?—for the unavoidability of the abyss.

The decision to tell the story of Aschenbach and Tadzio rather than that of Goethe and Ulrike von Levetzov,[158] an alternative Mann had seriously pondered, allows him to set a trap for unwary readers. Mindful of the sins of that famous "Somdomite," Oscar Wilde,[159] they might suppose Aschenbach to have fallen early, for his moral collapse to consist not in the failure to warn Tadzio's mother but in his obsession with a pubescent boy—or possibly even in his having "unnatural urges" long before they were ever expressed. Not only did Mann correctly judge that the novella would convince critics of his moral seriousness, but he explained to his friend Philipp Witkop that, any expectations to the contrary, he was not writing an "immoral" story: "I am hard at work: on a rather strange thing I have brought back from Venice, a novella, serious and pure in tone, concerning a case of "boy-love" [*Knabenliebe*] on the part of an ageing artist. You will say 'Hm. Hm.' But it is very respectable."[160]

Those inclined to greet Aschenbach with "Hm. Hm.," denouncers of "Greek love," could be allowed to think of the writer as thoroughly corrupt. The ambiguous formulation of his protagonist's moral collapse serves as protective covering for the author's own leanings, and it is easy to envisage Mann's ironic smile as he imagined the way committed homophobes would applaud his defense of rectitude and decency.

For the real moral collapse—Aschenbach's self-conscious decision not to warn Tadzio's mother—to have its full impact, and for the moralizing narrator to be able to present it as he does, readers must have advance knowledge of the discipline that is systematically and thoroughly undone. This episode in the writer's life, the journey to Venice and its aftermath, must be set against its previous pattern. Mann accomplished this with a brilliant structural idea, interposing between the opening chapter (the decision to journey south) and the implementation of that decision (the voyage and the stay at the lido) a chapter reviewing Aschenbach's life. That chapter has the style of an obituary, a summing up of the career of an eminent man.[161] Yet it cannot *be* an obituary, since to place it at the end, after Aschenbach's death, would make, explicitly or implicitly, some summary judgment about the worth of his life—and thus vitiate the philosophical project of inviting the reader to ponder what this life has meant. To open with it, on the other hand, would be to diminish the force of the portrait, for we need to feel our way into Aschenbach's current distress—the mind moving on in painful but profitless ways[162]— to appreciate the sensitivities that lie behind the eulogist's measured prose. The many indications of Aschenbach's suffering in the exercise of his relentless discipline—the allusion to the figure of St. Sebastian, for example—would provide an inadequate sense of what Aschenbach has been, done, and overcome, unless we came to them from an extended depiction of him at a moment of crisis, a moment when even his severe discipline has failed to overcome the obstacles he confronts—neither patient care nor a sudden inspiration will succeed. Placing this "obituary notice" where Mann does enables us to appreciate the condition from which Aschenbach's decline begins.[163]

Our readerly view of the intense discipline is purely retrospective: we do not see Aschenbach at work. Yet, as with the visit to Venice and the strong attraction to the boy on the lido, Mann's own experience as a writer undergirded his portrait of his protagonist's discipline. His decision to burn his early diaries[164] deprives us of his descriptions of the struggles, pains, doubts, and disgust that appear, sometimes day after day, month after month, in the records of his later years—but it is hard to imagine that life was easier in the period when he was still establishing himself. Long after success has come, many a morning is the scene of effort apparently unrewarded. Mann is frequently tired while he works and tired of his work; it goes forward only slowly, and he is dubious about its value.[165] His anxieties about what he is writing are periodically allayed through evening readings to family and close friends, who almost invariably respond in ways that reassure him: "I read Chapter XXIII (on Munich) [Chapter 23 of *Doktor Faustus*], with great effort, because still weak, 25 pages. The attention was great. Clever and moving comments of Werfel on the themes and original composition of this largely conceived and vulnerable book."[166] The entries on the succeeding days make it evident how important these occasions were for Mann: he writes that the reading and subsequent discussion have restored his faith in the book and remarks that "the encouragement of the recent reading was bitterly necessary."[167] Mann's strong positive impressions of the impact of his works, when they were read to his intimate circle and when they were presented to the broader public, sustained him through the frequently laborious and disappointing mornings—and it is interesting to speculate whether those closest to him took steps to ensure that he would always find the encouragement he so "bitterly" needed. Aschenbach, by contrast, has no such setting in which to hear the echo of his painfully crafted prose.

Aschenbach's afternoon walk follows, I suggest, a morning like many his creator had experienced and was to experience. Tired and strained, he has dutifully gone to his post (his desk) after breakfast—perhaps, like Mann, he has not slept well, but it is his duty to work, with or without sleep[168]—and he has failed to make progress with the literary problem confronting him. Because he is overwrought, the customary afternoon nap brings no rest, and he seeks refreshment from a walk through the English garden—where the oppressive weather matches his mood. As he waits for the tram that will take him home, a strange figure appears in the portico of the mortuary chapel, a man whose gaze challenges him and whose appearance inspires thoughts of travel.[169] Moved by the premonitory daydream of a tropical swamp with its "lewd" giant ferns, Aschenbach makes an impulsive decision to break with his routine, releasing himself from the exceptionless imperatives the "obituary" sees as governing his conduct. Discipline begins to break before he leaves Munich, and the fracture continues through subsequent episodes, through the unrewarding visit to the Adriatic island, the subsequent resolve to sail to Venice, the warning signals—ignored—of the fop and the gondolier, signals that might have alerted him to the fact that he is entering a world entirely alien to the orderly life he has lived.[170]

The strength of that discipline in its original, unrelaxed state is illuminated by Mann's own records of his struggles to craft his refined prose— but the clues are already present in the "obituary" account. Although the summation of Aschenbach's career opens with a catalog of the major works—the "clear and powerful prose epic" on Frederick the Great, the "novelistic tapestry" of *Maia*, the powerful story "A Wretch," and the passionate treatise on "Intellect and Art"—the focus turns quickly to the ways in which Aschenbach's development has been guided by heroic self-discipline. The review of his forefathers, with whom he will later identify himself, emphasizes the austerity of their lives, and the characterization of those lives as *"straff"* (literally: taut, tense, stretched) is echoed in the verdict rendered by one of Aschenbach's contemporaries: he had always lived as a clenched fist, never as a loose hand.[171]

We are told, however, of a period in which the young writer had pandered to the tastes of the times—and, it is suggested, precisely his inherited discipline enabled him to overcome this weakness. He identifies himself with the austere and respectable ancestors—like them, he serves "decent society," a soldier of a sort, protecting against hostile ideas that might attack its cherished values. (Mann sometimes emphasized the importance of the "soldierly spirit" in *Death in Venice*, commending those readers who perceived it.)[172] Rejecting bohemianism, Aschenbach embraced a life of solitude, of suffering, and of struggle, and the intensity of his self-sacrifice could be read in the lines engraved on his face by his dedication to his art.[173] Painstakingly, over weeks, months, and years of daily exertion, he crafted his masterworks out of innumerable small insights. The opening scene shows us a writer who has paid the price for his achievements, whose recent efforts have been thwarted, and whose discipline is—perhaps temporarily—exhausted.

Discipline dissolves through the progressive loosening of the connection between Aschenbach's will and its considered objective, by means of the substitution of a rival object. For much of the novella, he can convince himself that his aims are entirely compatible—as he becomes aware of the importance to him of the rival goal, being in Tadzio's presence, he thinks of it as part of the process of restoring his creativity. So he can endorse the substitution until the moment when he is forced to choose between his prior aims and ideals and the opportunity to gaze on the beautiful boy, when he must decide whether to warn Tadzio's mother. At this point, and only at this point, he self-consciously repudiates aspirations central to his earlier self. The initial resolve to travel south is not undisciplined because it implies some direct abnegation of his commitments—it might be necessary for him to rest from his labors and to recoup his strength, if he is to overcome the artistic obstacles before him. A good soldier can leave his post if, by doing so, he recognizes that he is advancing the broader cause. Yet Aschenbach's impulsive decision is not guided by any such disciplined considerations but is instead the product of a fantasy that erupts in him outside the mortuary chapel. We only fully understand that fantasy for the seduction it is when we look back on it from the perspective of the later dream. After the moral collapse, the deliberate substitution of Tadzio's presence for the aims that have guided his mature life, the conscious complicity in the guilt of those who mask the plague that has corrupted Venice, and the "lewd" ferns of the tropical swamp that initially beckons Aschenbach to go south have been transformed into the copulations, "mixing without boundaries," of the obscene creatures in the vision that possesses him.[174] The small lapse of discipline of the original impulse has given way to an abandon so complete that it can no longer be denied. Aschenbach can only acquiesce to what he has become and submit himself to the skills of the hotel barber, who will substitute an exterior rejuvenation for the artistic revival the writer has, officially, been seeking.

On the Adriatic island, on the ship to Venice, in the gondola, at the lido under the scirocco, Aschenbach deceives himself about the contributions his sojourn in an alien and disturbing environment will make to his central project, a potential recuperation that will enable him to resume the disciplined practice of his art. Standing at the rail of the unprepossessing ship that will take him to Venice, he has a sense of "dreamlike alienation"—but, at that moment, the voyage begins, and he reconciles himself to the course he has chosen, to revisit the "extraordinary fairy-tale" city for which he is bound.[175] His momentary suspicion that the gondolier who takes him to the lido may be a criminal arouses a brief residue of the old discipline—considerations of pride and duty, fleetingly recalled, impel him to question the strange and sinister boatman. His protest and queries, however, are easily brushed aside, and, once again, Aschenbach relaxes in acquiescence.[176] The Hotel des Bains initially promises the opportunity for the intended artistic rejuvenation: the mysterious gondolier (who operates without a license) gives way to the professionally welcoming staff; Aschenbach is shown to a well-appointed room with a sea view. He begins to recover from the disturbances of the journey, the observations he has made, "at once less focused and more penetrating" because he has traveled alone, begin to settle as he contemplates the sea. Fastidiously and carefully, he dresses for dinner, arriving, nonetheless, a little early in the hall. The guests, the proper clientele of an elegant hotel, have assembled. It is the moment at which recovery might begin.

Looking up from the newspaper he has casually selected, Aschenbach surveys the scene. The defender of bourgeois order can applaud the smooth operation of conventions and modes of dress; the novelist can appreciate the vivid diversity of the hotel guests. His activity of conjectural national classification is interrupted, however, by an arresting vision. Polish is spoken nearby, and Aschenbach looks toward the group: a governess with three girls and a younger boy. "With astonishment Aschenbach noticed that the boy was completely beautiful."[177] Struck by that beauty, he muses over dinner, not altogether coherently—the thoughts of the solitary traveler are, if penetrating, unfocused—on issues about art and beauty, finding at the end of his reflections that they resemble the apparent insights vouchsafed in dreams, appearing shallow and unprofitable in the sober light of day.[178] Here, in embryo, the next phase of his self-deception is already present. The beautiful boy can be seen as a means to Aschenbach's ultimate goal, an occasion for artistic inspiration within the domain of pure form and beauty to which he has, with self-conscious discipline, directed himself.

The next day, Aschenbach's wonted discipline begins to lapse in a small but telling way: seated at the beach, with his travel writing-case on his knee, he sets himself to the task of answering his correspondence, a chore that taxes him daily—"The forty-year-old writer, tired as he might be from the strains and vicissitudes of his creative work, still had to deal with a daily correspondence bearing postage stamps from around the world."[179] (Mann's own entries in the surviving diaries make clear the burdens he felt in the years of his success.)[180] After a quarter of an hour, Aschenbach sets work aside, neglecting part of his "duty," to survey the scene at the beach. At its center, of course, is the captivating boy, whose name—Tadzio—he soon divines and who increasingly attracts his "fatherly" attention.

"Fatherly," of course, is Aschenbach's own word, used to normalize his feelings as he looks on at the seaside panorama.[181] The attraction to Tadzio must be assimilated to the standards of bourgeois decency to which he has dedicated his literary gifts, either in the fashion of the dinner-table reflections, vague musings on form and beauty, or in the guise of permissible (paternal) admiration. Later in the day, however, as Aschenbach resumes his normal routine, taking tea on the Piazza San Marco and following it with the standard afternoon walk, he becomes dimly aware that Venice is not restoring him to a condition in which he can resume his labors. In another quick decision, he makes plans to leave—and the old discipline starts to revive in his resistance to the spell of the city.

On the morning of his departure, however, he delays, setting his own official plans at risk, and as he arrives at the station, his will is completely defeated by itself. Mann's narrative suddenly assumes the immediacy of the present tense, evoking Aschenbach's confusion and distress. "Completely torn, he enters the station. It is very late; he has no time to lose if he wishes to catch the train. He wants to [or wills to do this] and he wants not to [wills the opposite]. [*Er will es und will es nicht.*]"[182] To will contradictory things is to guarantee the defeat of the will, but the contingent misdirection of the baggage provides Aschenbach with the chance to fathom his deeper wishes, and he returns to the lido with "wild joy." From his hotel window, he sees Tadzio below on the beach and understands why the departure had been so painful for him. He raises his hands in a relaxed gesture of welcome and calm acceptance.

At this point, a reader might think that the failure of the trip to fulfill its original purpose ought to be evident to Aschenbach himself—but that is to ignore the strategies of self-deception that enable him to disguise the character of his feelings and thus provide further opportunities for the sapping of the will. Being in Tadzio's presence has come to be accepted as a goal, but, in the character of the musings at the first night's dinner, one that will promote his earlier object of restoring himself to artistic service. Self-deception survives the potential revelation of the confused attempt at flight. Aschenbach's frayed literary creativity, devotedly classical as it has striven to be, can be repaired and renewed by returning to the living source, to the joyous apprehension of pure beauty. The style of the fourth chapter, its classical allusions expressing Aschenbach's own sense of living a Greek idyll, enters into the form of his self-misunderstanding. Echoing Socrates, he tells himself that "only beauty is visible and worthy of love"—Mann amends only very slightly the words of the German translation of the *Phaedrus* he read[183]—and that the perception of beauty is the means to the work of the intellect (or spirit—*Geist*). Inspired by this thought, Aschenbach decides to write, his apparently new topic ("a burning problem of culture")[184] approached with erotic pleasure in language. The aftermath, however, finds him exhausted, as if after debauchery.

Self-deception begins to crumble, as the conception of his delight in Tadzio's presence as a pure renewal of sensitivity to classical beauty proves at odds with the feelings provoked. So, too, with the thought that Aschenbach's relation to the boy can be slid into the standard compartments of approved bourgeois conduct. On the morning following his sudden impulse to write, he forms the intention to normalize his connection to Tadzio, to lay a—fatherly?—hand on the boy's shoulder and engage him in brief conversation. His will fails him, and he becomes aware of an instinctive burning up of the discipline that has been central to his existence—the discipline recently imitated, or perhaps parodied, by his construction of a daily routine in which mornings are dedicated to the beachside contemplation of beauty.

The emotions felt in the wake of his writing and after the failure to speak to Tadzio—the sense of guilt, the agitation—echo the confusion Aschenbach had felt at the railway station. Try as he may to preserve the classical idyll, the mythical resonances turn in ambiguous and dangerous directions. Finally, after an evening on which the Poles have not appeared at dinner, Aschenbach is pacing restlessly in front of the hotel, when the family returns. Perhaps prompted by the older man's own unprepared expression of joy and admiration, Tadzio smiles at him, a smile that so shakes and disarms Aschenbach that, rushing into the garden, he confesses to himself his love for the boy.[185]

From the loosening of his will to pursue the central project of his life—his painstakingly crafted writing—Aschenbach has taken on the objective of being in Tadzio's presence as an allegedly secondary end, one that will restore his capacity for artistic service. The illusion is shattered by the smile. Henceforth, he must admit that his will is independently directed toward Tadzio, but, even as he modifies his behavior to follow the Polish family in their walks through the city, he need not yet concede that this objective takes precedence. Only when it becomes clear that remaining in Tadzio's presence requires an act of concealment on his part, only when he repudiates the attitudes that had constituted his mature self, by explicitly rejecting what he sees as a purifying and decent form of behavior, by explicitly endorsing the deceit of the Venetian authorities, and by recognizing his own complicity in their guilt, only then does he break with his earlier values. It is an open-eyed rejection of what he has been: "What were art and virtue worth to him, compared with the advantages of chaos? [Was galt ihm noch Kunst und Tugend gegenüber den Vorteilen des Chaos?]."

6

My presentation of Mann's anatomy of the breakdown of discipline deliberately highlights particular episodes and concepts, tracing the ways in which Aschenbach's *will* is directed and redirected and understanding the changes in terms of their deviations from his central conception of himself and of what is valuable. These formulations connect Mann with questions explored by Schopenhauer and Nietzsche, with the former's sense of the impossibility of realizing a vision of one's life that would give it worth, particularly with the diagnosis in terms of the blindness and rapacity of the will, and the latter's delineation of the difficulties imposed by culture and history on those who aspire to live well. My summary hopes to make plausible the thought that *Death in Venice* exhibits the second grade of philosophical involvement, that it can be read as simultaneously showing, in the milieu of haute bourgeois society, the inevitable failure and frustration of the individual will and the contradiction within the ascetic ideal.

Or something more . . . ? For Mann does not simply take over from Schopenhauer the idiosyncratic "correction" of Kantian metaphysics, nor does the asceticism exemplified in his protagonist quite correspond to the categories and judgments offered by Nietzsche. In Mann's Venice, the philosophical landscape is importantly—and ambiguously—transformed.

Schopenhauer founds his pessimism on a particular development of transcendental idealism, one that sees the world of our experience as an illusion—the veil of Maia, as he often calls it, with a gesture at the Indian philosophy that so impresses him. Behind the veil is the world of real entities, mischaracterized by Kant as "noumena" but properly seen as undifferentiated Will. Not only do Mann's annotations of *The World as Will and Representation* show no great interest in this heady and obscure metaphysical picture, but there is no trace of it in *Death in Venice*, not even when Aschenbach's ruminations are least well focused. Schopenhauer's "Will," undifferentiated and objectified in myriad ways from magnets to men, is replaced by the psychologically familiar will of a complex and sensitive human protagonist. Mann conceded that he had made use of philosophical ideas in ways that were foreign to his sources, and one of his important transformations was to turn Schopenhauer the metaphysician into "the psychologist of the will"—an eminently pardonable transformation given Schopenhauer's propensity to exploit the ordinary connotations of his chosen metaphysical term "Will."[186]

In fact, Schopenhauer can be read—or creatively misread?—in ways both less metaphysically charged and pertinent to the themes of the novella, specifically to the breakdown of discipline traced in the previous section. Book 4 of *The World of Will and Representation* oscillates between claims about the world's metaphysical structure and theses about the character of values: in Reality, the world is Will; values are constituted by the ethical stance, which transcends the boundaries dividing individuals to achieve deep and enduring sympathy. A reader sensitive to that oscillation, a reader who had been much moved by book 4—Thomas Mann, perhaps—might recognize an opportunity for "correcting" Schopenhauer, as Schopenhauer claimed to have "corrected" Kant. The world of experience, this reader might suggest, is one in which objects are marked as valuable, as worth pursuing: Aschenbach lives in a world divided, apparently naturally, into the worthy and the unworthy, the desirable and the undesirable, the beautiful and the squalid. To conceive the world in that way—as Aschenbach does, as Mann's readers do, and as Mann himself typically does—is an illusion. For the markings, the signs of "value" that prevail among any group of individuals or in any individual's experiences are the results of prior decisions and aspirations based on sympathies that are inevitably incomplete and partial. Instincts and desires press chaotically in different directions. Rival yearnings take precedence at different times. Desire once satisfied leads either to a new act of will or else to boredom. Nothing remains permanently or stably valued—the ideal condition of deep or enduring sympathy is unattainable. In consequence, any attempt an individual makes to force the will in a particular direction, to set a goal that will last, must bridle the conflicting desires that urge rival courses of action. Because of the strength of some forms of the will, particularly the sexual drive, disciplined control is impossible, and the best response is to rise to so clear an awareness of life as a condition of permanent striving, of endless suffering, that one recognizes the need for compassion with all those who experience the unceasing conflicts of desire, even if *feeling* that unbounded compassion and *acting from it* are impossible for us.

The philosophical view just outlined is not Schopenhauer's—it amends him in fundamental ways, just as he amended Kant (although by abandoning the basic metaphysics rather than reframing it)—but it retains important themes from *The World as Will and Representation*, setting them more univocally in the psychological idiom toward which book 4 so often tends. Instead of thinking of the human organism as permeated by the operation of Will at different levels, generating an "enduring struggle" between our higher aspirations and the "lower forms" of Will present in our physical and chemical constitution, the psychological conflicts that assail us can be recognized without dabbling in their "ultimate causes"—as Mann pointedly does by identifying the sexual drive as a paradigm of our internal division, interpreting Schopenhauer as "tortured" by the power of his sexual urges, which constituted a "diabolical disturbance" of his efforts to achieve pure contemplation and the abnegation of the will.[187] Schopenhauer often presents the thesis that the satisfaction of desire is transitory as a self-standing psychological claim: "possession takes the charm away: the wish reappears in a new form, the felt need recurs."[188] He declares that values arise from acts of willing that express the particular features of the individual: instead of recognizing something as good and wanting it on the basis of our recognition, our will leads us in various directions, and we label our (fleeting) ends as good.[189] To the extent that human beings can modify their aspirations through genuine understanding, they do so by taking on a condition of universal sympathy, in which the sufferings of all others are felt as keenly as their own, and, because this state is unbearable—it is as if we were forced to go over burning coals, with never an opportunity to rest in a cool place—the only option is asceticism, the abnegation of the will, and the first step is the conquest of the sexual impulses.[190] The metaphysics goes; the psychological theses remain.

Aschenbach does not operate in a world of illusory *objects*: the gondolas, the strawberries, and the red bow on Tadzio's swimsuit are all perfectly real. He lives, however, in a world permeated by values and attributed significance. The elderly fop is disgusting, and Aschenbach wonders how his comrades tolerate him; the scene at the beach, even before Tadzio appears, is peaceful and satisfying.[191] His fellow guests at the hotel and the large international public that applauds his writing would surely share these judgments, treating them as natural and "proper." Aschenbach, who has repudiated bohemianism, has thought more deeply about what is worthwhile and has made a conscious decision not only to endorse judgments of this kind but to articulate and to defend them, to make them clear and luminous for bourgeois society as a whole. He is, like his ancestors, a public servant, even a soldier, who guards the culture others take for granted, who understands possible challenges to it and dedicates his writing—and his life—to combating them. Or, to vary the comparison, he is akin to the Platonic philosopher-guardians whose informed judgments make the worthwhile life possible for the many who do not probe or question. He has taken some of the steps Schopenhauer envisages, guiding his conduct not by thoughtless assimilation of the values accepted around him but by considering and endorsing the cultural tradition in which he stands. Aware of the fragility of that tradition, he devotes himself to maintaining it and, in so doing, translates a broad sympathy for the unreflective *Bürger* (Tonio Kröger's "blond and blue-eyed ones") into a disciplined—ascetic—life.

Aschenbach treads a path to asceticism, but he does not reach the state Schopenhauer envisages. He does not abnegate the Will. Rather, he endeavors to force his will in a particular direction, one in which egoism gives way to concern for a wider form of human life and extended sympathies become frozen in a sense of duty. In his maturity, he acquiesces in the moral principles of his society, aspiring to an art that will support them, whose beauty will be a means of moral education and inspiration. The novella shows us how the asceticism is undermined. On a Schopenhauerian reading, we could view the anatomy of Aschenbach's decline as vividly exemplifying the claim that, even in a sensitive and self-conscious person, the orderly channeling of the will toward stably valued objects is impossible. It is, of course, especially apt, given the prominence of the destructive power of sex in Schopenhauer (especially as Mann read him), that Aschenbach's decline is brought about through the revival of his sexuality.

Similarly, Aschenbach's discipline, the asceticism that falters and collapses in Venice, can be read through a Nietzschean lens, even though it does not conform to any of the types into which Nietzsche divides the ascetic ideal. Aschenbach is a writer, an artist, but it would be uncharitable to characterize him as Nietzsche contemptuously does as a "valet of some form of morality or philosophy or religion."[192] Even if he serves as protector of the values of bourgeois society, the role has been deliberately chosen, alternatives have been canvassed and even experienced, before the turn away from "sympathy with the abyss."[193] Perhaps he has not thought things through with the keenness of that "steely-eyed knight," Schopenhauer, a man able to find his own self-conception, but Aschenbach, like Nietzsche's ascetic philosopher, sacrifices delights others take for granted to the daily demands of his routine ("his rigid, cold, and passionate duty"), thereby affirming his choice of role.[194] Like the ascetic priest, the writer dedicates himself to the care and cure of a potentially sick society—for him, the artist's role is to educate the community and to cure it of its moral ambiguities, its tendencies to laxity.[195] Aschenbach's striking discipline testifies to his faith in "the blessing of work" and the curative power of "mechanical activity," remedies prescribed by the priest-physician.[196] For Nietzsche's ascetic priest, of course, life is validated not through its mundane qualities but in its relation to something beyond, something transcendent, and the ascetic life becomes a "bridge" to this further entity. Although Aschenbach shares in the fin-de-siècle turn away from faith in transcendent deities, his Platonic sympathies incline him to a similar picture of his own life: the artist, too, points to "entities beyond," to wisdom and goodness, entities only apprehended through beauty. Artists search for wisdom, not what the world thinks of as "knowledge," "science," or "truth," for, echoing Nietzsche, Aschenbach has turned away from the fourth (and last) form of the ascetic ideal, perhaps the "noblest," but also one attuned to a society in decline, to people possessed by a propensity for self-belittlement, to an age in which it is all too easy to succumb to moral laxity: for the sciences offer a cheerless prospect of human life and worth, one that James captures in his bleak image.[197]

Aschenbach's discipline, his solitary struggles to serve as an artist— as his austere ancestors have served in their own roles—his attempt to achieve complete purity of language, his self-deceived recapitulation of Socratic views about beauty as a means, present him as a composite of exemplars of Nietzschean versions of the ascetic ideal. So, just as the novella can be read as a concrete presentation of Schopenhauer's theses about the will—shorn of their metaphysical underpinnings and developed psychologically—it can also be taken as a many-sided elaboration of Nietzsche's treatment of asceticism, one that vividly shows the self-mutilations asserted in the philosophical treatment. Better still, in accordance with Mann's own sense of the creative writer as making his own "strange brew" of ingredients borrowed from a passionate reading of philosophy, *Death in Venice* can stand as an original piece of philosophy, one that modifies and mixes themes from both influential predecessors and demonstrates their shared conclusion about the difficulty, if not impossibility, of finding value in human life. Aschenbach's iron discipline might be viewed as an attempt to live a worthwhile life—a *heroic* attempt, for Nietzsche recognizes the striving for self-affirmation that moves some of the figures he considers—but, in the end, it is undercut by the ways in which the culture and tradition in which he stands have framed the writer's efforts, foisted upon him ideals he cannot live by—and thus it inevitably fails.

So far, so plausible. Mann begins to emerge as an original philosopher, one who explores positions related to, but distinct from, those of the thinkers whose ideas he borrows. Yet there is more. The voice of the previous paragraph is, like that of the moralistic judge at the fountain, an explicitly philosophizing narrative voice. In this case, it presents the views of an outsider who observes the frailty of the lives of those who live lightly, and it assesses them from a vantage point to which they do not aspire. Voices of this sort are heard often in Mann's fiction, and they belong to figures who look on, hungrily, at a world from which they are excluded. Tonio Kröger's comparison should be remembered: they are like those "specially prepared" papal singers. Perhaps, then, there is room for ironic distance, a separation of the philosophical summary from the novella, a distance that will allow us to see what the case of Aschenbach actually *shows*.


7


In defending the idea of a third grade of philosophical involvement, I proposed that the important philosophical contribution of art, of fiction, or drama, or music might lie not in the *saying* but the *showing*. Connecting Mann's novella to themes in Schopenhauer or Nietzsche, revealing how he mixes and amends their ideas, is not itself problematic, but it easily seduces us into accepting a conclusion analogous to theirs. It is profitable to read Mann as *presenting* these themes for his readers' reflection, but I want to resist the thought that he should be taken to *endorse* them or that he intends his readers to make any such judgments. Our reaction to Aschenbach *might* be to conclude that he exemplifies the thought of the unruliness of the will, the inevitable failure of human attempts to define and pursue values, or some contradiction at the heart of the ascetic ideal. Before we arrive at that evaluation, however, we might reflect on the ways in which Mann frames the anatomy of Aschenbach's decline.

The "obituary" chapter informs us that Aschenbach already emerged as a writer in his late teens and early twenties. A decade later, his fame had grown to the extent of making it necessary to provide only short replies to the many letters addressed to him—and, in the dedication to his correspondence, there are already signs of that disciplined routine we associate with him. Supposing that the raw mistakes of his youth were made during this first period, it would follow that at least two decades of his life were devoted to the disciplined pursuit of his art and that these decades were those in which he produced the four major works attributed to him, through the daily accumulation of small insights, the painstaking and often painful crafting of exquisitely elegant sentences. Viewed more globally, then, this is a life dominated by *successful* application of a constant will, by an asceticism that maintains itself. The novella is largely devoted to a period of a few weeks, an epilogue to Aschenbach's career. It is an *episode*, one that surely does not fit well with the overall pattern of his career. Does the fact of a problematic ending necessarily invalidate the shape or nullify the worth of a human life? In what ways has Aschenbach actually failed, and in what precisely does his failure consist? What alternative, if any, is revealed in Venice to disclose the inadequacy of the values by which he has lived?

Those who think seriously about medical policies and about the best use of the resources provided by our increased understanding of the human body and its frailties often recognize the extraordinary disconnection between life and the process of dying, a disconnection that contemporary medicine permits and even encourages. With a tangle of tubes and a clutter of machines we strive officiously to keep alive people who have lost the psychological and physical capacities that were once central to their sense of themselves. They gain extra hours and days, even months and years, a prolonged existence sharply at odds with what they were, what they wanted to become, and with the reflective judgments they would have made about how medicine should be employed for human benefit. As the ancients already appreciated, part of living a good life is having a good death, and there is no doubt that some contemporary deaths are protracted enough to cast a shadow over the life that came before—many thoughtful people rightly fear the incongruity of a terminal mode of existence they could never endorse as their own.

To cast a shadow is not, however, to nullify the value of the person's life and its accomplishments. Those who observe the lingering of the shell of someone they have loved are rightly pained and appalled by the contrast between the vital past and the horribly diminished present— yet, when it is all over, the vivid sense of the beloved returns, and the person lives on in memory, defined by the aspirations and actions that preceded the mockery of the final stage. That stage becomes an episode, a regrettable period tacked on to a life whose value—or lack of it—is determined by quite other considerations.

Mann's sensitivity to life is at its sharpest in his sensibility toward death, and some of the most penetrating moments in his fiction focus on deaths at odds with the lives that came before. His novels contain relatives of the medical examples I have chosen in my efforts to liberate from premature philosophizing our thinking about Aschenbach's death: the death of the Frau Konsulin in *Buddenbrooks* and the lingering of Adrian Leverkühn after his collapse in *Doktor Faustus*. In neither instance, I suggest, does the character of the end of the life play a decisive role in assessing its worth.

Bethsy Buddenbrook, née Kröger, we are told, "made, like all the Krögers, an extremely elegant appearance"[198]—her early life is that of one of the great society ladies in the small but prosperous commercial town (modeled on Lübeck) in which she resides. After the death of her pious husband, however, she turns away from the social sphere, honoring his memory by her own new-found religious zeal. Her death begins quietly, with symptoms that might well signal an ordinary respiratory infection, but builds in a long crescendo of pain. As her trajectory toward death becomes undeniable, the family assembles at her bedside:

> The movements of the sick woman had increased. A terrible unrest, an inexpressible fear and sense of need, an inescapable feeling of being abandoned and of helplessness without limits, must have filled this body, destined for death, from the top of the head to the soles of the feet. Her eyes, these poor, beseeching eyes, complaining of pain and seeking relief, sometimes closed with the rustling motions of the head from side to side, sometimes opened with a

shattered expression or widened so much that the little veins of the eyeballs bulged red with blood. Yet there was no lapse into unconsciousness![199]

The hypersensitive Christian cannot endure the scene and stumbles out, appalled at the travesty of his mother's life displayed in its closing.

The grotesque death of the Frau Konsulin is entirely at odds with the elegance of her early life and the piety of her widowhood. Yet the discord between the living of her life and the painful mode of leaving it does not nullify its potential value. What we make of Bethsy Buddenbrook—and what those who survive her make of her—depends on the success of what came before. Was her care for her family and its elegant traditions, for the society in which she achieved her prominence, enough to make her existence worthwhile? Was her devotion to the charitable work of the church and to its evangelical mission sufficient? If the circumstances of her death are pertinent in taking up these questions, that is because they provoke reflections on the transience of some of the qualities she has exemplified: the woman whose head moves chaotically on the pillow has lost all the grace and elegance the Konsulin so carefully preserved; the piety appears to bring little relief in her suffering (although there are ambiguities in her final words to the beloved dead whom she thinks of herself as joining). The shadow cast by this death does not deprive the life of value but, at most, calls to our attention those features of it that *antecedently* undermined its worth: perhaps the ephemeral nature of the social distinctions the young Bethsy Kröger and Bethsy Buddenbrook had enjoyed, perhaps the shallowness of a religious commitment induced by modification of her social role. By the same token, the closing episode of Aschenbach's life might be viewed as bringing into prominence characteristics of his career that raise doubts about its success.

Adrian Leverkühn is, like Aschenbach, an artist, one whose life ends in an episode quite at odds with the twenty-four-year period of his creativity. After his collapse at the soirée whose official rationale is the presentation of his final oratorio—the *Lamentation of Faustus*—Leverkühn is delivered over to maternal care, first to his landlady and "surrogate mother," Frau Schweigestill, and then to "Jonathan Leverkühn's brown-eyed widow," who takes her "lost [literally, "gone astray"] son back to his childhood."[200] He lives on for ten years in his reduced condition. According to his biographer, Serenus Zeitblom, there are reasons to think that residues of the composer's former dignity caused him to be vaguely aware of his state and to be horrified by it, prodding him to attempt suicide.[201] Halfway through the decade in which he lingers toward death, Zeitblom sees him again, on the occasion of Leverkühn's fiftieth birthday, when the former composer presents to his long-time friend a face devoid of recognition, an "Ecce Homo face" whose mouth is "opened in pain" and whose eyes are "unseeing."[202]

There is little temptation to suppose that the terrible reduction of Leverkühn's last decade negates the value of his accomplishments any more than the similar fate that befell Nietzsche undermines the worth of the life preceding his collapse. These endings are travesties as grotesque as the close of the life of the Frau Konsulin, and they are far more protracted. Yet they raise no serious questions: rather, as Zeitblom accurately sees and rightly fears, what threatens the project of his friend's life is the possibility that his music will vanish, that the political circumstances of the times have deprived it of the chance to attain its proper place in the musical culture of Germany and the world. Moreover, unlike the death of Frau Buddenbrook, Leverkühn's collapse is not fortuitous: it is intimately connected with his artistic creativity, the reckoning he must pay for his extraordinary achievements.[203] Of course, readers must rely on Zeitblom's judgment that those achievements are the work of genius, but, whatever else this eminently decent biographer may have been deceived about, it is hard not to trust him on this point.

Aschenbach, by contrast, receives no such detailed account of his artistic works, and the voice of the "obituary" is measured and not that of a friend whose homage and dedication are unswerving.[204] Consequently, there is more space to wonder if this final episode exposes something lacking in the writings of his maturity, that the infatuation and the death to which it leads reveal that the "obituary" judgments are flawed or overblown.[205] Over ten years before conceiving *Death in Venice*, Mann had already explored the possibility that a final episode might undermine a life centered on dedication to art.

The eponymous central character of "*Der kleine Herr Friedemann*," left at the age of one month in the charge of a nurse with a liking for the bottle, fell from the changing table, and the accident distorted his physical development. Learning, as he grows through adolescence, that young women, however friendly and sympathetic, will never feel any romantic sparks for him, he reconciles himself to a life of physical comfort ministered to by his unmarried sisters, of respectable work, and, above all, of immersion in the arts. On his thirtieth birthday, as he sits in the garden with a book on his knee, looking up into the sunny sky, he reflects: "That has been thirty years. Now will come perhaps ten more, or even twenty, God alone knows. They will quietly arrive and pass by, just as years past have done, and I look forward to them with peace of mind [*Seelenfrieden*]."[206] Little Friedemann's serenity is shattered by the arrival in town of a married woman for whom he develops a violent passion. Thinking back on the contented musings of his thirtieth birthday, he understands the peace he has lost and knows that, despite his efforts to defend his quiet contentment, he is now gripped with an "irresistible force," one that will drive him into "the abyss."[207] There is no holding back. Conscious of his own folly, he reveals his adoration, is curtly rebuffed, and, in humiliation and self-disgust, drowns himself.[208]

Friedemann's life *is* negated by its ending. He sees—and the reader understands—that the serenity he had worked to acquire was a second best, that he had reconciled himself to a "twilight existence" without light and shadows.[209] The fatal passion exposes that.

Does the same hold for Aschenbach, too? Was Mann recapitulating themes from his pre-*Buddenbrooks* period, albeit on a larger and more complex scale? There are important differences, both in the patterns of the previous life and the character of the passions evoked at their ending. Little Friedemann is an amateur, a consumer of the arts, whereas Aschenbach has been a distinguished creator; Friedemann's yearning is for a relationship that might have all the dimensions of a marriage, that might have proved the enduring center of the life he might have had (but for the negligence of the nurse and the crippling fall); Tadzio points to nothing similar.[210] Once we have freed ourselves from the overly simple idea that Aschenbach's response to the boy's beauty reveals the Dionysian tendencies he has repressed, tendencies essential to Truly Great Art, there is no basis for concluding that the incidents on the lido disclose the worthlessness of the disciplined work of creation that has filled his mature years.

Yet, as I have recognized (in section 5), for a period toward the end of his life, the discipline is broken. Like Friedemann and Leverkühn but unlike the Frau Konsulin, Aschenbach is active in his own decline. At the moment when he gives precedence to remaining in Tadzio's presence, he explicitly disavows the values he has hitherto embraced. That is, to be sure, a blotch on his life, a disfigurement that detracts from its overall worth and success. We might consider, however, whether this is decisive for negating *all* value. Here it is instructive to compare Aschenbach with a fourth example from Mann's fiction.

Whatever the ambiguities of *Der Zauberberg* — and they are legion[211] — the verdict on Hans Castorp's cousin, Joachim Ziemssen, seems secure. Joachim dies as a "good soldier," and he is honored, in the flatland, by a military salute fired over his grave.[212] Throughout the early chapters, like Aschenbach (and his ancestors), Ziemssen shows an impeccable discipline, following carefully and conscientiously the steps prescribed for the cure of his tuberculosis. Hans's flexible responses to the alluring but morally ambiguous Frau Chauchat contrast with his cousin's determined resistance to the charms of their tablemate, Marusja, of the swelling bosom and the orange-scented handkerchief. Yet the discipline is broken. As his "sentence" to remain in the sanatorium extends, he becomes impatient to take up his military life. Advised by Hofrat Behrens that he must "serve" another five or six months, he announces his decision to leave. Behrens is blunt about Joachim's condition and about the risks he is incurring: he tells the impatient young man that he is "throwing down his arms" and "deserting."[213] Joachim persists. He joins his regiment, begins his military duties, takes part in maneuvers — and becomes sick, intermittently at first. Then his mother telegraphs that she is bringing the young soldier back to the mountains. He dies there.

Despite the Hofrat's blunt words, Joachim's single revolt against discipline cannot be seen as a fatal undermining of the value of his life. Even if imperfect, his devotion to duty — his discipline — is admirable. He dies as a good soldier. In its contours, the pattern of his life is strikingly akin to Aschenbach's: there are years of self-denying dedication to a chosen ideal — and a single fatal lapse from duty. Why, then, suppose that the cases are to be evaluated differently, that the distinguished author's decades of devotion to his art are invalidated by the brief seduction of the last weeks?

Aschenbach's moral lapse is, in fact, inconsequential. He does not gain from it what he had unrealistically fantasized (if it should even be seen as a serious fantasy), a Venice in which only he and Tadzio were left alive; indeed, he obtains no more than a few days' reprieve before the Poles depart. His failure to warn has no impact on their well-being. Indeed, one could have suspected as much, for Tadzio and his sisters are under the watchful eye of a governess, so that the chances of their eating contaminated food—overripe strawberries, for example—are extremely low. Joachim Ziemssen, by contrast, drastically curtails his own life by his decision to leave the sanatorium. If we see this, as we should, as an *excusable* rebellion against his high ideals of service, can we simultaneously suppose that Aschenbach's concealment of the truth signifies a form of corruption that negates everything he has done and been?

Joachim's life goes on after the impetuous decision to return to the "flatland." Equally, so does Aschenbach's after his moral and physical collapse. The coda to *Death in Venice* reveals him learning of the impending separation from Tadzio. He nods, acquiescing, and, with what can be viewed as the renewal of his discipline, resumes his place on the beach. Horrified by Jaschu's subjugation of Tadzio, he wishes finally to intervene, but, at just that moment, the boy is released. As Tadzio stands on the sandbar, Aschenbach looks on, "*as at first*,"[214] when he had originally exchanged glances with the boy. In these last moments of his life, there are hints that the frenzy has passed, of a calmer mood and a return to his former self.

Hints only. I shall have more to say in chapter 3 about this closing scene, but for now I want to note a significant feature of the novella. It is framed, in the first sentence and the last, with a reference to Aschenbach's, *von* Aschenbach's, eminence. The coda abandons the moralizing—scornful—voice of the previous sentences. It begins with a recapitulation of his ennobled status and ends with the "shocked respectful world" learning of his death. In a sense, nothing has changed. This episode leaves no reverberations. Aschenbach has written virtually nothing more, one and a half pages on the "burning cultural problem," and his reputation remains unaffected.

Unless, of course, he has, like Mann, confided his yearnings to *Tagebücher*, or until, some decades later, an aging Polish gentleman discloses his identity.[215] The final piece of prose, apparently, betrays no change. It is certainly good, remarks the moralizing narrator, that the literary world only recognizes the beautiful work and not its sources—having, of course, just divulged the circumstances of and inspiration for Aschenbach's last writing.[216] We can, I suggest, distance ourselves from this earnest voice, with its determination to bring into the foreground of the writer's life its last few weeks; we can insist that the life be seen as a whole and be grateful that these closing disfigurements occurred in a confined, even a quarantined, space.

To do that is to read Mann as responding to the complex of problems he adopted from Schopenhauer and Nietzsche but to see him as offering his own distinctive treatment of it. We can interpret him as making his own modifications of their judgments and evaluations, as providing his own seductive presentation of a conclusion akin to theirs, and as inviting us to reflect on his vivid example, to test the pessimistic assessment that comes so easily. Perhaps the test will prompt us to rethink. Perhaps it is *hard* to live a worthwhile life, but there is no inevitable disruption of the will, no contradiction in the ascetic ideal. Perhaps Gustav von Aschenbach is not to be conceived as a failure: the events of his death might be a minor deviation from the hard-won but triumphant perseverance of his life. We are easily persuaded into concluding that this death, so intricately presented to us, must negate what went before—but the larger invitation is to reflect on the exquisite presentation and judge Aschenbach for ourselves. If we accept the invitation, we may discover that *Death in Venice* is a more ironic work than is usually supposed. The disciplined life, even the imperfectly disciplined life, may be worth living.

# TWO

# Beauty

1

Early in Ibsen's *Pillars of the Community*, the schoolmaster Rorlund borrows a famous New Testament phrase to characterize the large towns of the modern era: they present a beautiful exterior, but it only serves to conceal the rottenness within—they and their most respectable citizens are "whited sepulchres" full of "uncleanness."[1] Even if the suggestions of the previous chapter might permit the judgment that Aschenbach's *art* lends worth to his life, important questions about his social persona are left unanswered. For Aschenbach is not only the celebrant and defender of bourgeois values but one who has claimed to embody those values in his conduct. His obsessive passion for Tadzio reveals him to be a sham, an unworthy descendant of those severe ancestors whom he has attempted to emulate—as with Ibsen's protagonist, Karsten Bernick (and many other Ibsen characters), the pleasing appearance masks the "uncleanness": Aschenbach is distinguished from Bernick only by the fact that his mumbled and self-serving "confession" at the fountain is far less honest and courageous than Bernick's forthright final acknowledgment of what he has done and been.

A less moralistic narrator, one who did not repudiate the maxim that "to understand all is to forgive all,"[2] might appraise the mismatch between the writer's desires and his conduct differently, not diagnosing any "foulness within" but seeing instead the deformation wreaked upon a sensitive but potentially healthy individual by a rigid and uncomprehending society. Aschenbach would emerge as a victim, a man forced to conform to prejudices about the limits of acceptable human nature and permissible conduct. His own acquiescence in the prejudices, the identification with the ancestors and the narrow values they defended, would be seen as emphasizing the intensity of the forces working to confine and distort him and the depth of their penetration.

Yet wherever the fault is taken to lie, in proclivities so "unnatural" they must be concealed or in social judgments so uninformed by understanding of human psychology and so inflexible in their application that they twist the lives of those unlucky enough to be at odds with them, the envisaged unity between artist and citizen, at least in this case, has broken down. Aschenbach fails to advance beyond Tonio Kröger's predicament — he does not achieve that deeper identification in which the writer not only endorses and defends the bourgeois values but successfully lives them as well.

Mann's two writer-protagonists reject Nietzsche's condemnation of the "decent citizens," the *Bürger*, as inevitably limited and crippled, part of a herd whose lives are worthless. To the figure of Zarathustra dancing on the mountains, Tonio counterposes the images of Hans Hansen and Ingeborg Holm dancing in a Danish resort. Even to have written *The World as Will and Representation* or to have composed nine symphonies (presumably Beethoven's) would pale, Tonio Kröger thinks, beside the achievement of their living.[3] These joyful bourgeois figures, Hans and Inge, are oblivious to the higher beauties art claims to discern or to create (Hans, rightly, reads books about horses rather than Schiller's *Don Carlos*), but they embody beauty.[4] Observing them, Tonio Kröger is moved to his Credo: although he, the artist, has seen the confusion of human life, its tragedy and absurdity, his deepest love is for those who are unconscious of these realities, for the "lightly living ones" whose philosophically innocent lives are beautiful. For Aschenbach, too, the elegant lives he observes on the lido and in the strange, ambiguous city appear as parts of an elysian landscape to which he has been magically translated, where a wonderful lightness of living is given to humanity—and where beauty is embodied in Tadzio.[5]

*Death in Venice* apparently follows *Tonio Kröger* in presenting the split between artist and citizen, a split reminiscent of Plato's famous story of the division of humankind related in the *Symposium*.[6] The artist is sensitive to the sources of value in human life, able to contemplate life's beauties and to create beautiful representations of them. The citizens who live well embody those beauties in their lives—lightly, thoughtlessly, carelessly. No individual can manage both—even those who live well, live incompletely. Hence any attempt to go beyond what Tonio, the self-conscious outsider, already achieves must involve pretense, must be a confidence trick—a visit behind the scenes to the actor's dressing room would reveal the repulsive spots under the costume. Aschenbach cannot be the good citizen he seems.

Important to the success of the novella was Mann's skill in allowing his readers to observe the split from either side. His sardonic reassurance to Philipp Witkop that his story was "very respectable" expresses itself in a narrative voice, that of the moralistic "second narrator," who issues the orthodox judgments and permits readers to think that Mann, like Aschenbach, buttresses the Approved Moral Point of View.[7] Yet the novella can be read—probably always has been read by those with a less intolerant view of Aschenbach's latent predilections—as a depiction of the deformation of a once-vulnerable youth who has been compelled, throughout his life, to confine and deny central elements in his character. Those who combine this latter interpretation with a reading of Mann's surviving diaries will understand how closely Aschenbach's sense of self-distortion resembles that felt by his creator. They will recognize Mann's fidelity to the demand that the writer who is to be of service must place himself on trial.[8]

Connected though it surely is with his earlier fiction, *Death in Venice* should not, however, be regarded as a simple reprise of themes Mann had presented before: it is no more a recapitulation of *Tonio Kröger* (the Artist, even one who admires the Bourgeois World, is inevitably an Outsider) any more than it is a repeat of *"Der kleine Herr Friedemann"* (Discipline undone by Passion—again). If the later novella goes further, it is (as the last chapter proposed) because there are significant differences between Aschenbach's years of discipline and their fruits and the tepid serenity Friedemann attains—and because *Death in Venice* probes a relation *Tonio Kröger* takes as given. From the first tense moments in which Tonio fears that Hans Hansen will not join him for the walk home from school, Tonio is presented as an outsider: it is no surprise when his letter to Lisaweta confesses that he stands between two worlds.[9] Aschenbach successfully masquerades as a bourgeois—he "passes" well enough that the unctuous manager of the Hotel des Bains ascends with him to show him his room. On the face of it, however, the writer's failure to fit into conventional society, for all his apparent success, has nothing to do with his role as *artist*: the incompatibility between artist and citizen, presupposed by Tonio Kröger (and by *Tonio Kröger*), is irrelevant to the issue. The elements of Aschenbach's life do not fit together; his literary work and its aims are concordant with the persona he presents but not with the person he is—but the clash stems from his repressed homosexuality. Mann apparently decided on a change of theme, turning his attention to the plight of the closeted homosexual (or bisexual) male in prewar Wilhelmine Germany.

Or did he? In turning from the disciplined artist to the socially embedded man, I have already slightly amended the philosophical perspective that dominated the previous chapter: there the focus was on potential sources of value in human lives; here the issues have been posed in terms of values in general and of a specific value—beauty. Echoing the most famous sentence of Nietzsche's first work—"Only as an aesthetic phenomenon is existence and the world finally justified"[10]—I have suggested the quasi-Platonic split: the artist *perceives* value and its beauty and *renders* what is valuable beautifully visible; the "blond and blue-eyed ones" *live* beautifully. *Death in Venice* explores the tension between artist and citizen, a tension taken for granted in *Tonio Kröger*, in terms of this perspective on the central philosophical question, a perspective that understands worthwhile lives as possessing beauty, as being themselves works of art. Citizens and artists whose lives appear to go well stand in different—complementary—relationships to beauty, but the relations necessarily exclude one another. To reveal the inevitability of exclusion, *Death in Venice* presents an apparent possibility of transcending the split between artist and citizen, a possibility heavily dependent on ideas in

Plato and his successors,[11] one that must ultimately fail. Although failure can be dramatically exhibited in an older man who is drawn to the beauty of a boy—a case of *Knabenliebe*—the homoerotic resonances only heighten the drama. The plot Mann discarded, the story of the seventy-four-year-old Goethe's infatuation for the teenage Ulrike von Levetzov, would have sounded, if less strongly, the same tones.

The attempt at transcendence rests on transforming the roles of artist and of citizen. Instead of thinking about the attitudes of *actual* citizens, cramped as they may be by widespread prejudices, we can envisage an *ideal* citizen, one whose evaluations and whose conduct conforms to the civic virtues, those virtues that allow human beings to lead worthwhile lives in harmony with one another. These ideal citizens may live as lightly as Hans and Inge, responding to the pull of what is just and good and beautiful without deep understanding of how their actions should be directed; thanks to their natural dispositions and the circumstances in which they are placed, particularly because they have been given a wisely crafted education, they grow into people who will naturally behave gracefully and well. Their accomplishments would be subverted were they to try to probe the psychological complexities of human behavior: that is why Hans should not read *Don Carlos* and why Aschenbach *rightly* turns away from "knowledge." Actual citizens, although they may approximate the ideal of unselfconscious virtue, may sometimes be led astray by the faulty ideas about virtue current in their societies—in this respect their education fails them, and they deviate from the civic ideal. Consequently, real-life counterparts of Hans and Inge, who have unfortunately absorbed the prejudices of prewar Wilhelmine German bourgeois society, may misunderstand and scorn some of the passions of the Tonios and the Aschenbachs, may even be moved to talk of "whited sepulchres" or to applaud the judgment of the moralizing narrator who comments on the writer's fall.

One philosophical tradition that descends from Plato—and opposes its founder in making peace with the arts—takes the problem of understanding "wisely crafted education" as central.[12] Dewey writes, provocatively, that "if we are willing to conceive education as the process of forming fundamental dispositions, toward nature and fellow-men, philosophy may even be defined *as the general theory of education*,"[13] and he claims that attempts to work out a wise approach to education properly draw on the arts as well as the sciences (broadly construed).[14] Similar ideas are present in Schopenhauer and Nietzsche—although they are far less explicit and directed very differently (to say the least).

Nietzsche's early essay "Schopenhauer as Educator" ("*Schopenhauer als Erzieher*") was a work Mann read with considerable care and interest.[15] In it, Nietzsche begins by formulating the ancient philosophical question: we are, he claims, conscious of our finitude and recognize that we only have a brief span in which "to show why and to what purpose we have come to be."[16] Unlike the philosophers who have emphasized participation in and contribution to society as an educational goal, Nietzsche focuses on the individual, on "the law of your individual self":[17] "Your true teachers and educators reveal to you the true original sense and fundamental substance of your being, something ineducable and unformable, but, in any event, difficult of access, imprisoned, paralyzed: your educators can be nothing else than your liberators. And that is the secret of all real education . . . "[18] To contribute to the real goals of civilization, this liberation should bring forth exceptional individuals ("geniuses"), not docile servants of the state. Scorning contemporaries who replace the serious problem of how to live with issues about the reform of political arrangements, Nietzsche rails against "the doctrine, preached from the rooftops nowadays, that the state is the highest goal of humanity, and that there can be no higher human duty than to serve the state: in which I recognize, not a return to paganism, but a return to stupidity."[19] Schopenhauer, unlike most of the learned occupants of professorial posts, including Kant,[20] is a genuine philosopher, someone who can serve as educator for exceptional people, someone who can enable those people to find themselves.

In transforming the role of the artist, Mann borrowed from Nietzsche the idea of the educator in the fullest sense, the *Erzieher*, the discoverer and communicator of insights that free people to live in their own worthwhile individual fashions, attributing to the artist the power to take on this invaluable work. At the same time, he ignored the Nietzschean suggestions that the work can only be for the few, that it must produce individuals whose projects override the interests of their communities, that if it gives rise to good citizens it must ipso facto have failed. Mixing features of Plato's philosopher-guardians with characteristics of Nietzsche's ideal educators, he envisaged artists identifying enduring values and making those values apparent to all, thus contributing not only to the success of individual lives but also to the publicly pervasive assessments made within the ambient society. This is the goal he assigns to Aschenbach, who sees his own writerly service as following in the tradition of his ancestors.[21]

There was one significant further borrowing from Nietzsche's conception of the educator. Schopenhauer was distinguished among others bearing the title "philosopher," suited to be a "teacher and disciplinarian,"[22] because his thoughts permeated his life. Nietzsche explains how Schopenhauer could be *his* teacher: "I recognize a philosopher to the extent that he is able to provide an example.... But the example must be given through his outward life and not merely through his books, and thus in the way that the ancient philosophers taught, through demeanor, behavior, clothing, food, and customs more than through what they say or even what they write."[23] So the role of the ideal artist-educator—Mann's counterpart for the Nietzschean philosopher—is properly discharged if the insights discerned and communicated are reflected in the life of the *Erzieher*, as, according to the "obituary," they do seem to be in Aschenbach's case: for, unusually for an intellectual, he lives in "honorable upper-class bourgeois status."[24]

Mann's sympathy for this view of the artist's role is apparent from the notebooks he kept at the time of his early writings. During the tempestuous period in which his notebooks reflect on his friendship with Paul Ehrenberg, the object of intense homoerotic yearnings, he writes that the truly eminent writer (*Dichter*) must build "beautiful bridges" to the world of his contemporaries and that his life, too, must be seen, in its entirety, as a work of art.[25] Goethe figured as an exemplar here, a poet who served as advisor—even cultural czar—for the Weimar of his day: Mann paid careful attention to Nietzsche's attempt to transform Goethe into a purely contemplative "inactive" presence.[26] The conception of the artist-educator was also exploited in *Königliche Hoheit*, the immediate predecessor of *Death in Venice*, where the pinched and limited life of the "poet," Axel Martini, is used to cast doubt on his suitability for the role for which he is publicly honored.[27]

This chapter began with two simple approaches to Aschenbach the decent man and honorable citizen. Readers inclined to say "Hm. Hm" on hearing the theme of the story but then reassured by its "respectability" approve the unmasking of Aschenbach as a sham, the opening of the "whited sepulchre" to disclose the foulness it contains. Others, less prejudiced, find the story poignant in its revelations of the deformations societies inflict. The novella, I suggest, allows a different and more complex reading. There are transformations of the roles of citizen and artist allowing for the apparent possibility of joint embodiment. An ideal artist may live after a fashion that prompts the disapproval of actual citizens—but that is because the deprecating judges do not recognize the virtues to which the artist responds, the virtues present in his life and conduct: like the moralistic narrator they are possessed by prejudices, indoctrinated by an inadequate education, one devised, perhaps, by a "bureaucrat-philosopher," a truncated Kant lacking all traces of genius. Ideal citizens, Hans and Inge if they are wisely educated, will appreciate the virtue the artist perceives and embodies, just as he responds to theirs. Artist and citizen will be at one in the understanding of virtue—and beauty.

## 2

Aschenbach, *von* Aschenbach, is introduced to us as one who has dedicated his art to moral education, although we do not know the extent to which he has refined the norms current in his society. His life, too, insofar as it is lived in public, moves gracefully through the bourgeois world. We might worry a little about the circumstances under which the finely chiseled prose is generated—and not just that final page and a half on the beach—the hours of dedicated and often painful struggle. Perhaps the contrast between the grace of the surface and the austere discipline behind it is itself a kind of confidence trick. The major question to Aschenbach's successful reconciliation of the roles of ideal artist and ideal citizen is, however, posed by the embodiment of beauty in Tadzio not, in the first place, because of the direction of the longings evoked but because of the moral obfuscation to which it leads. One moved by beauty to perceive the good would not connive at the venal deceptions of the Venetian authorities.

The perception of the boy convinces—or perhaps reminds—Aschenbach that there is a kind of beauty—call it "higher beauty"—to which his prose has hitherto been inadequate. Even in the presence of that higher beauty, Aschenbach fails to capture it—and recognizes his own failure.

On the evening when he waits anxiously for the Poles to return, the evening that will extort from him the self-confession of his love for the boy, that awareness is painful. "He [Tadzio] was more beautiful than it is possible to say, and Aschenbach felt, with pain as on many previous occasions, that words can only praise the beauty conveyed through the senses [*die sinnliche Schönheit*] but cannot fully reproduce it."[28] The struggles of the past decades have been so hard precisely because Aschenbach has striven to find the closest verbal approximation to higher beauty, persevering even though his efforts always disappoint (*"Durchhalten!"*). Tadzio's presence is an opportunity to pursue this task, perhaps an impossible one, yet further, and the newly felt pain is not merely the result of a lover's fears (Has the beloved left Venice?) but the realization that his words cannot match what is directly before him.

A very specific conception of the artist-educator, the *Erzieher*, is at work here. Art, at its greatest, is not simply the free creation of beauty but the creative response to a prior perception of higher beauty, a response that itself makes beauty accessible to those who have not had such perceptions. To play the role fully, a writer must reproduce higher beauty completely. Even though gestures and approximations may convey something, more is always demanded.[29]

The "obituary" chapter provides enough clues to attribute this self-conception to Aschenbach during the decades in which he crafted the works that have brought him renown. After his encounter with Tadzio, however, the conception is focused with ideas from Plato he may never previously have made explicit. Greek references begin to appear in his private characterizations of the boy, as Aschenbach sits at breakfast the morning after he first observed Tadzio: the rest of the family is assembled, but the "little Phaeacian" is late.[30] When he does appear, the writer studies the "godlike beauty" of the youth, whose head is that of Eros. Later, Aschenbach observes the comradeship of Tadzio and Jaschu as they stroll along the beach with their arms around each other (each other's shoulders?), and Jaschu bestows a kiss. The observer rehearses a playful warning, quoting the words Xenophon attributes to Socrates when Critobulus supposedly stole a kiss from a beautiful young man—an occasion for the philosopher-educator to remind his interlocutors of the importance of self-discipline and restraint in the presence of beauty.[31] Aschenbach's thoughts move from a generalized characterization of the youth in terms of Greek mythology to the perspective of Socrates, first as rendered by Xenophon and then by the influential teacher's more prominent disciple—Plato.

After the return from his abortive attempt to flee Venice, Aschenbach plunges into his Greek idyll, and, seated on the beach, he muses on the role of the senses and of the beauties they disclose in the most intellectual endeavors. He looks toward Tadzio, and he seems to be looking on Beauty itself. The Platonic allusions flood in. Thoughts that the sun diverts the attention from the intellectual to the physically embodied give way to the judgment that observation of physical things is necessary for the spiritual quest:

> Only through the help of the body is the soul able to lift itself up to higher reflections. Surely the love-god does as the mathematicians do, when they show untalented children pictures of the pure Forms: so too the god deploys the figure and color of human youth to make the spiritual visible to us, using form and coloration as tools in prodding our memory, by decorating them with all the sheen of Beauty itself, so that the sight of them will consume us with pain and hope.[32]

Plato's vision of the world of Pure Forms, observed before birth and recalled to us as we are cleverly prodded to remember what we once saw— as, in the *Meno*, Socrates leads the slave boy to geometrical knowledge— is already in Aschenbach's mind, and it becomes explicit almost immediately. The sound of the sea and the glitter of the sunlight transport him in thought to a Greek landscape, scene of the only Platonic dialogue set *al fresco*. Using fragments of the *Symposium* as well as of the *Phaedrus*, he reflects on love and virtue and beauty.

According to the *Phaedrus*, higher beauty is associated with the most fundamental values, with wisdom, justice, and goodness, so that the perception of higher beauty is simultaneously our way of having access to these values: beauty, unlike wisdom or goodness, can be perceived with the senses. Hence, in apprehending and communicating beauty, the artist would fulfill his function as educator—he would build those "beautiful bridges" of which Mann wrote in his *Notizbuch* ruminations. The ideal artist would seek out the objects in which higher beauty is most manifest, for reproducing *their* beauty is the optimal way to carry out the artist-educator's appointed task. As he sits on the beach, calling up the Platonic tradition offers Aschenbach a reassuring identification of those privileged objects.

Higher beauty is most accessible in the human form, indeed in boys and young men. For, on the Platonic account, sensible manifestations of higher beauty should kindle love, love not simply directed at the object perceived but at the qualities it embodies.[33] Erotic yearnings are bound up with the recognition of higher beauty, but the erotic response must be of a special sort, one that is not debased or corrupted. Supposing that the perception of higher beauty generates love facilitates Aschenbach's conclusion that other human beings are especially suitable as tools for prodding our recollection of Beauty, and it is not hard to understand the specific focus on the young. Less easy to understand is the step that takes us to the young (postpubescent) *male* as the ideal vehicle for the perception of higher beauty.

In the *Symposium* and *Phaedrus*, the dialogues most concerned with the exploration of love, the dialogues Mann studied as he was writing *Death in Venice*, the priority of homosexual love is simply taken for granted.[34] The *Phaedrus* discussion is, however, as we have already seen (in section 4 of chapter 1) much concerned with distinguishing between properly disciplined love and the undisciplined love that consumes those who are profane, loose, and corrupt: this is the point of the simile of the team of horses that runs through Socrates' second long speech.[35] If there is an argument for giving precedence to homosexual love in the apprehension of higher beauty—rather than simply the expression of a fashionable aristocratic Athenian prejudice—it lies, I suggest, in the thought that, while the perception of higher beauty must kindle love, the love so inspired must be controlled and disciplined.

Two strands in ancient thought elevate the love of men for youths by emphasizing the incompleteness of heterosexual love. Women are taken to lack the qualities of intellect and character essential to the full erotic relationship. Thus, in Plutarch's *Dialogue on Love*, one of Mann's important sources, Protogenes, the spokesman for the superiority of homosexual relationships, characterizes desires for women in unflattering terms: "even if they turn out well, one may enjoy only physical pleasure and the satisfaction of a ripe body."[36] Intercourse with women is viewed as a tiresome necessity, something that cannot be avoided if humanity is to continue but, because of the intellectual and moral inequalities between the partners, can be nothing more than a physically satisfying act. Diotima's speech in the *Symposium* obliquely makes that point when she emphasizes the superiority of that form of reproduction in which the "souls" of "descendants" are shaped by the ideas and example of a great teacher.[37] Thus homosexual love is superior because it is not reducible to mere physical release and also because it cannot be aimed at the inferior sort of "immortality," that obtained through begetting children.

These background ideas impose demands on the character and expression of homosexual love, demands that Aschenbach appears to accept. If the superiority is to be taken seriously, the homosexual relationship must be one in which the lover educates the beloved, "urging him on the path to excellence."[38] Physical contact, should there be any, is only justifiable if it is bound up in this educational mission. Hence, the emphasis on disciplined restraint, an ideal condition made vivid in Alcibiades' description of his night with Socrates. Plato makes it clear that there is no doubt of Socrates' delight in the youth's beauty or of his love for Alcibiades. Despite Alcibiades' open invitation to sexual relations, his lover remains aloof, and Alcibiades concludes his account of their night together by remarking that he might as well have slept with his brother or his father.[39]

Aschenbach wants to practice this severe discipline. His failure to normalize his relations with Tadzio, to place a hand on head or shoulder and to begin conversation with him, indicates his failure to achieve the Socratic condition. Instead, as he apparently discovers, his perception of the boy's beauty entangles him in erotic yearnings of the classically despised kind, yearnings that overwhelm him and ultimately challenge his self-conception as moral educator. After the physical collapse at the fountain, he returns to Socratic language, this time in parody, arguing the anti-Socratic conclusion that perception of higher beauty inevitably involves submission to erotic mastery and thus moral corruption. At the end, Schopenhauer's suspicions about the power of the sexual impulse triumph over Plato's vision of a form of love that will guide the artist-educator to the perception and communication of beauty.

So it seems. Aschenbach was deceived into thinking he could combine disciplined restraint with the perception of Tadzio's beauty. Well and good, but surely too blunt. For we must ask: Is this because of some flaw in Aschenbach? Or is it, as the Socratic parody supposes, because perception of higher beauty engenders irresistible erotic yearnings that corrupt their possessor? More fundamentally, is there really some notion of higher beauty? Is what makes it higher some connection with the most basic values? If it exists is it embodied only, or most completely, in human beings, particularly in young men?

Or, more fundamentally, isn't all the philosophizing evasive, stemming from strategies to cover up what is held, under repressive social conditions, to be disreputable and disgusting? The Platonic ideas are too implausible to survive in a world that has overcome the prejudices confining Aschenbach and his creator. So my attempt to explore a reading that will "transcend" the split recognized in the first section of this chapter may seem entirely too hifalutin' and elaborate, an unnecessary way of avoiding what we, if not Mann's contemporaries, can see as the simpler—sexual—reading. Immediate post-Wildeans may have needed the disguises in which Mann swathed his homoerotic leanings, the classical references and the philosophical superstructure; we do not.

Mann himself shed those disguises posthumously, allowing the few *Tagebücher* he decided not to destroy to be edited and published, after a safe interval.[40] Even the volumes that passed his censorship made his complicated sexuality apparent. Besides the references to specific episodes in which one or other "pretty young man" attracted his attention, the overall tone of the language reveals his preferences. The adjective *hübsch* (pretty) is overwhelmingly likely to be attached to young men, although there are occasional periods, particularly in Mann's later years, in which a few women have the privilege of its application.[41] Chance visions of young men, sometimes interestingly enough, at the beach, are registered with appreciation and even delight—to the extent of inspiring the thought that Mann's liking for the sea stemmed from the opportunities offered for observing the male body relatively unclad: he was disappointed, it seems, with a stay at the seaside in Holland, because the young men he saw were insufficiently attractive.[42] His explicit references to the "real passions of his life" betray a lifelong fascination with actual counterparts of Tadzio.[43]

So why not recognize that something more elementary than "Greek Love" is at stake? Why not elaborate a "sexual" reading of *Death in Venice*? Aschenbach is fascinated with Tadzio's beauty, because he is a closeted homosexual. The writer's marriage and family life is long in the past, and it was probably always an attempt to conform his sexuality to approved standards. The challenge of the stranger at the cemetery, with his direct stare, can be read as a sexual invitation; the imagery of the vision of the south in Aschenbach's reverie is explicitly sexual (the overgrown ferns are described as *geil*, voluptuous perhaps, but more literally lewd) and primarily phallic (thrusting roots and hairy palm trunks are only the start); the elderly fop disturbs Aschenbach because of the serious possibility that this is a version of himself (as eventually it will be). Even the fop's parting words of "compliments to your little darling" use the suspiciously neutral word *Liebchen*. Before he arrives at the lido, the attentive reader can see through Aschenbach's disguise.

His repression, we might assume, has affected his art, turning it toward formalism because only careful choices allow him simultaneously to conform to the bourgeois conventions and engage passionately with his subject matter: perhaps it is no accident that the great prose epic centers on Frederick the Great.[44] On the lido, however, his powers of repression are broken, simply overwhelmed by Tadzio's beauty, and, because the feelings have been held in check so long, they erupt with a force that makes artistic shaping of them impossible. All Aschenbach's defenses are destroyed, and his passion leads him to violate the conventional standards that have held him in thrall.

So the challenge: *Death in Venice* may come in elaborate trappings, echoes of Nietzsche and Schopenhauer, allusions to Greek mythology and play with Socratic dialogues, but it is tempting to suppose that these are disguises Mann considered necessary to mask a more basic story about the social distortion of sexuality and its costs. Freed from the conventional prejudices Mann accurately ascribed to his contemporaries, readers today can recognize the novella for what it is.

The next two sections will attempt a pair of complementary responses to this challenge.

## 3

From his youth on, Mann had cherished the melancholy poems of August von Platen, recognizing with sympathy Platen's yearning for love, love typically doomed to remain unexpressed and, when timidly ventured, brusquely rebuffed. Born into the threadbare aristocracy, Platen was sent to the boarding school for cadets in Munich shortly before his tenth birthday. During the next few years, he became aware of his sexual orientation: "I grew accustomed to devote my hopes and dreams to members of my own sex, and sought to achieve in friendship with them the very same goal that lovers seek in marriage."[45] During the years he spent in military training, with an interval of service as a page at court, his feelings were directed at a number of young men—typically his contemporaries—whom he admired from a distance: sometimes the passion flared before he had exchanged a word with the object of his desires, or at a time when he was only rewarded with monosyllabic responses, but it was important for him to gaze on the beloved, to have the opportunity of being in the other's presence.[46] In his early twenties, Platen fell in love with a young man to whom he was able to declare himself—he guessed, apparently correctly, that his beloved was also primarily attracted toward men—but the relationship was stormy, with only occasional moments of reassurance and relatively chaste fulfillment. The episode ended when the beloved, Edward, returned Platen's correspondence and the poems he had written, with "a horrible letter" (*"une lettre horrible"*); the conclusion gives the tone: "Never dare to write even a single line to me again, or, if I should be in your presence, to speak a single word to me. For my own part, I shall avoid you as a pestilential sickness. Otherwise you could place yourself in danger of being treated just as someone deserves, who has completely abandoned human worth."[47] Later, after he had left the army and devoted himself to a nomadic life in Italy and Sicily, Platen appears to have had fleeting sexual liaisons. Reciprocated love seems always to have eluded him.

How many of the details of Platen's life did Mann know? In the absence of the diaries he kept in his early years (and destroyed in the 1940s), we cannot discover just which parts of Platen's own copious journals Mann read. A note from 1898 or 1899 records his intention to read Platen's *Tagebücher*, which were transcribed and published between

1896 and 1900.[48] Assuming he followed through on his intention, virtually *any* sampling of the 1,900 printed pages would have confirmed the portrait he had already constructed from reading the poetry—and from knowing Heine's famous gibe about Platen's "effeminacy." In the essay on Platen ("Platen-Tristan-Don Quichotte") Mann wrote in 1930, he refers to Platen's love "that saturates every poem"—"an unending and unquenchable love, one that flows into death, which is death, because it finds no satisfaction on Earth."[49] Reflecting on that essay almost four years later, Mann exclaims at how Platen's "spiritualized and overerotic passion fired my blood" when he himself was in love.[50]

Mann's admiration and his sense of kinship with the unhappy poet, who had preceded him by three-quarters of a century, would invite a comparison between Aschenbach and Platen, whether or not Mann had carried out his plan of reading the diaries. Perhaps Mann knew already that Platen's own visit to Venice had liberated him, that he had overstayed his leave, had suffered (mild) punishment for doing so, and that the experience inspired him to quit his military career and take up life in the south. Platen's most famous poem—"Tristan"—quoted in full in the 1930 essay, points toward Aschenbach's collapse at the fountain: the one who has "gazed on beauty," the third stanza tells us,

would like to dry up like a spring,
to suck poison from every breath of the air,
to smell death in every flower.[51]

Mann might well also have known that Platen's last years were spent in restless, unfulfilled, wanderings around Italy—Aschenbach's obsessive pursuits of Tadzio, on a far larger scale—and also, maybe, that these peregrinations ended when, fearing cholera (which had broken out in Sicily), Platen misdiagnosed himself, took the wrong medicines, and died of a violent intestinal infection.[52] Most important for present purposes, however, is a connection made clear by Mann's reference to "spiritualized and overerotic passion": Platen's recapitulation of the Platonic tradition.

Whether or not Platen had studied the *Symposium* or the *Phaedrus* or Plutarch's *Dialogue on Love*,[53] his efforts to come to terms with his own emotions work through the same conceptions and construct the same defenses. The early confessions to his diary surround his passions with allusions to religious devotion, some of them explicitly Christian ("So I was able to gaze on him, uninterruptedly, fixedly, as the pious do when they pray to the picture of the Savior, before which they lie in the dust"), some steeped in classical allusions ("O come back, happy days, I beseech you; let me at least taste your Olympian nectar once again!").[54] He rehearses the ancient view that women cannot be objects of the highest forms of love, because of their intellectual (or spiritual?) limitations ("I believed that the cramped spirit [*beschränkte Geist*] of a woman would not be capable of captivating me long, and that the vast majority of the fair sex are spoiled through affectation").[55] He echoes Diotima's account of the priority of intellectual/spiritual reproduction ("nobody was so besotted with his children as a poet").[56] He confesses that his homosexual passions developed during a period when he was unaware that any "criminal relationship could exist between two men" and that he only later paid attention to writings on same-sex love, noting that, in his own earlier readings of Plutarch, he had entirely overlooked this theme.[57] The most important recapitulation, however, is the struggle to identify homosexual love as the highest form of friendship. In March 1816, when he was nineteen, Platen characterized friendship in a way of which the ancients would have approved:

> I feel that this inclination [toward his current love, "William"] is something noble and forms itself in a noble fashion in me. Its endeavor is to make its object as worthy as possible, and, where possible, to ennoble and improve the errors and weaknesses of that object. It would be my highest triumph to make my William the best of men. It is no blind, no irrational, inclination, for it is grounded on the deepest and best human feelings.[58]

Later in the same year, a reading of Brandes's *On Women* prompted an extended identification with the Greek perspective:

> The author defends the practice of homosexual love among the Greeks. He believes (as I have always believed) that such love among the Greek aristocrats never degenerated into vice, even if outer appearances aroused it or contributed to it. He shows

what great deeds proceeded from this love, how two men could be everything to one another, and how they alone were able to exchange thoughts and feelings. These considerations did not leave me indifferent. I have come to feel stronger in my sense of the probity of my inclinations, which I have always felt as noble and directed towards goodness. I cannot take it as a reproach to have sought the human ideal always among my own sex, and I consider this inclination all the more pure, the more I recognize how different the love of men for women is and how it eventually degenerates into mere sensual satisfaction. The conflict between love and friendship within my breast is resolved. I feel that they [love and friendship] can be united, even if I shall never find a man to whom I can give both.[59]

The resolution, however, was only temporary: about a year later, Platen lamented a fall back into the folly of love. "I am of an age that demands love, and cannot be satisfied with mere friendship. . . . I can dull my feelings by means of serious occupations, but I cannot silence them."[60] Opposing his earlier thought that women are too limited to serve as objects of the deepest love, he envies those whom he has previously loved who have been "saved" by marriage—and hopes wistfully for a future marriage for himself ("Respect and friendship would draw me to my wife, and these would, perhaps, give birth to love").[61]

The turn away from the Greek ideals and defenses is accompanied by an increasing awareness of the slide from sense to sensuality, of the power of the sexual drive, and of a sense of human suffering that echoes Schopenhauer. Platen asks if "the best existence is not a constant suffering" and sees the ideal of love as lying in devotion to another, fulfilled in ameliorating the beloved's fate.[62] Pessimism pervades his thinking in the passage, in which he distinguishes between love and friendship. That entry concludes:

There can be no love without a sensual component. But never, in any fashion, did Federigo awake in me a merely sensual impulse. But suppose it should come to that for me in other cases! Then the abyss would swallow me up. I should be lost. I would wretchedly gnaw at myself, I would never achieve my purpose and would even shudder to attain it. I know already how easily a noble love can lead to the edge of corruption and desperation; but I have not yet experienced how dreadfully sensual ardor can destroy the whole person; I have, however, a grim premonition of it. There is so much in the world that makes me wish I had never been born.[63]

The Greek ideal that section 2 attributed to Aschenbach was present for long periods in Platen's own efforts to come to terms with himself—and, as with Aschenbach at the fountain, there are moments at which it cannot be sustained, moments at which the abyss threatens.[64]

Mann's immersion in his predecessor's melancholy lyrics enabled him to divine this pattern in Platen's thoughts and feelings. Poetry in which the author figures as a rejected friend (or possibly rejected as something more than a friend), in which the friend/beloved steals off to a girl while the poet broods over a pile of books,[65] hardly conceals the circumstances in which Platen sometimes found himself:

> Friend, it was an empty, mad longing
> that our spirits would find one another,
> that our glances would spark understanding,
> that our tears would mingle . . . [66]

Particularly important, however, is "Tristan," from which I quoted above, a three-stanza poem Mann made central to his essay on Platen. Literally (and clumsily) translated, it runs:

> Whoever gazes on beauty with his eyes
> is already at home with death,
> and will be suited to no earthly service,
> and yet will tremble before death,
> whoever gazes on beauty with his eyes.
>
> For him the pain of love endures forever,
> for only a fool can hope on this earth
> to satisfy any such impulse:
> Whoever has been struck by the arrow of beauty
> for him the pain of love endures forever.

Ah, he would like to dry up like a spring,
to suck poison from every breath of the air,
to smell death in every flower:
Whoever gazes on beauty with his eyes,
Ah, he would like to dry up like a spring![67]

Mann had already cited this poem in an earlier essay (on "Marriage in Transition"), where he suggested that beauty and form were connected not with life but with a critical attitude toward life, an attitude "most profoundly bound up with death and infertility": Platen's poem was viewed as encapsulating the essence of "aestheticism", and the homoerotic impulse the core of "erotic aestheticism."[68]

There is an important last aspect of Platen's attempt to construct a sexual identity with which he could rest, to wit the prominence of vision in his yearnings. As I have already noted, his feelings could easily be kindled from a distance: without words, without knowledge of the young men who attracted him, he could blaze into passion, torturing himself with plans for seeing more of the beloved, reproaching himself for wasting chances to come closer to them.[69] During his original stay in Venice and throughout the restless wanderings of his final years, *sight* is paramount: in Venice he scurries from church to church, entranced by the wealth of paintings, but the sounds, tastes, and smells of the city (of Venice!) leave little impression. Later, in Naples, he finds bathing in the sea particularly agreeable, since it brings him into the company of the local youth.[70] The apparently clumsy repetition of references to the eyes in the opening line of "Tristan" reflects his openness to *visual* beauty, and here again Platen recapitulates the ideas of the ancients. In the crucial section of the *Phaedrus* in which Socrates describes the earthly apprehension of beauty, he is explicit about which sense is involved: "Beauty, as I said, was radiant among the other objects; and now that we have come down here we grasp it sparkling through the clearest of our senses. Vision, of course, is the sharpest of our bodily senses."[71] Platen, I suggest, accepted this Socratic idea so deeply that he made it central to his understanding of homoerotic expression.

The pessimism of 1817 reaches its nadir in the fear that his erotic yearnings will drive him into the "abyss." Just over a year later, in the grip of the passion for the young man he identifies as "Adrast"—later revealed as Edward—he reassures himself: "His beauty enchants me, but sexual craving has never sullied me."[72] As he comes to know Edward, he suggests that he would be the "happiest of men" if "heaven" would give him "an unchangeable purity of soul," and he rejoices that "their esteem for each other" increases every day.[73] It was not long before their arms found each other's shoulders and waists, and Platen reports that their "cheeks often touched."[74] Yet, in accord with his wish for purity, he hopes that God will help them to emerge from "this abyss" (*"cet abyme"*).[75] Even after Edward's declaration of his own feelings, Platen can reassure himself:

> We were no more than a single soul, and our bodies were like two trees whose branches are tightly interlaced, intertwined forever. Nonetheless, I can swear without deception that my longing has been enhanced, and that it has also gained in purity what it has gained in ardor, since when true love, reciprocal love, lifts itself up to a high degree, sensuality is diminished.[76]

In retrospect, after recurrent storms and difficulties—probably caused by Platen's yearning for a combination of profound spiritual union and restrained physical expression—he looks back on this particular day (June 24, 1819)—"the day that remains in my memory as the most beautiful and the most tender."[77] The height of their sexual contact seems to have been attained on the day when they separated: "As he started to leave, he embraced me again tenderly and our lips touched in a long kiss. I accompanied him through the streets and before we separated we embraced each other one more time. I no longer feel my ardent love, I only feel the purest and most lasting friendship [*amitié*]."[78] For Platen, apparently, gazing at the beloved was primary and could permissibly lead to ardent conversational exchanges, embraces, and, as apogee, a kiss. Love was to be separated from the lower part of the body.[79]

At least in the early part of his life, Platen sought to adapt his homoerotic feelings to conventional ideas about sexual expression, by limiting the forms of contact allowed to those that might "pass" as exuberant expressions of deep but "pure" friendship. There are even hints that, at this stage of his life, he foresees a role for himself as educator, as *Erzieher*, someone whose writings will assist sensitive young men who come after him, youths who discover that they are attracted to men and not to women. He considers the possibility of composing an extensive discussion of "Friendship between men"[80] and, more prophetically, imagines his diaries as helping sensitive youths—"of my own leanings"—who might learn to avoid his own mistakes.[81] The poetry, if not the diaries, surely comforted one such youth, the author who attributed Platen's acute, conflicted, Platonic homoerotic identity to Aschenbach.

A "sexual" reading of *Death in Venice* is too simple because it ignores a primary way of coming to terms with the "love that dare not speak its name," one elaborated in the poetry and in the life of a writer who spoke intimately to Thomas Mann.

## 4

Yet Platen's example—as well as Mann's own—should prompt a deeper response to the charge that "elevated" philosophical references are solely cover for more elemental impulses. In supposing that the complex of ideas about beauty and the role of the artist are parts of Aschenbach's attempt to hide his own sexuality from himself, and equally parts of Mann's concealment of his central theme from censorious readers, an over-simple picture of human psychology is taken for granted. We are invited to think of a drive that is in place, fully formed quite independently of the ambient social environment, a drive that cannot be faced directly and is masked by complex cultural constructions. Nietzsche falls victim to this picture when he supposes that the task of the educator is to liberate the "real self," the "true original sense and fundamental substance of your being,"[82] as if there were something completely formed before any educator had gone to work. Platen is less sure, even about the direction of his longings: he wonders if he might have been attracted toward women if his early environment had been different, had he not been sent to military school and grown into adolescence in an all-male society.[83] Reasonable skepticism about that particular hypothesis is compatible with appreciating a more general point: cultural complexes of ideas—the cluster of themes about "higher beauty," for example—might play a double role, giving direction to a more elementary, previously unformed impulse and, at the same time, providing a guise in which that impulse could be accepted. Aschenbach deceives himself when he supposes his fascination with Tadzio stems *merely* from his apprehension of higher beauty, embodied in the boy—but that does not mean that his homoerotic yearnings are not shaped by a conception of higher beauty and of some ideal relation to it.

What exactly does Aschenbach want from Tadzio? If we assume that he wants, though he dare not admit it, full homosexual relations with the boy, then the self-deception of the Greek idyll is complete. Classical allusions and Socratic paraphrases are just cover for something more carnal. There is, however, an alternative. We may consider whether the same disciplined restraint of his sensibility to beauty, the restraint that underlies his two decades of success as a mature artist, is also felt in the shaping of his erotic yearnings. In the novella, Aschenbach makes increasingly strenuous efforts toward two goals, to observe Tadzio and to elicit from him glances and smiles of recognition. Those goals might be viewed as intermediate aims, first steps toward some more intense intimacy. Or they might not. We can think of Aschenbach as someone whose desire is simply for the sight of Tadzio and for the pleasure, the intoxicating pleasure, he receives when the boy smiles at him. Like (the young) Platen, he may want no more than to be able to gaze on the beloved, to exchange confidences and tears, to give and receive the occasional embrace, to "touch lips" on parting.

*Death in Venice* records Aschenbach's daily routine but does not show it. We know that the writer's life was mostly solitary, but it involved a daily walk, and we can presume that he sometimes encountered youths whose beauty attracted him—*hübsche Jungen*, as his creator would have called them. Should we suppose the pleasure those visions gave him went unnoted or, at least, was left unanalyzed? Not necessarily. We can imagine him attributing to himself an ambiguous desire, the wish to place a hand on head or shoulder, say, to stop for casual conversation—just the intentions formed when he thinks of "normalizing" relations with Tadzio. Perhaps, on the lido, the attraction is more intense, engendering a sudden recognition of what the ambiguous gesture would mean for him—a recognition brought about in part by Tadzio's exceptional beauty, in part from the loosening of Aschenbach's severe discipline.

Aschenbach's literary development is only sketched, and his psychosexual development must be a matter of complete conjecture. One hypothesis, however, merits exploration. Imagine the young Aschenbach, delicate and intellectually precocious, educated at home, growing into adolescence without many opportunities to play with other children.[84] His incipient sexual feelings are directed toward other boys, whom he sees from a distance but with whom he can have little contact, and the desires he forms are pervaded by the pious discipline of his family and the classical education he receives. He forms a synthesis of ideas, combining elements from bourgeois orthodoxy and the Platonic tradition, and the synthesis defines the human relations he wants: a respectable and respectful marriage, without passion; love in the contemplation of beauty—or, at most, in modest contact with it. Aschenbach is a homosexual—we can apply that label if we choose—but his homosexuality takes a specific form, one dominated by the wish to fit his unformed yearnings into orthodox culture, to transcend the split between artist and citizen. That form is as central to his "true original sense" as the first springs of attraction toward those distant boys.

Why should we take that particular hypothesis seriously? For a variety of reasons, some of them resting on clues in Mann's fiction, some stemming from the form of sexuality revealed in the surviving diaries. Let's begin with two examples from the fiction.

*Death in Venice* was, as already noted, a replacement for a novella about Goethe's late infatuation with a teenage girl. Mann was to return to Goethe later, and, when he did, he avoided the depiction of passion in favor of ruminations on the expression of love. For the first two-thirds of *Lotte in Weimar*, Goethe is the absent presence, dominant in the conversations of the other characters but offstage. Charlotte Kestner (née Buff), the alleged original for "Werther's Lotte," now a widow in advanced matronhood, arrives in Weimar to visit one of her sisters, an event that causes a flurry of visits to her in the Hotel Elephant—in the manner of *Tristram Shandy*, the Main Event, the reunion apparently envisaged by everyone, is deferred for six (out of nine) chapters, as the kindly and tolerant Frau Kestner is unable to escape the hotel.[85] At the very end of her final interview—with the poet's son—the young man remembers the reason for his visit and issues the invitation with which he has been sent. So, at last, we come to Goethe.

We meet the great man in the early morning, in bed, as he muses to himself, in a long chapter punctuated by conversations with a servant and with his son. The *Meister-Erzieher* meanders through large thoughts, present aspirations, and past events until the smell of raspberries elicits a connection:

> It's a truly lovely aroma and the berries are charming, swelling with juice under the velvety dryness, warm from the fire of life, like women's lips. If love is the best thing in life, so too in love the best is the kiss — the poetry of love, the seal of ardor, sensual and platonic at once, the middle of the sacrament between the holy beginning and the carnal end, a sweet act, completely in a higher sphere than that [the consummation in intercourse], and with the pure organs of breath and speech — spiritual because still individual and thoroughly differentiated — between your hands the unique head, tipped backward, under the lashes the smiling serious evanescent look into your eyes, and the kiss says "You I love and adore, you lovely unique creature, expressly in the whole creation, you!" — for copulation is anonymous and animal, fundamentally without choice, and night properly covers it. The kiss is happiness, copulation debauchery, God gave it to the serpent. To be sure, you imitated the serpent [*du würmtest*] energetically at times, but your proper métier is rather happiness and the kiss — the fleeting touch of self-aware passion on evanescent beauty. It is also the difference between art and life, for the abundance of life, of humanity, the making of children, is not a thing of poetry, of the spiritual kiss on the raspberry lips of the world . . . [86]

Mann's Goethe, citizen and artist,[87] offers a view of restrained fulfillment we might easily ascribe to the character who replaced him in the early novella. Goethe adds to the complex of ideas about higher beauty the thought that the truly spiritual erotic response is individualized, concentrated on this being, here and now, in which beauty is, for the moment, most forcefully realized. Tadzio is almost the only human figure in Aschenbach's field of vision who receives a name.[88] Tadzio is the focus of that vision, the object of the gaze, Goethe's "holy beginning" of the "sacrament." The writer who gazes might share with the character he displaced the view that the sacrament would be fulfilled in a kiss.

Or consider a much earlier work, the immediate predecessor of *Death in Venice*. *Königliche Hoheit* is rightly seen as a fairy tale, one that retells the story of Mann's courtship of Katia Pringsheim. Mann himself figures as the prince, Klaus Heinrich, born with a withered arm that he tries, with disciplined determination, to conceal; Katia becomes the heiress Imma Spoelmann, the daughter of a wealthy man who has made his home in America but who returns to the declining principality because its mineral waters seem good for his health. The prince woos and wins, convincing Imma to give up her mathematical studies[89] to join him in discharging his royal duties, and the old gypsy prophecies are fulfilled: that a prince with one hand would "give more to the nation than others could with two" and that, on a day of great jubilation, the old stock of roses will no longer bloom with a scent of mould and decay but will give off "the most natural and the loveliest" fragrance.[90]

If we take Mann seriously in claiming that the elite writer puts himself on trial, it is not hard to recognize aspects of the Manns' long marriage—its successes as well as limitations—behind the fairy tale. A pivotal moment in the relation between Klaus Heinrich and Imma is his admission to her of his deformity. As he stands in front of her, with his usual oblique stance so that the withered arm and hand can easily be concealed behind his hip, he observes the direction of her gaze:

"Have you had that from birth?" she asked quietly.
   He went pale. But with a sound, that seemed a sound of release, he sank down before her, while he embraced the strange [*seltsam*: singular] figure with both arms.[91]

Imma's "singularity" at this moment is less odd than the phrase Klaus Heinrich utters at a moment of apparent redemption: he calls her "little sister."

Those words have come to the prince earlier, as a private designation of Imma[92]—and they will recur, in the conversation when she accepts his courtship—a "strange" agreement to marry: "'Little sister,' he said with a serene expression, and held her a little more tightly in the dance, 'little bride.'"[93] Even as she goes to the altar on her wedding day, that description resonates not in the prince's words but in those of the narrator: "Her strange little child's face (*Kindergesichtchen*) was pale as mother-of-pearl."[94] Imma is taken as a partner, a wife . . . but not, it appears, as a fully grown woman.

The sexlessness of this relationship is reinforced by the mode through which Klaus Heinrich wins his bride. His first proposals are resisted, as Imma confesses her sense of the distance that the pomp of royalty—in which the prince has been so carefully coached—conveys to her, the coldness he radiates. In true fairy-tale style, he is set a quest, but, faithful to the character of their situation and of his courtship, it is a prosaic one: he is to learn to immerse himself in the affairs of his people. Full redemption comes to Klaus Heinrich through a course of study, particularly in economics, in which Imma participates. He is to become a different kind of prince, one attuned less to protocol than to the issues and policies that affect his subjects. Romance is even subtracted from the fulfillment of the gypsy prophecies. The prince gives greatly to his people because the dowry paid by Imma's father frees the country from the economic disorder of the recent past. The roses yield their true scent when they are replanted outside the confining mold-infested walls of the palace courtyard, when they are given light and sun.

This marriage may provide happiness, a "severe" or "demanding" happiness, as the final words of the novel suggest,[95] but that happiness is founded in respect, in cooperation, in commitment to a wider duty. That is no bad foundation. It might have served a more fortunate—or more venturesome—Platen. It might have been the marriage Aschenbach had, a disciplined partnership unfortunately truncated by his wife's premature death. It seems to have been a marriage of the sort the Manns lived through their five decades together.

At the core of Klaus Heinrich's marriage is the moment of revelation, of release, of redemption, when his inborn disability (*Hemmung*) is disclosed and Imma accepts it. Katia came to terms with the secret her husband took pains to conceal—a secret that plainly tormented him during the period of threatened exposure[96]—the fact of his attraction toward young men. Her memoirs touch lightly on the visit to Venice during which Mann was struck by the "charming, picture-pretty (*bildhübsch*)" boy: "He had an immediate weakness for this boy, who pleased him beyond measure, and he always observed him on the beach with his playfellows. He didn't pursue him around Venice, that he didn't do, but the boy fascinated him and he thought about him often."[97]

The surviving diaries are even clearer about the extent of Katia's knowledge and acceptance. On October 17, 1920, Mann recorded his appreciation of his wife's understanding: "Gratitude towards K., because she is not in the least disconcerted or troubled in her love, when she is finally unable to arouse any desire in me and when lying beside her cannot equip me with desire—that is, complete sexual desire—for her. The peace, love, and equanimity with which she accepts this is truly admirable, and thus I do not have to be unnerved by it."[98] That entry was written shortly after Katia had returned after an absence of nearly two weeks—on an evening when Mann had seen his elder son, Klaus, naked, and had been confusedly aroused.[99]

A few weeks earlier, after celebrating his mother-in-law's birthday, the couple had come home late, and an attempt at intercourse had failed. Mann had apparently visited his wife's bedroom.

> I am not completely clear about my condition in this respect. It can hardly be called real impotence, but more a matter of the usual confusion and unreliability of my "sex life." No doubt it's an annoying weakness, brought about by wishes that are directed "to the other side." How would it have been if a boy "lay before me"? In any event, it would be unreasonable if I let myself be depressed by a failure, whose grounds are not new to me.[100]

Several months later, in the spring of 1921, Mann again expresses his appreciation for Katia's acceptance of him. After an evening out, " . . . embraces with K. My gratitude for the great kindness in her response to my sexual problems is deep and warm."[101]

It is not hard to understand how, at the time of his great distress over the possible publication of the earlier diaries—possibly even more ardent and candid than those of 1918 through 1921—he could be comforted by sitting for hours with Katia, hand in hand, or how through the years for which we have records, his sleeplessness, whether bound up with self-doubt or unwelcome sexual stirrings, could lead him to her room, perhaps to place his head on her shoulder, perhaps to sit by her bed in a chair.[102]

Yet it is worth asking: what if a boy had lain before him? With the exception of the diaries from 1918 to 1921, all those that remain belong to a period after the threat of exposure, and prudence may have made the later records of his longings less vivid.[103] Nevertheless, the entries do not *conceal* Mann's sexual proclivities, although they do give it a particular form. They recapitulate the vision-centered restrained expression of homosexual desire hypothesized for Aschenbach. Here is one extensive explanation of a common type of incident. On his daily walk, Mann was gripped by a vision; he saw with "great joy"

> a young lad at work in the garden-shop, a little cap on his head, very pretty [*hübsch*], naked to the waist. The uplift I felt at this so ordinary, so everyday and natural "beauty," the chest, the swell of the biceps, led me to think again afterwards about the unreal, illusory, and aesthetic character of this inclination, whose aim, it seems, lies in looking on ["gazing"] and "adoration," and, although it is erotic, neither reason nor the sense aims at any sort of further consummation. It probably consists in the influence of the sense of actuality on the imagination, which allows delight, while holding it fast to the visual image.[104]

Again and again, through the years of the surviving diaries, young men who attend Mann's lectures, or who come to interview him, or who are children of friends or friends of his children—or who are simply seen on his walks—stir his visual imagination. More than a decade after the observation of the youth at the nursery, he records an unwelcome sexual excitement, partially caused by medicines but partly the result of an "image by the wayside."[105] That phrase was first used several months earlier, when on a walk he had been "captivated by an image at the wayside"—on subsequent days, he saw the "image at the wayside, dressed" ("*Das Bild am Wege, dressed*"), the "image, undressed," and the "image, in bright colors."[106] The southern California climate was conducive to these welcome opportunities—as was the seaside.

It is impossible to know the character of the sexual expression Mann wanted or allowed himself in his early romantic attachments, but the diaries do contain comparisons among episodes. Early in 1934, he read the records he had kept in 1927, when, on a family holiday to the island of Sylt, he had made the acquaintance of the seventeen-year-old Klaus Heuser. The Heuser and Mann families encountered one another on the beach, and Mann was sufficiently charmed to invite the youth for a visit to Munich. Recalling these events he finds himself "excited, touched, and captivated" by the memory, viewing them as occasions on which he attained what is truly rare in human life, Happiness. Reflecting on his earlier amorous adventures, he understands them as "taken up in the late and astonishing fulfillment," so that his previous loves are "consummated, expiated, and made good" in this (last) episode.[107] The (apparently positive) effects of his evening reading of passages in his diaries, recording the time Klaus Heuser had spent in the house in Munich, were still felt the next morning.[108]

A few months later, he returned to the contrast between his relationship with Klaus Heuser and the more "melancholy" romantic experiences of his youth. Thirty years on, he is able to declare that he has "lived and loved," that he has attained happiness and been able to "enfold within his arms that which he desired," and that the later passion was "more mature, more considered, happier" than those of his earlier life.[109] In 1942, he revisited the episode:

> I read extensively in the old diaries from the Klaus Heuser time, when I was a fortunate lover. The most beautiful and touching parting in Munich, when I realized my dreams, and laid his temples against my own. Yes, I have lived and loved. Black eyes that shed tears for me, beloved lips that I kissed—it happened, I too had this, and I shall be able to tell myself that when I die.[110]

As with the young Platen, the fulfillment of sexual desire comes with a kiss.[111]

We return to the sensibility of Goethe's morning musings, to the conception of a purified and acceptable sexuality grounded in the visual apprehension of beauty. So: *what if* a young man had taken Katia's place in bed? If Mann had held true to the thoughts he had formulated and the feelings he had reflectively endorsed—very little. Of course, discipline might have broken down: as we shall see, he was all too preoccupied with that possibility. Throughout his life, he wanted to distinguish his own inclinations from what he saw as the "orgiastic release" of a homosexuality much more developed than his own.[112] He distinguished his own novella from his son Klaus's coming-out novel (*Der Fromme Tanz*).

FIGURE 2.1. *Kinderkarneval*, Friedrich August Kaulbach, 1888. The five Pringsheim children. Thomas Mann cut this picture out and kept it.

Klaus's own diary commented on the difference between his own sexual identity and that of his father: "the theme of seduction is so characteristic of 'Zauberer' [magician; the family name for Thomas Mann] — in opposition to me. The seduction motif: Romanticism — music — Wagner — Venice — death — 'sympathy with the abyss' — pederasty. . . . Different for me."[113]

The entangling of his homoerotic desires with aesthetic fulfillment was central to Mann's conception of his own sexuality. To the end, he longed to separate love from the lower part of the body. That love flowed in two directions — toward young men, through his enraptured gaze, consummated, perhaps, in a few embraces, a kiss at parting — but also to the woman he married. He saw her first in a picture, posed with her four brothers, all in pierrot costumes. Katia records that, in his youth in Lübeck, "he saw the picture in a magazine. It pleased him so, that he cut it out and fastened it with drawing-pins over his desk. Thus he had it always before his eyes."[114]

Five children, all attractive with similar features, four of them boys, wearing costumes that elide sexual differences . . . that is what is shown in the picture Mann chose. Nevertheless, whatever the grounds of the original attraction, whatever the vicissitudes of his sexual difficulties, despite the often-noted lack of interest in the diaries about what "Katja" wore or said or did (in marked contrast to Mann's preoccupation with minute details of his daily life), there can be little question of the strong bond with his wife.[115] Besides the gratitude expressed for the understanding she showed and the comfort she supplied, their marriage embodied their devotion to a common purpose—*his* purpose—prefigured in the depiction of Imma and Klaus Heinrich. A diary entry from 1933 uses a different figure from his fiction in her praise. Reading the proofs of the first volume of the *Joseph* tetralogy, Mann

> was again moved to tears by Rachel's death, as in the writing and as inevitably recurs on each rereading. The origin of this character in my relationship to K. plays a role in this. It isn't for nothing that she loves the story of Jacob and Rachel so much. She recognizes it as the idealized, mythical, representation of our lifelong companionship.[116]

For all the intensity of his focus on himself, for all the effusions about the beauty of the young male body, it would be wrong to conclude that the creator of Rachel was incapable of at least some form of heterosexual love.

Aschenbach may be confined by the society to which he belongs, but his complex sexuality is also shaped by it. That sexuality, refracted for the reader through the Platonic tradition, through Platen's poetry and attempts at self-definition, through Goethe's musings and Klaus Heinrich's marriage, and, above all, through Mann's wrestling with his own inclinations, is molded into a form Aschenbach can accept. We should reject the idea of some "core identity" in Mann or in Aschenbach (or in the young Platen), a biologically fixed drive that continues to yearn for complete homosexual intercourse, something that is opposed and eventually repressed by the pressures of the ambient society. Thought about human behavior and the inclinations and capacities that underlie it is all too easily distorted by hypothesizing some fixed nature that socialization may combat or foster or even liberate.[117] The specific form of homosexual desire attributed to Aschenbach and to his creator, desire that is satisfied in gazing on the beloved or that culminates in an embrace or a kiss, expresses their real selves—it is no façade erected to mask urges that cannot be confessed. Given the social worlds in which they have grown to adulthood, these are the people they have come to be. When, in a late diary entry, Mann asks rhetorically "How can one sleep with men?" he is completely self-conscious and sincere.[118]

Nevertheless, without lapsing into the myth of the preformed self, the idea that the social environment has confined a person retains its sense.[119] Imagine Thomas Mann growing up a century later, perhaps in Hamburg rather than in Lübeck, able to express his attraction to other men, experiencing joy in full homosexual intercourse. Comparing this imaginary figure (a happier Klaus?) with the real thing, you may be inclined to envisage possibilities of greater fulfillment, even to judge that the actual Thomas Mann's life was diminished by the prejudices of the society that shaped him—he could, it seems, have had a richer, deeper set of sexual desires and could have satisfied them. Judgments of this kind rightly identify the depth and intensity of full sexual relations—just as Klaus Mann confided to his diary—but they raise questions that are hard to answer. The actual Thomas Mann (and the Aschenbach he created) forgo particular profound pleasures they might have had, but it does not follow that they are—overall—less fulfilled, that—as a whole—their lives are rendered less worthwhile. Global comparisons of the value of lives across different environments are not easy, even though there may be one respect, even an important respect, in which one regime of socialization precludes a central and rewarding form of human satisfaction. We do not need to make a global comparison, however, to ground a judgment that society has confined a person's life: it is enough to point to a major part of human experience and to features of the social environment that prevent full and fulfilling exploration of that domain.

To claim, as I have done, that a particular form of sexual identity, attributed to Aschenbach or to his creator, goes "all the way down" allows for the possibility that the expression of that identity, in some episode of attraction or infatuation, might involve self-deception or pretense. Aschenbach's desire to gaze on Tadzio's beauty, even to yearn for an embrace, expresses entirely and completely his sexual character. When he thinks, however, of laying a "fatherly" hand on the boy's shoulder, or when he imagines himself playing Socrates to Tadzio's Phaedrus or Alcibiades, he is indulging a comfortable illusion: what, after all, would they have to say to each other?[120] In these respects, Aschenbach is as deluded as countless other lovers, fictitious and real.

To understand a sexual identity is not necessarily to endorse it. We may well regard Aschenbach and Mann as curtailed in their sexual development, unable to reach out for the intense pleasures that should have been available to them, as importing fantasies into their self-confessions in affairs of the heart, and we may view the limitations and deceptions as effects of intolerant and prejudiced societies—all this is consistent with reconstructing their longings as I have done. That reconstruction is crucial. For the danger of harboring those very particular yearnings is central to one important aspect of the novella. Mann used Aschenbach to dramatize a possibility he feared: to maintain this form of sexuality requires a stringent discipline, one that may border on the superhuman—for it is vulnerable to the very beauty it celebrates.

5

On the "sexual" reading of Aschenbach, he is thoroughly self-deceived, refusing to acknowledge his sexual inclinations until their violence forces him to do so. I propose, instead, that his self-deception is only partial. What he wants from Tadzio is simply more of what he actually gets, a continuous opportunity to look on, to gaze, to smile and be smiled at—or, perhaps beyond that, conversation, openly exchanged looks of mutual understanding, or a gentle touch, a modest embrace, and a chaste kiss. Society may *actually* frown on these desires or their fulfillment, but it *should* not do so. Aschenbach's conception of the ideal citizen includes the possibility of responding to beauty as he sees himself responding to Tadzio, and his conception of the ideal artist-educator favors the project of making beauty manifest so that narrow prejudices are undone. Thus the supposed tension between artist and citizen is resolved: Aschenbach is clear about his own attractions to boys and young men (Tadzio, and any predecessors who featured along the writer's walks or who attended his public readings), clear about the proper limits of homosexual expression, and clear about the integration of these inclinations with his (now past) life as husband and father.

On this reading, he would recognize, from the beginning, the erotic character of his delight in Tadzio, seeing the content of his underlying desires as directed at being in Tadzio's presence, exchanging glances with him, and so forth. Indeed, he would be right about that. His error would lie in believing that such disciplined eroticism is safe, that it could not invade other areas of his psychological life and undermine his moral commitments. Seen in this way, he is not deceived about the *content* of his sexual desires but only about their *scope* and *power*.

When Aschenbach confesses his love for the boy, he is prompted by a smile. He characterizes that smile as that of Narcissus, enchanted by his own reflection in the mirror. The mirror in which Tadzio has seen himself is Aschenbach, surprised and overjoyed by the sudden appearance of the Polish family. To view the writer as the mirror of Narcissus is to understand him as the passive recipient of beauty, whose sole activity consists in creating opportunities for the expression of beauty.[121] We might even say that his erotic love is not directed primarily at Tadzio but toward the feelings and images that the boy impresses upon him. Tadzio becomes an "image at the seaside"—a *Bild am Meer* rather than a *Bild am Wege*. In his notebook for the period in which he was writing *Death in Venice*, Mann copied out Spinoza's definition of love: an excitation accompanied by the idea of an external thing.[122] Aschenbach cannot leave Venice and must pursue Tadzio not because he wants physically to possess him but because of his insatiable desire for the excitation produced by an external object, the boy whose life does not really touch his own.[123]

To be a perfect mirror of Narcissus is to be exquisitely sensitive to beauty, and that sensitivity brings danger. In his parody of Socrates, Aschenbach contends that the perception of beauty leads inexorably to intoxication and desire, to actions that flout moral strictures, and so to corruption and "the abyss" (*der Abgrund*).[124] The argument the writer rehearses, to be examined shortly, aims to uncover a deep tension between the roles of citizen and artist, even in the idealized form that aspires to transcend the split. The resolution Aschenbach hoped to have achieved is inadequate not because he has repressed homosexual desires but because the sexual identity he has fashioned and its integration with the quest of the artist-educator, the pursuit of beauty, can only be combined with the conduct of the ideal citizen through a discipline so fierce and severe as to be unsustainable. Aschenbach's homosexual desires heighten the drama of the undoing of his discipline precisely because that discipline is so central to his life not only as a writer but also in the shaping of his sexual self. Those inclinations have been recognized and channeled toward a proper object—beauty—to be gazed at, captured in words, touched modestly, perhaps at last with a "spiritual kiss on the raspberry lips of the world": the need for self-control has been thoroughly absorbed. To think that is, however, self-deception. Discipline is undone by the lure of beauty.

Mann was preoccupied by the theme, perhaps because of his sympathy with Schopenhauer's thesis that the "higher" objectifications of blind will are in intense conflict with those that are more basic: the struggle between spiritual striving and sexuality being particularly acute.[125] From his early stories on, he explores the ways in which human self-conceptions, even human lives, may be undone by the lure of beauty and the desires it elicits. Those desires do not have to be homosexual or even socially forbidden, merely at odds with the previously chosen self, and the power of the lure of beauty will be most clearly revealed when the subject is already forewarned—a writer, for example, who has reflectively endorsed limits to the expression of desire and who polices those limits with strict discipline.

Little Friedemann falls victim to the lure of beauty. His youthful experiences convince him that fulfilled romantic love is not part of his lot, and he turns to the arts, achieving what appears to be a disciplined serenity. That is disturbed by the arrival of the beautiful Gerda von Rinnlingen, whose charms Friedemann struggles to resist. Resistance finally breaks down at a performance of *Lohengrin*, where she is his neighbor in the box: she drops her fan, and they both stoop. "Their heads had been quite close together, and, for a moment, he had had to breathe in the warm scent of her breasts. His face was contorted, his whole body shook, and his heart beat so appallingly heavily and violently that his breathing stopped."[126] The combination of surging romantic music and enforced proximity to female beauty is too much for Friedemann. His disciplined acceptance of quiet joys—the static pleasures recommended by Epicurus—is acutely felt as insufficient. He must strive, against all his good judgment, hopelessly, ludicrously, for more, and when the inevitable rejection comes, he sees no alternative to death. The effects of the lure of beauty are more pronounced in Friedemann's case than they are in Aschenbach's—despite the fact that the desires beauty provokes in him are socially permissible, even if absurdly quixotic: Friedemann's life is curtailed; Aschenbach's probably is not.[127] Both characters deploy the same metaphor to describe the breakdown of their discipline, both refer to the "abyss" (*Abgrund*).[128] With a little exaggeration, we could say that Friedemann ends there.

A second example of the preoccupation with the lure of beauty, far more extensive, many sided, and profound, occurs in the *Joseph* tetralogy. Mann draws the material for an extensive episode (almost two hundred pages) from fourteen verses of Genesis.[129] The source tells merely that the wife of Potiphar, whom Joseph serves, invites him to lie with her; he flees, leaving his "garment" behind. On the return of her husband, she accuses Joseph of trying to seduce her, and Potiphar sends Joseph to prison.

Mann gives Potiphar's wife a name and an extensive character. She is Mut-em-enet, Potiphar's "titular wife,"[130] known for her purity and chastity, the "nun of the moon" (*Mondnonne*), whose participation in sublime religious rites is much admired. The appointment of Joseph as Potiphar's steward brings a beautiful young man daily into her presence and disturbs her unfulfilled marriage. Aware of the passion that arises within her, she struggles to resist it. Over a period of three years, she attempts to have Joseph dismissed, even pleading with her husband to send him away. Potiphar refuses. Irresistible desires grow within her, driving her to grotesque and demeaning rituals.[131] Eventually, abandoning both chastity and dignity, she attempts to seduce Joseph. Rejected, she emerges from the palace, bearing his clothing, and calls the Egyptians of the household to hear what the foreign slave has attempted. Joseph is bound and taken away. Mut sits on the ground before the palace and awaits her husband's justice.

Yet Joseph is partially complicit in these events. He is aware of his own charms, delights in them, and refuses advice to avoid Mut's presence. His actions amplify the corrupting effects of his beauty. In this, he further develops aspects of Tadzio that Mann presents only fleetingly—for example, the Narcissus smile that wrings from Aschenbach a confession of his love for the boy. The lure of beauty applies to the bearer of beauty himself, and, because of that corruption, the corruption of others proceeds more easily. Tadzio's future decay—his corruptible mortality—is touched on only fleetingly, when Aschenbach takes note of his pallor and of his teeth.[132] Joseph's self-corruption by his own beauty receives extensive treatment: we are introduced to him as he lies, in a state of provocative undress, under the moon—thereby eliciting the rebuke of his father.[133] His delight in the coat his father has favored him with leads him to carry out the mad plan of parading his beauty and distinction to the world, which prompts his envious brothers to strip him naked and cast him into a pit.[134] In the face of Mut's unbounded passion for him, he decides to carry out his supposed "duty" of inspecting that part of the palace in which she is alone.[135] Justice requires that Joseph be punished—that he be thrown into the pit a second time.

Potiphar delivers justice. Arriving home, he hears the accusations, listens to the pleas of Joseph's longstanding foes that the young foreigner be mutilated, observes Joseph's silence (which he praises), and offers a swift and sure verdict. Joseph is not to be killed or even subjected to bodily damage. Instead, he is to go to a labor camp in the Nile delta. This is Potiphar's finest hour. A figure previously portrayed as genial but lazy, cultured but inclined to dilettantism, a master of the ceremonies and leisure pursuits of aristocrats, emerges as an impartial and fair judge—even in a case in which jealousy might inspire harsh and partial judgment.

Why is this? The secret of Potiphar's achievement as a judge is the secret of his earlier failure as a husband, the secret of his imperviousness to Mut's pleas for Joseph's dismissal—and the secret of his uncomprehending suggestion to her, in the aftermath of the trial, that, since she has held herself in the house throughout the festival day, they might now enjoy the evening together in celebration (a wonderfully ironic close to the third part of the tetralogy).[136] In Mann's version, Potiphar is a eunuch. As Joseph learns, before he even enters Potiphar's service, the noble boy received a "little snip," a penance paid by his parents, brother and sister, whose incest created him.[137]

If "Friedemann" can be taken as a simplified miniature of the lure of beauty that overwhelms Aschenbach, the breakdown of Mut's extraordinary resistance reveals it on an epic scale. Mann wanted his readers to appreciate the possibility that the lure of beauty is irresistible, that the

Socratic restraint that so impressed (and perhaps disappointed) Alcibiades is a myth. Only those who have been freed from sexuality entirely, who have come to Potiphar's condition, can emerge unscathed from the encounter with beauty.[138] That is one way—the only way?—to separate the lower body from love, or as Mann wrote in a (slightly later) letter to Grauthof, urging his friend to develop discipline with respect to the urges that troubled him, to "fasten the dog in the basement to his chain."[139]

Aschenbach's anti-Socratic murmurings at the fountain elaborate this attitude. They oppose the possibility, presented (maybe regretted?) by Alcibiades, of the Socratic discipline that can both apprehend beauty and restrain the associated erotic desires, allowing the lover to become a genuine moral educator and friend in the fullest sense. They also contest the idea of some route to artistic insight independent of the perception of beauty and thus freed of the lure that would corrupt any discipline of which human beings are capable. In explanation of his own fall, Aschenbach presents a Socratic dilemma. There are two potential routes to artistic insight. One—a path the obituary chapter tells us Aschenbach rightly abandoned—involves deep and intimate knowledge of the human condition. Those who follow this path recognize and communicate the detailed circumstances of human actions and thereby bring readers to understand, to sympathize, and to excuse: the moralizing author of the obituary praises Aschenbach for avoiding this "sympathy with the abyss," for refusing a route that leads to the laxity of thinking that all is to be forgiven.[140] The alternative path focuses on beauty, attunes itself to purity of form. Yet, as Aschenbach's own example has shown, the development of the capacity to apprehend beauty makes the artist vulnerable to erotic passions of such power that they cannot be resisted. The more fully developed the sensitivities that suit the artist for his ideal role—recognizing beauty and serving as a perfect mirror of Narcissus, reflecting beauty in fullest form—the greater the power of the erotic longings: the dog can no longer be kept on its chain. The lure of beauty leads to intoxication and desire and an equally ineluctable descent into the abyss.

It is easy to dismiss this supposed dilemma as sophistry, even to think of it as deliberate sophistry, intended to reveal Aschenbach's debasement in a bitter but unsuccessful effort to rationalize his predicament. I pointed earlier to the complex of ideas involved in Aschenbach's original conception of the artist and to the questions they raise, and now, faced with the alleged dilemma, it seems vulnerable to critique on any number of grounds. Why should we endorse the background idea of the artist as perceiving something "higher" and communicating it to society? Why suppose that there are just these two routes to this "higher" insight? Why take them to have the features Aschenbach attributes to them? Why suppose, in particular, that the perception of beauty must always be erotic? Only someone in the grip of a particular version of Platonism would be moved by the reasoning Aschenbach presents.

Just as philosophers continue to find insights in Platonic dialogues, so too I think here. Provided we take one step with Mann, endorsing his basic conception of the artist—or the poet-philosopher—as an educator in the fullest sense, an *Erzieher*, we can reconstruct an interesting line of reasoning. This educative role is not to be fulfilled by some iconoclastic act, a revaluation of values that will expose and undermine the commitments of bourgeois society and its "light-living" members.[141] Rather, the poet-philosopher's deeper insight into the human condition makes the worth of those commitments clearer, makes them more stable, perhaps refines them. What forms might the communication of insight take? One possibility is the deeply psychologistic novel or drama, in which motives are thoroughly probed and in which readers are led to sympathize with figures who see circumstances from different perspectives. A paradigm would be Schiller's *Don Carlos*, the work the young Tonio Kröger wants Hans Hansen to read and one the mature Kröger rejoices that he hasn't read. The recognition of the psychological complexities promotes sympathy with varied perspectives and thereby weakens the force of bourgeois commitment to simple principles and values. Indeed, it may weaken the commitments of the poet-philosopher, making him unfit for the society whose educator he is supposed to be.

The *Joseph* tetralogy illustrates the phenomenon. Its elaborate and speculative psychology for the mythical characters of the book of Genesis leads to forms of sympathy for which the simple biblical narrative provides no basis. We come to view Joseph, Mut, and Potiphar from different angles and thereby to suspend unrestricted praise or unrestricted condemnation. As one of the narrative voices explains at some length, we have to rethink the much-lauded chastity of Joseph. So, in one of Mann's brilliantly sly passages of "religious commentary" (a higher "higher criticism"), seven different motives are given for Joseph's resistance to Mut's seductions.[142] The discussion leads to an obvious question:

But why did he dare to go so far? . . . In a word: why did he not rather avoid the lady completely, but let things go between him and her, as far as it is known to have gone? Yes, that was making eyes at the world and showing a taste for curiosity about what is forbidden; there was also a certain corruption of thought with respect to his posthumous reputation and the divine disposition which he recognized in himself; there was also something of cocksure overconfidence, his reliance on the fact that he could flirt with danger—he could always retreat, if necessary; it was probably also, as the laudable flipside of this, the will to challenge himself, the ambition to put himself to severe test, not to protect himself but to push himself to the uttermost, in order to emerge triumphant from the temptation—to complete a virtuoso performance of virtue and to be more true to the spirit of his father than after a predictably easier trial . . . [143]

Or possibly, as the chapter concludes, because he foresaw the coming events. In any case, for those who have learned the commentator's details, Joseph can no longer serve as an uncomplicated paradigm for human conduct—inspiration has given way to opportunities for reflective deliberation. That is a loss for those good citizens who need the right patterns to "live lightly." Better for bourgeois society, perhaps, to stay with those fourteen verses of Genesis.

So the art that educates through careful and detailed presentation of complexities is dangerous. The alternative, pursued by the mature Aschenbach, is the presentation of what is valuable as beautiful. If writing of this sort is to be effective, however, it requires the development of aesthetic capacities on the part of the poet-philosopher and possibly also among his readers, capacities that are themselves problematic. For the lure of beauty depends on the fact that sensitive attunement to the beautiful requires the capacity for erotic arousal by it, and those with this capacity may transfer the passion from what is enduringly worthwhile to things that are more suspect—as Aschenbach's passion is turned to Tadzio. The effect of that turning is the reinforcing of a desire, the wish to gaze on beauty, that is not problematic in itself but equipped with such power that it distorts moral judgment: Aschenbach is not Mut, for whom sexual impulses are to be expressed in intercourse, but the intensity of his erotic emotions leads him to moral compromise: he remains silent about the epidemic. The crucial premise for the quasi-Socratic argument maintains that developed sensitivity to beauty must have some such disruptive effect—sex must out in some fashion or other: it is a thesis that greatly interests (and perturbs) Mann but one we may not wish to endorse.[144] Is it a matter of psychological fact that the refinement of sensibility is always accompanied by the flowering of sensuality? Does attuning yourself to beauty inevitably arouse the dog in the basement? Is the only "solution" Potiphar's—to neutralize the lower body and thus forcibly separate it from love?

Aschenbach's reasoning can thus be detached from the explicitly Platonic framework in which he develops it. When reformulated, it may not compel assent, but it should engage our interest. To be sure, the conclusion is more limited than the one Aschenbach draws. Slumped at the fountain, he abjectly concludes that the synthesis for which he has striven is impossible: the conception of the artist as *Erzieher* and good citizen simply falls apart. On the revised account, that conception is endangered. Only with careful, possibly heroic discipline can the poet-philosopher find ways of apprehending and communicating insights that will not lead him or his readers to forms of moral relativism or moral nihilism. His development of his own sensibilities must be carefully controlled, his explorations of the details of human life not so extensive as to disturb a precarious equilibrium. The cultivation of refined perceptions must be accompanied by a studied development of bluntness, a resistance to the lower forms of blind Will, an ever tighter attachment of the dog to its chain. It is a kind of confidence trick after all.

In his despair, Aschenbach takes himself to have failed completely. That is an overreaction: for two decades he has brought off the trick with great virtuosity. If the episode in Venice discloses his failure, readers need not accept his pessimistic verdict—nor, for that matter, the judgment of the moralizing narrator. Even if the complete identification Tonio Kröger envisaged has eluded him, Aschenbach has come close. Perhaps his creator did, too.

## 6

For a different perspective on the material of the novella and the themes of the previous sections, it is interesting to turn to the last opera of a great twentieth-century composer, a man much more at ease with his own sexuality than Mann had been, even open about his interest in adolescent boys.[145] Perhaps Britten's *Death in Venice* should be seen and heard as more resolutely pursuing the sexual interpretation: concentrating on the deformations society exerts on a sensitive artist whose sexual inclinations are not to the public taste. Yet, Robert Tear, one of those who has sung Aschenbach, recognizes the extent to which Britten follows Mann in embedding the protagonist's yearnings within a philosophical frame, one apparently intended to make them more respectable or at least more tolerable. Tear comments: "Musically, it's a masterpiece. But there's a cop-out. It mustn't be called sexual lust. It's Beauty, or it's Greek. And that's a cop-out."[146] Two of Tear's points are absolutely correct: it is a musical masterpiece, and Britten does embed the sexual themes within the aesthetic and philosophical framework of Mann's novella. Nevertheless, I shall suggest that Britten places *less* emphasis on the aesthetic and philosophical issues than Mann does and that his opera is consequently *closer* to the sexual interpretation of the original story.

Just as critics have sometimes castigated Visconti for his departures from the novella,[47] they have rightly praised Britten and his librettist, Myfanwy Piper, for their fidelity to Mann.[148] When Britten was exploring the possibility of the project, Golo Mann wrote to him about his father's admiration for him.[149] Although Mann may have previously heard of Britten — perhaps from conversations with Auden during the period shortly after his eldest daughter, Erika, married the British poet and thereby obtained the right to enter Britain[150] — his first introduction to Britten's music seems to have come when he listened to a recording of the *Serenade for Tenor, Horn, and Strings*.[151] He was sufficiently impressed to listen again, in Erika's company, and to compare one of Britten's settings with the music of the central figure (Adrian Leverkühn) in the novel he had recently finished (*Doktor Faustus*): "Blake's 'sick rose' could well be by Adrian."[152] Golo Mann's letter recapitulates the idea of that connection: responding enthusiastically to Britten's request for permission to set *Death in Venice*, he relates his father's view that Britten "would be the composer" to attempt a "musical illustration" of *Doktor Faustus*.[153] On the face of it, the connection is inappropriate: Leverkühn's compositional ideas are modeled on those of Schoenberg (for whose music Mann had little sympathy),[154] and the idea of twelve-tone music is attributed to Mann's fictional protagonist; Britten's own musical idiom is far more conservative and free of the rigorous constraints both Leverkühn and Schoenberg emphasize; interestingly, however, the German film version of *Doktor Faustus* follows Mann's thought and uses passages from Britten, particularly from the *War Requiem*, as examples of Leverkühn's music.[155] The adaptation of *Death in Venice* was thus an unusual one in that both writer and composer knew the other's work and admired it.[156]

From the opening moments of the opera, it is evident that Britten is attuned to the artistic difficulties Aschenbach faces. The gnawing motif, "My mind beats on," makes musically vivid the unproductive pulses that continue after the writer has left his desk, capturing the psychological state described in the novella's opening paragraph. Similarly, the moment of illusory resolution—"The boy Tadzio shall inspire me"—provides a nervous bravado well suited to this stage of Aschenbach's progress. These are only two of many examples in which Britten's sensitivity to nuances of the text, beyond the homoerotic themes, is matched by extraordinary skill in what one might have thought was almost impossible— operatically adapting a work whose main arena is the central character's mind. Despite all these efforts, the opera is, even had to be, a differently oriented work than the novella. The aesthetic-philosophical questions are directed differently in Britten's treatment, and, despite Tear's complaints, the homosexual passions are given a more central place than they are in Mann.

Most obvious is the sensuality of the music, the opulent orchestral coloring and the lushness of some important motifs (prominent examples are the "Serenissima" and "View" themes).[157] This musical backdrop creates a context in which Aschenbach's fascination with Tadzio cannot be heard as anything other than erotic. The possibility of a disciplined artistic perception of beauty is never present: from the moment he encounters Tadzio and we hear the exotic vibraphone motif that accompanies the boy, Aschenbach must be understood to be in the grip of passions he refuses to acknowledge. The sexually ambiguous voice of Apollo, sung by a countertenor, enhances the effect. That voice is first heard in the "games of Apollo," a ballet scene Britten uses to stand for Aschenbach's Greek idyll (the period in which he officially contemplates Tadzio as an embodiment of pure beauty), and the quality of the voice invites us to conceive it as a homoerotic festival to which Aschenbach responds with delight.

Because of the evident difficulty of matching the quasi-Socratic passages to convincing music, Piper and Britten effectively eliminate the first of them—the games of Apollo ballet stands in—but the second, the anti-Socratic ruminations at the fountain, could not be omitted. Musically and dramatically, it would have been impossible at this point to introduce a spare and angular setting suited to the bitter argument of the text. The focus would have to be on the *logic* of Aschenbach's attempt to diagnose his predicament, and it is hard to envisage how any music could do that—and if the words were simply *spoken*, they would lack the force appropriate to this moment. Britten solved the problem by changing the quality of the reflections, providing Aschenbach with a hauntingly tender song of farewell, his last extended music in the opera. It is a threnody for a love Aschenbach has had to confront but that he cannot endorse, and it is simultaneously an adieu to Tadzio, easily identified as the "Phaedrus" to whom it is sung. It is impossible to hear in it Aschenbach's austere and embittered attempt to think through the questions about beauty and art that have preoccupied him. Consequently, the scene is shifted away from his failure to be the type of artist he has aspired to be and toward the expression of his unfulfilled love.

There are other respects in which the unacknowledged intensity of Aschenbach's passion is given greater prominence. Uncharacteristically, Britten struggled with the score, and, even after the early performances, there were cuts and changes.[158] One problem he confronted was that of shortening the music of the first act to allow a balance with the second.[159] The resolution was to break the opera at the point of Aschenbach's self-confession and thus to give even more prominence to this moment. Indeed, it is easy to hear it as the climax of the first act, the point to which Aschenbach has been tending from the beginning, his sudden awareness of who he is and what he most profoundly desires.

Practical considerations, this time of staging, led Piper and Britten to make another significant modification. In the novella, Aschenbach's repudiation of his felt duty to warn the Poles is immediately followed by the terrible dream. The opera replaces the violent Bacchic orgy with the appearance of Dionysius—sung by the bass-baritone who has played earlier menacing and disturbing figures—who engages Apollo in a struggle for Aschenbach's allegiance.[160] The assignment of the various nameless figures to a single voice makes excellent musical sense, but it invites the thought that Aschenbach is encountering a single force, his repressed desires, ultimately unmasked when the singer shows himself as Dionysius. In the vocal duel—a contest for Aschenbach's soul?[161]—Dionysius triumphs, and Apollo leaves, singing "I go, I go now," words echoed in Aschenbach's farewell to Phaedrus/Tadzio. Deserted by Apollo, Aschenbach too must leave, and the reappearance of the bass-baritone as the hotel manager makes the nature of this departure clear: the "time of politeness and welcome" is over; "who comes and goes" is the hotel manager's affair.[162] By giving the manager a prominence not envisaged in the novella, Britten confirms him as the last of the messengers of death, indeed as the powerful Dionysius to whom Aschenbach has given himself and who will now decide his fate.

The final scene of the opera, focused on games that turn into the serious fight between Tadzio and Jaschu, stands in obvious relation to the "games of Apollo" of Aschenbach's Greek idyll. Apollo has departed, and these can only be the games of Dionysius, passionate, violent, and cruel. In Britten's setting, the mood established in the threnody to Tadzio/Phaedrus continues through the somber pronouncements of the hotel manager to culminate in the bleakness of the deserted beach, on which the last bare rites of unmasked passion are enacted. The music seems to make inevitable Aschenbach's agitation and his final collapse, and, at least in my seeing and hearing, the closing measures of the score and the final tableau do no more than remind us of how he has descended to his death. The coda of the novella is thus woven into the previous scenes, understood as the continuation of the tragic decline to death. Tear was wrong to think that Britten avoided the reality of Aschenbach's sexuality—for the "cop-out" in the invocation of classical ideas is exposed in the cruelty of the Dionysian rites. He would, however, have been right to claim that Britten's focus on the destructive power of unacknowledged passion was one-sided.

Despite its astonishing evocation of the ambiguity of Venice, Britten's opera, seen without reference to the original novella, is relatively unambiguous. It is the tragedy of a gifted and sensitive man torn apart by the force of erotic desires he has struggled to avoid or repress. As in so many of Britten's earlier works, our sympathy with the central figure results from recognizing him as a victim, someone whose predicament is brought about by the failure of others to recognize the value of what he is and wants. Despite Aschenbach's worldly success, he belongs in the world of Mann's outsiders, of Christian Buddenbrook and little Friedemann and Tonio Kröger: the envisaged identity that goes beyond Tonio to fuse artist and citizen is shattered. The world we are presented with is also that of Britten's outsiders. Aschenbach is another version of Peter Grimes, with the difference that Aschenbach does not have the conventions of the Borough thrust upon him but instead absorbs them deeply within himself.

## 7

If that were all there is to say about Britten's opera, then it would pay the price of its dedicated fidelity, standing as a vivid translation of a specific way of reading the novella into music of great beauty. Yet, just as some ideas in Mann's novella can be illuminated by seeing them in light of his other works—we can view the preoccupation with the lure of beauty in the stories of Friedemann and of Mut—so too with Britten. If one comes to the opera *Death in Venice* after concentrated hearing of *Peter Grimes*, the effect will be to underscore the interpretation I have sketched. *Billy Budd* provides a different perspective.[163]

There are two remarkable affinities between the operas. One is the explicit discussion of Beauty in both.[164] In Britten's version, Billy is referred to as "Beauty" both by his admiring fellow sailors and by his adversary, the master-at-arms Claggart. He is seen as the embodiment of virtue and goodness, the moral attributes connected to the aesthetic ones, just as they are in Aschenbach's Greek meditations. The second affinity lies in the motifs Britten uses for the confessions of three major characters: Claggart, Captain Vere, and Aschenbach. Each of them makes a declaration in similar words.

I, John Claggart, master-at-arms upon the *Indomitable*, have you in my power, and I will destroy you.

I, Edward Fairfax Vere, captain of the *Indomitable*, lost with all hands on the infinite sea.

I, Aschenbach, famous as master-writer, successful, honored, self-discipline my strength . . .

(a) Vere

(b) Claggart

Figure 2.2, *continued next page*

(c) Aschenbach

FIGURE 2.2. Three declamations (Vere, Claggart, Aschenbach).

Yet it is not just the similarity of the word structures but the musical setting that unites these lines. In each instance, Britten assigns the singers (Vere, like Aschenbach, is a tenor; Claggart a bass) a sequence of repeated notes, high in the singer's range, with a shared, distinctive, rhythmic pattern.[165] He thus invites us to consider the kinship between Claggart and Vere and, for those who come to *Death in Venice* with *Billy Budd* in their ears, the kinship of both to Aschenbach.

How can this be? Claggart is threatened by Billy's beauty, moved to a desire to destroy it. For the recognition of "beauty, handsomeness, goodness" is a reminder of what he is not, a disturbance of the precarious equilibrium he has fashioned for himself. His attempt to convict Billy of treason and mutiny leads to a confrontation in which the youth, unable to speak because of his stammer, answers with his fist. Claggart falls dead, and it is left to Vere to administer justice, to condemn Billy to death and so to complete that destruction at which Claggart had aimed.

Vere makes his declamation at the moment when he has just committed himself to carrying out the sentence of death; Claggart's comes as he announces his intention to achieve that end. Claggart and Vere, then, are bound together in the destruction of Beauty, the one because of its threat to him, the other with great reluctance and guilt. As Vere sings: "I was lost on the infinite sea."

In Britten's *Death in Venice*, the roles are reversed. Aschenbach does not destroy Beauty but is himself destroyed by his perception of it. If, however, we consider the final scene of the opera, there is a trio of figures: Aschenbach, Jaschu, and Tadzio. In these Dionysian games, Jaschu rises up against Beauty, overthrowing Tadzio, while Aschenbach, like Vere, looks on, helpless. We can even conceive this witnessing of the defeat of Beauty as the immediate cause of Aschenbach's death—assuming we do not take it for granted that the writer succumbs to cholera.[166]

Billy Budd has a flaw, the fatal stammer that prevents him from replying to Claggart's accusation—and so, too, with Tadzio. In Mann's version there are physical imperfections: on his first sight of the boy, Aschenbach wonders whether the pallor of his skin connotes sickliness, and his later observation of Tadzio's teeth reveals them to be jagged and unhealthy. Concluding that the boy will probably not grow old, Aschenbach has feelings of satisfaction—as if he were secretly glad that this embodiment of Beauty will perish prematurely.[167] This is not Claggart's wish to smash and destroy, but it is an echo of it, one that will be heard further in Aschenbach's fantasy of a diseased Venice in which he and the boy linger on, perhaps in some hoped-for *Liebestod*.[168]

Britten's opera omits the physical flaws but highlights Aschenbach's fantasy of a world in which he and Tadzio are left alone. It also develops further the moral flaws that Aschenbach is pleased to observe in the boy—the proud petulance and the narcissistic joy in the regard of others. (Britten's Tadzio is more coquettish than Mann's, although he is an amateur compared with the extraordinary flirt Visconti depicts.) With the earlier opera in mind, we might understand these flaws as background to the final scene, as spurs to Jaschu's revolt, indications of coming destruction that is prefigured in the wrestling match (the culmination of the Games of Apollo in act 1). Like Vere, Aschenbach must look on at the fragility of Beauty, must recognize its transience, must understand that he is powerless to prevent its passing.

Mann's novella is framed by announcements of von Aschenbach's eminence and by the worldwide reverberations of his death. Britten's *Billy Budd* is also framed by monologues, an opening in which the older Vere remembers the pivotal events on the vessel he commanded, events that changed his sense of self, and a coda in which he recalls how the Beauty and Goodness he helped destroy proved able to restore him, how he found his way again.

The Vere who opens *Billy Budd* is an old man, one who "has experienced much." The good he has seen, he tells us, has never been perfect—there has always been "some stammer in the divine speech." Although he has tried to work for the good, his efforts have been confused. He has been "lost on the infinite sea," and he asks: "Who has blessed me? Who saved me?"

The answer, of course, is Billy Budd, the young man whom he sentenced to death. Vere needs to work through—surely not for the first time—the events of 1797: the opera unfolds in the mind of an old man searching for reconciliation with what he has been and done. In the epilogue, the older Vere is on stage again, asking the same questions. Now they have answers.

> O what have I done? O what, what have I done? But he has saved me, and blessed me, and the love that passeth understanding has come to me. I was lost on the infinite sea, but I've sighted a sail in the storm, the far-shining sail, and I'm content. I've seen where she's bound for. There's a land where she'll anchor for ever. I am an old man now, and my mind can go back in peace to that faraway summer of seventeen hundred and ninety-seven, long ago now, years ago, centuries ago, when I, Edward Fairfax Vere, commanded the *Indomitable* . . .

Even before Vere sings of "the love that passeth understanding" it is overwhelmingly obvious that Billy is a representative of—or a vehicle for—Christ,[169] that his willingly accepted suffering absolves Vere of guilt, that the depth of the goodness he embodies (even if it is flawed with a stammer) enables his captain to find peace. So, it might seem, the crucial difference between *Billy Budd* and *Death in Venice* lies in the character of their theologies. The God of Love presides over the events on the *Indomitable*—the lido is the scene of struggle between Apollo and Dionysius, a struggle inevitably won by an unforgiving, blindly passionate deity, the epitome of Schopenhauer's Will. Hence, Vere can find redemption, whereas Aschenbach must discover failure, humiliation, and a bleak death. Once beyond the Christian world, there is no alternative to destruction.

Perhaps not. For the Platonic connection between Beauty and Goodness is central to the figure of Billy. The stammer mars his physical grace, but *moral* beauty shines through all his actions, even the blow that fells Claggart. Were we to understand Vere as inspired by the apprehension of Beauty, in counterbalance to Claggart's immediate urge to destroy it, we could *humanize* the action. Billy is not Christ—he is a mortal young Englishman in whom the capacity for forgiveness attributed to Jesus manifests itself. A flawed captain is confronted with beauty and goodness, expressed in an extraordinary gesture: "Starry Vere, God bless you!" Billy sings at the moment of execution. That confrontation enables Vere to find peace. Could Aschenbach, conscious of his own flaws, of his straying from the Socratic path that leads through Beauty to Goodness, achieve anything similar? Could Tadzio's walk into the sea, the turn back and the beckoning gestures, lead Aschenbach too to some sense of reconciliation? That is not the operatic ending Britten wrote as he attempted to be faithful to Mann's story, but, as chapter 3 will explore, he might have concluded with something akin to it.

### 8

Vere's anguish and confusion express his sense that he has acted wrongly: he has been complicit in the destruction of goodness. He might be viewed as facing a classic moral dilemma, caught between the duties of his office (that require him to condemn Billy) and his recognition that the murder of Claggart is an act in which evil is eradicated. The deeper self-reproach lies in an awareness that his own conduct has been inadequately sensitive to the sufferings unjustly inflicted upon his men— in his concern to avoid insubordination and possible mutiny, he has allowed the master-at-arms to practice cruelty in the name of discipline. However the etiology of Vere's judgment of Billy is understood, however the morally suspect moments in it are given greater or lesser weight, one thing is clear: the decisions and actions have grave consequences, and the ultimate outcome is one Vere rightly regards as the sacrifice of an innocent.

Mut's seduction by the lure of beauty is similarly consequential. Although Joseph, "chaste Joseph," and even Potiphar may share responsibility for what occurs, she has not only made an assault on Joseph's virtue but also slandered him, thereby exposing him to possible death or mutilation and to an actual unjust imprisonment. It is possible to imagine an extension of the fourth part of Mann's tetralogy, or even an opera based on it, in which Mut's subsequent penitence culminates in a scene in which she receives from Joseph, in his role as Pharaoh's vizier, explicit forgiveness and redemption.[170] The potential opera might even be framed by the anguish of the elderly Mut, just as *Billy Budd* is framed by that of the elderly Vere.

The case of Aschenbach, however, is entirely different. His capitulation to the lure of beauty has no actual consequences for anyone's well-being except, perhaps, his own.[171] To be sure, he fails to warn Tadzio's mother of the cholera that has infected Venice, but it is hard to estimate the difference his moral lapse makes to the chances that any member of the family will fall ill: as already noted, the children are well supervised and thus unlikely to eat contaminated fruit, mother and governess may already have better information than the socially isolated writer, and even an attempt to report the epidemic might fail to convince, because he would be viewed as trafficking in unsubstantiated rumors. Readers rarely blame Aschenbach for not trying to broadcast around Venice the report he hears from the English clerk—a course of conduct he never considers—even though that might be viewed as the behavior of an ideal citizen: tolerance surely rests on thinking that any attempt of the kind would be quixotic.

Aschenbach's failure is *internal* to his own life. By the standards of Greek perfectionism, a life succeeds or fails according to its fit with a proper pattern, a pattern that fully develops the person's nature; a post-Enlightenment modification would abandon the emphasis on individual "natures" in favor of a criterion of autonomous choice—a proper pattern is one that embodies the person's free selection, provided that the selection respects the equal autonomy of others.[172] Lives that bring grave consequences for others will often be undermined by doing so, but this is not the only way in which things can go awry. Internal failures may arise from the absence of any pattern, or from a pattern that suppresses part of the person's nature, or from a chosen pattern to which, because of propensities that cannot be restrained or confined, the person cannot conform. On any of the readings we have been considering, *if* Aschenbach fails, he does so in one of the latter two ways. Were this to be counted as an ethical failure, it would belong in a different range of the ethical spectrum from those lapses that adversely affect others—it is tempting to echo Nietzsche's early dictum and conclude that Aschenbach's life is unjustified as an aesthetic phenomenon. For, apparently, he does no harm.

Britten writes eloquently ambiguous music for the Venice in which he sets his central character. The "master-writer" is imposing, like the Venetian palaces—but the pilings beneath are pressed by weight and lapped by foul water. The beauty in Aschenbach's life masks the strains below, and it is inevitable that the foundations must crumble. When they do, the apparent beauty is nullified: on this, Britten is unambiguous. Mann, I suggest, was more ambivalent. His hero succumbs to the lure of beauty, but we should ask how deeply that affects the worth of his life. If Vere—and perhaps Mut—can find "redemption," why suppose that Aschenbach's apparently inconsequential lapse from his self-chosen discipline, the odd but insulated behavior of his final days, is weighty enough to undermine the worth of all he has been and done?

Britten could not have known how eerily his portrait resembles Aschenbach's creator. Moving elegantly through the world of well-to-do Munich, the young author of the brilliantly successful *Buddenbrooks* captured the fairy-tale princess Katia Pringsheim. Together they had six children—Erika, Klaus, Golo, Monika, Elizabeth, and Michael—and lived in public as exemplars of bourgeois well-being. After *Death in Venice*, there were more masterpieces to come, including, at least, *The Magic Mountain, Joseph and His Brothers*, and *Doctor Faustus*. Along the way, he won the Nobel Prize for literature—and was, apparently, considered for a repeat award because of the brilliance of his later work.[173] His prominence in resisting Nazism made him the voice of "healthy" Germany. In the end he became a monument.

The costs are not immediately visible—even today, the majority of Mann's readers know little of the life behind the writings. Without the surviving diaries and letters, there would only be external clues to the pains, the severe depressions, the repressed desires, the sleeplessness,[174] the sexual difficulties—all the things that could move Mann to declare, on his thirty-third wedding anniversary, that he would not choose to live his life again. *His* miseries, however, are not the principal concerns about the worth of his apparently so brilliant career. They might even be viewed as part of his triumph, his fidelity to the motto—"*Durchhalten!*"—he attributes to Aschenbach. Aschenbach's turmoil, as we have seen, does no damage to others. Mann, by contrast, was sustained by a family, on whom his troubles—and his successes—took a severe toll. Even in the rosiest vision, offered in prospect in *Königliche Hoheit*, what is predicted is "severe happiness," a combined effort in which disabilities must be overcome, deformities accepted, and, most importantly, sacrifices made.

Imma Spoelmann's sacrifices are beyond the horizon of the early novel, to be guessed as readers take leave of her at the dawn of her marriage. Katia Mann's selfless devotion to the *Manngesellschaft*— Thomas Mann Enterprises, Inc.—can be glimpsed in her "unwritten memoirs" and gleaned from what her husband's diaries say and do not say. She is the organizer of the household, often invisible but especially appreciated when she falls ill or when the presence of guests or the absence of servants increases the strain.[175] Her duties include picking her husband up from his walk, taking him to his various medical appointments, writing letters from his dictation, listening to and providing constructive comments on his readings of works in progress—as well as occasional jobs like attending to the needs of an increasingly decrepit brother-in-law (Heinrich).[176] Her memoirs make it clear that she rejoiced in the success of her "Tommy"—*mein Mann*. His diaries make it equally evident that she made the everyday routine of his life possible, responded to his sexual failures with compassion and comfort, tolerated his attractions to young men, and, perhaps, even helped him keep them within the bounds of his own disciplined homoeroticism. A recorded exchange between them reveals how they were able to discuss those inclinations—how, like Imma Spoelmann, Katia was able to look on her husband's "deformity" and, perhaps, help him to accept it. In May 1948, after a walk together, they had lunch at a favorite café, where Mann observed the "picture-pretty" (*bildhübsch*) teenage son of an "unattractive Jewish man."[177]

> I said: "Sad that beauty is only for a moment. In a couple of years, he will be so like his father, that it will have quite disappeared." To which K. responded, to my comfort: "Why? Maybe his mother is a beautiful woman."[178]

Aschenbach, of course, lacks any similar helpful presence.

Mann's awareness of that help was fleeting—although sometimes he became conscious of how little notice he had taken of his wife or of their marriage. On February 11, 1945, his diary entry begins: "Cooler weather. K. had to remind me that today is our *40th wedding anniversary*. Ended the article for *Free World* to my satisfaction . . . "[179] Celebrations of her birthdays often seem centered on his own projects: "K.'s 56th birthday. In the morning on the beach I *finished* the *seventh chapter* of Lotte in Weimar on p. 104 with a short dialogue, and on the subsequent walk I turned my attention to the eighth chapter. . . . In celebration of the day, I read K. the last 20 pages of the seventh chapter."[180]

Yet his frequent moments of depression, self-doubt, and unrest make his debt to her apparent to us—as it was to him. "Sleepless until 3 a.m. and longer. A whole Phanodorm [a sleeping medication Mann commonly used in this period] with only belated effect. Some time in K.'s room in the chair. Walk around the room. Towards morning a few hours of rest."[181] "Tired and sad. Sat on the sofa, my head on K.'s shoulder."[182]

Occasionally, his gratitude became public, as when, on her seventieth birthday, he declared that "she would live on," by his side, in any posthumous celebration of his work.[183] Most of his audience would not have known how much lay behind the conventional praise—maybe not even Katia herself, whose famous remark, "Never in my life have I been able to do what I would have liked to do," is made as if this is simply a social fact about the condition of daughters, wives, and mothers (at least in her period and milieu).[184]

If she signed on to the *Manngesellschaft* as a willing partner, the sacrifices demanded of the six children were less obviously voluntary. External clues already raise questions about their parents' success in equipping them to live worthwhile and independent lives of their own. There were two suicides—Klaus, the second child and first son, and Michael, the third son and last of the six.[185] Klaus's death came after a previous attempt had failed: in July 1948, he had been visiting his parents in California and tried to gas himself. As Mann's diary records, Katia went immediately to the hospital and gave her husband a report on her return. The next day, Erika visited her brother, and Katia seems to have gone back and forth between hospital and home. The diary entry continues: "Distracted work, interrupted by reports from K. Drove out with her a little to Santa Monica. Handwritten letters to (Lavinia) Mazzuchetti, Adorno, and others. Heinrich to dinner."[186] The following afternoon, Mann accompanied his wife to visit Klaus in the home of the Bruno Walter family. He was "touched" by his son's "sensitive" nature—and very, very tired after the visit.[187]

The entries for the subsequent days reveal that the work (interrupted or not) went on: he continued to write his account of the composition of *Doktor Faustus*.[188] A month after the incident, when Klaus was ready to return to Europe, Mann's primary thought seems to have been that his son might undertake a mission on his behalf. "Evening with Klaus to say goodbye before his departure to Amsterdam. Good wishes. Emphasis on my interest that he should work with Marton and Korda in London on the *Magic Mountain* project [a proposed film that never materialized]."[189] Was the emphasis on participation in one of his father's artistic ventures meant as encouragement? Were the "good wishes" accompanied by expressions of how Mann felt about the near-loss of his son? We cannot know, but there is an odd tone to this farewell, the conspicuous absence of any expressed concern that a vulnerable young man might try again—and succeed.[190]

When Klaus did just that, his father, mother, and elder sister were on a speaking tour in Scandinavia. After a discussion among them, they decided to continue with a reduced version of the engagements planned—Mann would deliver the promised lectures but would cancel the social events. Katia and Erika were evidently more affected than Mann himself, and he records his "sympathy" with them and his attempts to comfort them.[191] Almost three weeks after Klaus's death, Erika flew to Nice and went on to Cannes, the scene of his suicide. The only one of the family who had been there before her was Michael, who was fortuitously in Europe at the time and who played a viola solo at the funeral.

It has sometimes been suggested—although the idea has been sharply challenged—that Klaus suffered from three great burdens: he was a drug addict, he was homosexual, and he was the son of Thomas Mann, and that the greatest of these was the shadow cast by his father.[192] Certainly, Klaus's own diaries sometimes complain of paternal coldness, and, in a letter to Herman Hesse, Mann acknowledged the "shadow" he felt he had cast on his son.[193]

The relation between father and youngest son was also difficult. Before Michael's birth, Mann had meditated on the merits of having a sixth child. His diary dispassionately considers the economic and cultural situation of postwar Germany, and the deliberation concludes: "Apart from considerations of K.'s health, I really have nothing against it [allowing the pregnancy to continue to term], except that the experience for 'Lisa' [Elizabeth, the fifth child] (she is, in a certain sense, my *first* child) might be influenced and diminished by it."[194] After the birth of the new baby—known initially within the family as *Beisser* (biter) and later as Bibi—Mann confessed his emotional distance: "I continue to feel estrangement, coldness, even dislike towards our youngest, about the arrangements for whose baptism I wrote yesterday to the parson who teaches Erika religion."[195]

Although his early career as a violist was apparently successful, Michael decided, shortly after his father's death, to obtain a Ph.D. in German literature. In 1975, Mann's diaries were finally available for others to read, and his youngest son, now a professor at Berkeley, read the passages just quoted, apparently during a visit to Europe where he was participating in celebrations of his father's centenary.[196] His reading probably confirmed what he had already felt.[197] The suicide came a year later.

Despite Mann's sense that his fifth child was really his first, that with the birth of Elizabeth he had discovered paternity, his diaries show significant interest in and admiration for his eldest daughter. In the early weeks of the Manns' exile, Erika showed the organizational skill and helpfulness that would be so thoroughly developed later—and Mann also showed paternal pride in her writing.[198] At that stage, Erika was very much an independent force in the cultural world—her satirical cabaret, *Die Pfeffermühle* (*The Peppermill*) had won considerable acclaim for its witty attacks on Nazism. The independence occasionally led to sharp differences between father and daughter, especially concerning the ways in which the German writers who had emigrated should publish their work. An early dispute in 1933 was much amplified in 1936, when Erika wrote her father a critical letter about his "Protest," published in the *Neue Zürcher Zeitung*.[199] At this stage, she was very much aligned and allied with Klaus, to whom she had always been close. During the next two decades, she was increasingly drawn into orbit around her father, especially after the Second World War, in which she had played an active role as a correspondent. The visits to California became longer, and her intelligence, organizational skill, and command of English proved especially valuable. The diaries reveal her deftness in turning Mann's German into speeches and lectures for an English-speaking audience and in coaching her father on his delivery.[200] Her advice in fashioning and refashioning his writings, articles, lectures, and *Doktor Faustus* was constant and much appreciated.[201] Gradually, she took over the role of principal sounding board and managing director of the *Manngesellschaft*. Three days before Klaus's suicide, Mann could write of "the priceless help of Erika and K."[202]

As the sibling to whom he had been closest became ever more involved in his father's work and life, Klaus may have experienced a sense of betrayal. After his suicide, Erika's principal intellectual endeavors were divided between service to a living father and to a dead brother. The independent voice of her youth became an amplifier—a most valuable amplifier, to be sure—of the work of others.

The youngest of the three daughters, Elizabeth ("Medi"), through whom Mann discovered paternal love and to whom he wrote his hexameters (*Gesang vom Kindchen*), did achieve independence. She married, suddenly and young, Giuseppe Borghese, a man thirty-six years older than herself. Her father found the wedding day painful and oppressive, nor did his view of the marriage improve.[203] After the death of her husband in 1952, she embarked on a successful career as a political scientist, with special interest in environmental issues, raising two daughters who went on to professional lives of their own.

The diaries record Mann's continued affection for Medi, although, with the years, her primacy is undermined by his increasing gratitude toward and love for Erika and his enchantment in his grandson Frido.[204] They also reveal shifting attitudes toward the two middle children, often overlooked and almost always less prominent. Monika, the fourth child and second daughter, initially appears as one among many, only occasionally distinguished—as on Christmas Eve 1918, when she was particularly pleased with her presents.[205] Her birthday (the day after her father's) in 1920 rates a perfunctory mention but goes unnoted in the following year.[206] By the time the extant records resume, "Moni," now in her twenties, has clearly become a problem, making difficulties for her mother.[207] So it continues. There are discussions of Moni's "oddness," of the *Problem Moni.*" She remains in her room during the Christmas Eve sharing of gifts—yet it is "the happiest Christmas and New Year for years."[208] After 1940, Monika's difficulties increase: married in 1939 to Jenö Láni, she settles with him in London; during the blitz, the couple resolves to travel to America, but the ship is torpedoed and, while she looks helplessly on, her husband drowns. The parental home provides little sanctuary: her presence is a problem requiring bright ideas from parents and siblings; Mann has to bridle his "bitterness about her existence."[209] Her intellectual efforts are slighted—"Manuscript from Moni, embarrassing"; "Wrote critically to Moni about her little manuscript."[210] After her father's death, however, she does manage to achieve some personal happiness and, contrary to his judgment, even some success as a writer.

Then there is Golo—Angelus Gottfried Thomas, to give him his full name—the only one of the siblings for whom the family nickname became the public appellation. Teased, possibly even tormented and humiliated by his elder brother, he figures early on as a cross between gnome and clown in the family drama, careful, it seems, to avoid too much parental scrutiny or parental discipline.[211] Through the 1930s and 1940s, his father's diaries show Golo's stock rising. Unlike Monika, he is a serious partner for serious conversation; although never achieving the intimacy allowed to Erika (or even to Klaus), he earns his father's respect. After Mann's death in 1955, his own career as writer, academic, and intellectual begins to flourish, as if he were finally liberated. He becomes a distinguished man of letters in his own right—in my judgment, the only one of the siblings whose works would be widely read if their authorship were entirely unknown.[212]

His personal life was shrouded from public view. Golo never married, although he adopted a son, and he spent his final year in the home of his widowed daughter-in-law. *If* as is often supposed, he was homosexual, he was far less open about his preferences than those—Britten among them—with whom he once shared a house in Brooklyn. It seems probable though not certain that he never found fulfilling romantic love. Eventually, he inherited his parents' last house, in Kilchberg just outside Zürich, and, like them, he is buried in the Kilchberg cemetery. In accordance with his explicit instructions, his grave is placed at the maximum distance from that of Thomas and Katia Mann.

9

There was probably no moment in Mann's life at which he intentionally did something that caused serious harm to his wife or to one of his children or when he deliberately acted to limit the value of their lives. In that respect, he is quite unlike Mut or Vere. Nevertheless, a review of the lives of his children cannot avoid raising questions about the costs imposed by the disciplined life he led: this is not a matter of ascribing blame—that would be pointless and silly—but of recognizing that the achievement of some kinds of value puts others in jeopardy. The *Manngesellschaft* produced wonderful things, masterpieces of world literature that continue to illuminate, delight, and even transform those who read them. Yet the conditions of production cannot simply be wished away or ignored.

Whatever the strains he felt in uniting the roles of artist and citizen, Mann succeeded as the Artist-*Erzieher* he aspired to become. The discipline imposed on himself had costs, but they are trivial in comparison with the triumphs—as Goethe's imitations of the serpent, his "energetic wormings," although by no means poetic, do not detract from his life—the discarded novella about his late infatuation ought to have been a comedy.[213] The more serious problem comes when other lives are conscripted, joined to a larger enterprise without any reflective choice, when those lives are confined or truncated or blossom only when the period of conscription is over. For all Mann's commitment to reading Nietzsche ironically, the achievement of the *Manngesellschaft* recapitulates the Nietzschean thought about the proper relationship between birds of prey and lambs—sacrifices are needed for the full triumph of what is noble and strong.[214] Whole lives are devoured in bringing about a greater end.[215]

With the enduring quality of Mann's fiction clearly established, its artistic eminence fully recognized, those whose lives felt the impact of the efforts required in accomplishing it—however the losses are finally identified and the causes finally understood—might well retrospectively acquiesce in the contributions they made or even in the interferences with their own development. Katia and Erika apparently did exactly that. As the events recede into history, the perceived costs to individuals diminish. Looking back, grateful readers do not worry about the conditions of production—or, if they do, they focus on the aesthetic balance in the life of the author: was *Mann's* life justified as an aesthetic phenomenon?

From the beginning of this chapter, the central concern has been with parallel questions about Aschenbach. Does he succeed in fitting the disparate elements of his identity together? Is his life invalidated by his capitulation to the lure of beauty? Must the artist inevitably succumb to that lure? For Mann, these were crucial questions, and the creation of Aschenbach was part of his long exploration of them, part of his lifelong endeavor to put himself on trial. Juxtaposing Mann's Aschenbach with Britten's, with Mut and with Vere, *and with Mann himself* may lead us to wonder if these are the right—or the only—questions. Aschenbach, so far as we can tell, does no serious harm. There is nothing to suggest that his marriage curtailed another life or that he cast a long shadow on his daughter. As I suggested earlier, the novella simplifies the philosophical predicament precisely through leaving other human relations unaddressed—on the one hand we have Aschenbach's austere discipline, resolutely maintained for more than two decades, and the literary accomplishments it has made possible; on the other, the brief final lapse, the entrapment by the lure of beauty, personified in Tadzio. No baneful effect on others complicates the picture. Assuming that the literary triumphs are comparable to Mann's own, *Aschenbach's* life appears easier to vindicate.

The maxim he rejects—"To understand all is to forgive all"— overstates a sound thought, that understanding may lead sometimes to forgiveness. We can "see life foully," in Joyce's apt phrase, and reconcile ourselves to it. In the wake of Klaus's suicide, Mann invoked a similar thought, as his distraught daughter quarreled with an old friend: "Her bitter distortion of things, including what concerns Klaus and his life. Humiliating in its rigor, and even more in its half-truth. But too much character makes one unjust. Of course, tolerance is probably not allowed today."[216]

I read these words as a half-articulated defense against a charge Erika never made explicitly, one Mann was inchoately conscious of but would not look fully in the face. The perspective is quite contrary to Aschenbach's official stance—even though considering it would be valuable for him as he sits, slumped and humiliated at the fountain. Equally it is apt for us readers as we think about Aschenbach—and about his creator.

# THREE

# Shadows

1

In the spring of 1912, Thomas Mann wrote to congratulate his brother Heinrich on the completion of a play, adding: "I would be glad to report something similar about my novella, but I cannot find the ending."[1] What exactly was the difficulty? Could Mann have been uncertain about whether Aschenbach should live? Was he torn between cleaving more closely to the actual events of his own visit to Venice and the version in which his protagonist dies there? Almost certainly not. The premonitions of death, the shadows that fall across Aschenbach, are already marked in the earliest pages of the story, and there is no reason to think that these were added at a late stage in writing, after Mann's thoughts had settled on an ending—his constant method was to work slowly and steadily, almost doggedly, making only small revisions.[2] Furthermore, an earlier letter to Heinrich makes it evident that death itself could not have been the issue, since the novella already bears the title—*Der Tod in Venedig*—by which we know it.[3] By the time of the letters, he had clearly reached the final chapter, for, despite his surmise that Heinrich might not approve of the whole, he expected his brother to warm to parts of it, citing, in particular, the "classical chapter" (*"ein antikisierendes Kapitel"*; chapter 4). The problem he faced could not have been that of deciding *if* Aschenbach should die but rather *how*. The difficulty was to discover the *right* death for his protagonist, a death that would show what it—and the life that preceded it—*meant*. Perhaps Mann wondered if the story should continue after the collapse at the fountain—and solved his problem by writing the coda?

Death hangs over Aschenbach from the beginning. It is already present in the traveler who suddenly appears at the cemetery chapel, whose pose is that of Hermes, bearer of souls to the realm of the dead: this manifestation of Hermes is malign, threatening, and challenging, and Aschenbach is duly disturbed (as we shall see, the harbinger of death can come far more gently).[4] Death appears too in the mysterious gondolier, whose "strange vessel" reminds Aschenbach of a coffin and conjures up in him thoughts of an easy, even pleasurable, end.[5] Tadzio's delicate appearance reinforces the idea of premature death, and, as Aschenbach lingers in the plague-ridden city, he is conscious of death as a possibility for the boy and for himself. By assigning many different characters to a single singer, Britten intensifies the idea that they are all emissaries of death, the last of whom, the hotel manager, prefigures Aschenbach's imminent end by claiming powers to decide matters of mortality: "Who comes and goes is my affair."

Aschenbach must die—but how? The question comes in a mundane form, "What is the cause of his death?" and a more interesting one, "What is the significance of the coda to the novella, the ending Mann ultimately chose?" The latter will be a principal focus of this chapter, but it cannot be addressed without explicit consideration of the more pedestrian issue. Readers, commentators, and critics rarely ask what causes Aschenbach's death because they gravitate to an obvious diagnosis. Just before his collapse at the fountain, the writer eats a strawberry, a reckless, irresponsibly foolish gesture, presumably made in the fever of his passion.[6] Cholera is in Venice—*hence*, the fruit is contaminated, Aschenbach is infected, and, after a few days, he succumbs. The coda is only needed to give the period of grace the bacillus needs. As noted earlier, if this were Mann's preferred account of his protagonist's death, the strawberry could easily have been introduced on one of his previous pursuits of Tadzio—after the service in St. Mark's, for instance—and the collapse at the fountain could end the novella. The burning of his head, his sweating and shaking, his intense thirst—symptoms felt just before he slumps on the steps of the fountain, *and, indeed, before he has eaten the strawberry*—could then be interpreted as manifestations of the disease.

There is a satisfying neatness to the diagnosis. Aschenbach's feverish obsession with Tadzio leads him to abandon the prudent care of himself that has always been part of his discipline: the boy is the ultimate cause of his death. Complicit in the corrupt decision to conceal the plague in Venice, Aschenbach himself falls victim to it. His own internal decay foreshortens the life that was apparently so successful and respectable. When he dies, cholera must be the prime suspect: it has means (it is frequently fatal), opportunity (it could be transmitted by the strawberry), and motive (it highlights Aschenbach's obsession and corruption).

Except that, as Mann knew very well, any competent examination of the patient would be far more circumspect.[7] What exactly do we know about Aschenbach's symptoms? On the morning of his death, he suffers from dizziness, and that might be explained by the low blood pressure that often comes with cholera—but the episodes of light-headedness are only partly physical (*"nur halb körperlichen"*), and they are accompanied by violent feelings of anxiety (even before he has learned of the Poles' planned departure).[8] He has had other ailments before, and the symptoms described just *prior* to eating the strawberry—especially the shaking and the terrible thirst—are *more diagnostic* of cholera than the features reported for the day of his death. His original decision to leave Venice (canceled on the pretext of the misdirected luggage) was prompted by sensations that might well give a middle-aged man cause for alarm: difficulties with vision, constriction in the chest, throbbing in the head, feverish sweating.[9] Were Aschenbach to consult a doctor about these episodes, it would be advisable for him to present the ominous judgment of the "biography" chapter—he was not a robust child, and "medical precautions" led him to be educated at home.[10]

On the day of his death, Aschenbach does not present the symptoms of the most common form of cholera. As medical sources—both those available in 1911 and those current today—invariably report, the primary sign of a dangerous cholera infection is "diarrhea of the most violent character": patients who die of cholera typically undergo episodes of evacuation and vomiting, bringing forth a characteristic "rice-water" fluid; they become dehydrated and suffer failure of vital organs (often the kidneys). Mann's protagonist surely does not suffer this sort of unpleasantness, for it strains credulity to think of so fastidious a man straying far from his hotel room if he were undergoing purgations with increasing frequency. Instead, with feelings of dizziness, partly products of anxiety and a sense of hopelessness, Aschenbach "goes"—the verb is unmodified—to the beach.

Nor is this spare description of the writer's final hours the product of Mann's ignorance or confusion.[11] His notes for *Death in Venice* contain an extensive summary of the medical wisdom of the time on the subject of cholera, covering geographical patterns of diffusion, symptoms, postmortem analysis, modes of transmission, and treatment.[12] The summary differs very little from the accounts offered by medical sources today—the most prominent deviation lies in the estimates of mortality: Mann's source gave an estimate of 60 to 70 percent for cholera epidemics, while contemporary figures are more optimistic. Yet there is one part of the summary, brought into prominence by Mann's underlining, that does mark his account as dated—the use of an old-fashioned term for a rare variant of the disease.

*Cholera sicca* ("dry" cholera) occurs when the fluids drain into the intestines rather than being evacuated through the rectum or through the mouth. Patients with dry cholera (*sicca* is a somewhat archaic usage) also suffer dehydration and the consequent stresses on vital organs, they feel intense thirst, and their abdomens are greatly distended. If anything, the course of the disease is quicker for them and more violent.[13] Mann's underlined sentence sums up the essential features, noting the rarity of this variant, its relative intensity, and the temporary paralysis of the intestinal canal.[14]

*If* Aschenbach dies from cholera, the more likely hypothesis would be that he is infected with dry cholera. Yet this would be extremely improbable, and not only because dry cholera is rare. A patient about to die from dry cholera would be swollen from the retained fluid, would experience harrowing thirst, would be chilled, and would have a weak heartbeat—he would not have a brief conversation with the hotel doorman and then simply "go" to the beach—unless, of course, he were profoundly insensitive to the state of his own body.

Mann, the great ironist, the master of ambivalence, allows his readers more than one possibility for Aschenbach's death. Once he reveals that cholera is rampant in Venice, the threat of death is omnipresent, and he supplies a few clues *consistent* with the conclusion that his protagonist is infected with the dry form of the disease.[15] Yet by presenting this death as so atypical of *cholera sicca*, he invites us to explore alternatives to what initially appears as the most obvious cause. We do not have to suppose that—somehow, improbably—Aschenbach reaches the state of dehydration that immediately precedes death from cholera without experiencing any of the violent processes that usually bring about dehydration, shock, and organ failure. Consequently, we do not have to conclude that he dies prematurely because of his participation in the corruption of Venice, that his death is intimately bound up with his obsession or with his moral decline—the apparently neat web of symbolic connections thus falls apart. A different pathology is easy to find: Aschenbach dies of heart failure.

The alternative liberates our reading in two ways. Perhaps Aschenbach dies not prematurely but as might be anticipated in light of traits that have been longstanding features of his life. Perhaps, too, the final spectacle on the lido plays a role in his death.

## 2

Luchino Visconti's film *Morte a Venezia* ends with Dirk Bogarde as Aschenbach, hair dye and makeup streaming down his face, apparently suffering cardiac arrest on the beach—from which he is carted unceremoniously away by two attendants. The slow zoom out, with the figures becoming ever smaller and more anonymous, adds an ironic touch of Visconti's own, a homage to Mann's manner, even though both the ungainly configuration of the body—more like a heavy sack of fertilizer than the remains of a respected visitor—and the reduction of Aschenbach to a small speck seem quite at odds with the writer's regained dignity in the novella's final sentence. Yet the closing scene is hardly the most provocative of the many deviations Visconti allows himself. Although they are generally sympathetic to Britten's opera,

Mann's most ardent admirers sternly criticize the film for its departures from the novella.[16] Purists can find many occasions for becoming irate at the liberties taken.[17] Visconti turns Tadzio into a flirt who returns Aschenbach's gaze at their very first meeting and who, on the walks through Venice, lingers behind his sisters as if to give the pursuing Aschenbach the chance to catch him. Aschenbach himself is portrayed as petulant, fussy, and often childish—a prime example being the incident of the misdirected luggage. In the closing fight between Jaschu and Tadzio, there is no moment of genuine danger in which Tadzio's face is pressed into the sand, and the catalog of sins could be extended much further. Visconti's principal innovation, however, is to replace the *writer* von Aschenbach with a composer of the same name, a composer plainly modeled on—if not identical with—Gustav Mahler.[18] Instead of being moved to travel by a disturbing encounter at the Munich cemetery, this composer goes to Venice for reasons of health. As the film opens, we see him, muffled and frail, on the deck of the boat that will bring him to Venice.[19]

The philosophical reflections Mann attributes to Aschenbach are plainly hard to transfer convincingly to stage or screen. Britten and Piper worked around the difficulty by including relatively few of them and, in the case of the final anti-Socratic musings, by modifying their character.[20] Visconti endeavors to solve the problem by introducing flashback scenes in which the composer discusses broad issues about art, music, and life with a younger figure, Alfred, apparently a student or assistant, perhaps to be identified with Schoenberg.[21] Some of these flashbacks are effective in using allusions to Mahler's life and work to explore Aschenbach's intimations of mortality. One scene shows him with his wife and young daughter in an alpine meadow—recalling Mahler's summer retreats to the mountains he loved, where, relieved of the burdens of conducting, he could devote himself to his own compositions. Another shows grieving parents at a child's coffin, an obvious reference to the death of Mahler's beloved elder daughter (Maria, known in the family as "Putzi"), who, in 1907, succumbed to a combination of scarlet fever and diphtheria. Three years earlier, in the year his younger daughter (Anna, or "Gucki") was born, Mahler had completed the *Kindertotenlieder*, prompting his wife, Alma, to accuse him of "tempting Providence."[22] Viewers who know the song-cycle well can easily draw a connection between the two flashbacks: above the family in the sunlit meadow towers an alpine peak, beyond which are threatening clouds—a reminder of the fourth song, in which the singer vainly hopes to find the children "on the heights" (Höh'n), and of the fifth (and final) song, whose first part protests the raging storm in which the children were allowed to go out.

In contrast to Visconti's skill in condensing allusions in these scenes, the interpolations involving Alfred are heavy handed to the point of absurdity. Mahler took considerable interest in younger composers and explored literary and philosophical questions with them—and the respect appears to have been mutual: for Schoenberg, Mahler embodied "the highest artistic ideal," and the group of young musicians and intellectuals around Schoenberg viewed the older composer as a "Saint."[23] The scenes in which Alfred lectures, hectors, and berates Aschenbach are thus entirely at odds with the identification of the composer as Mahler—but the far deeper and more damning problem with them lies in the fact that no student or junior colleague, no matter how independent, would, in the social-intellectual world of prewar Vienna, address his *Meister* in any such way. In the last of these scenes, when Alfred exults at the boos and catcalls that have greeted Aschenbach's conducting of one of his own symphonies, the almost sadistic savagery of the young man's attack is, given the social-cultural setting, ludicrous. Yet the profoundly unrealistic manner in which these dialogues unfold is matched, even outdone, by the jejune judgments that slide out of the mouths of these supposedly engaged intellectuals. Mann's Aschenbach is literate and subtle—as we have seen, not only is the philosophical background to the novella rich and complex, but the thoughts attributed to Aschenbach, even when unfocused, have depths that merit exploration. By contrast, Visconti offers two pretentious interlocutors who exchange slogans of a sophomoric grandiosity: "I reject the demonic nature of art," "Evil is a necessity." Even on a charitable view of what these characters are trying to express, the scenes are entirely inappropriate as a debate about the music one has written and the other derides. In recent decades, the older view of Mahler's songs and symphonies as formless, as rich but undisciplined juxtapositions of very different types of motifs and material—the interlacing of folk songs and dances with sober, even searing, themes—has given way to detailed musicological analyses that have revealed intricate patterns in keys, melodies, harmonies, and rhythms.[24] Yet, subtle and complex as the forms of Mahler's major compositions have been found to be, no serious critic—or hearer—could ever charge the songs and symphonies with the "pure passionless form" Alfred cites as the fatal flaw of Aschenbach's music.

Visconti's skill in offering opulent images of early twentieth-century Europe is beyond dispute, but the film often gives the impression of an undisciplined dramatic imagination, offering provocative possibilities without any clear focus. Aschenbach voyages to Venice on a ship named *Esmeralda*—and those familiar with Mann's *Doktor Faustus* will immediately recognize the name Leverkühn gives to the prostitute through whom he contracts his fatal syphilis.[25] The ship that brings Aschenbach to Venice is marked as the vessel of his destruction. Yet Visconti elaborates the allusive complex further. After Aschenbach's failed attempt to "normalize" his relations with Tadzio, the score gives us Mahler, not the Adagietto from the Fifth Symphony, which is the film's dominant music, but the finale of the Third Symphony, the setting of a poem from Nietzsche's *Zarathustra*, "O Mensch! Gib' Acht." The words—"O Man! Take care!"—are surely appropriate warnings to Aschenbach at this moment, if not earlier. Visconti then has Mahler give way, in the next scene, to Beethoven: Aschenbach observes Tadzio playing the right hand of *Für Elise* on a piano in the hotel foyer. The piece recalls to him an earlier scene in his life: a prostitute in a brothel is playing *Für Elise*; she leaves the piece unfinished and begins to undress for him. This flashback alludes to the scene in *Doktor Faustus*, reported by Leverkühn in a contorted and stylized letter to his friend Zeitblom, in which the student composer is taken, by mistake, to a brothel, a brothel with a piano, where he first encounters "Esmeralda."[26] Mann adapted the scene from the account of Nietzsche's contraction of syphilis,[27] so the film connects Mahler, Aschenbach, Leverkühn, Nietzsche, Tadzio, and Esmeralda. Suggestive as the associations might be, it is not clear that they contribute to any coherent reading of Aschenbach and of his fate—beyond the rather obvious identification of Tadzio as another vehicle of his destruction (Tadzio is to Aschenbach as Esmeralda is to Leverkühn and some unnamed prostitute is to Nietzsche).

Nevertheless, although mention of Visconti in discussions of the novella is typically an occasion for negative, even scathing, comments,

FIGURE 3.1. The newspaper photograph of Mahler from which Mann worked. The published edition of his notebook for the novella preserves the placement of the photograph in the middle of Mann's notes on cholera.

the film deserves defense not simply for the qualities students of film rightly emphasize but also for its illuminating perspective on Mann's story. The kernel of Visconti's insight, expressed already in the opening shots of the frail Aschenbach and most fully in the depiction of heart failure on the lido, lies in his emancipating the writer's death from the obvious diagnosis. Visconti's Aschenbach is not a victim of the cholera that plagues Venice. Instead, he dies as the result of a condition that has been with him for a long time, possibly for his whole life. Although the core conception, the identification of Aschenbach with Mahler, could only be pursued coherently by making quite substantial departures from the novella, its shifted gestalt on the causes of death and on the protagonist's attitudes toward death will modify our understanding of Aschenbach's death—and perhaps of death more generally.

Fusing Aschenbach with Mahler was always a relatively obvious and alluring possibility. Not only did Mann give his protagonist the composer's physical features,[28] but he made little secret of the fact that he had done so. His working notes for the novella contain a newspaper photograph of Mahler, and the composer's physiognomy was presumably beside him as he wrote.[29] Mann had met Mahler in 1910, after he had attended an open rehearsal for the Eighth Symphony, which the composer was conducting in Munich; Katia's family had been acquainted with Mahler, making an introduction possible. The encounter impressed Mann, who described the composer as the first man of genius with whom he had been directly acquainted.[30] In 1911, during the trip to Venice with Katia and Heinrich, he followed the reports of Mahler's terminal illness and death—after what originally seemed to be influenza had suspended Mahler's conducting of the New York Philharmonic, an astute diagnostician discovered that he was suffering from bacterial endocarditis; the trip home to Vienna, where he died on May 18, was extensively chronicled in German-language newspapers.[31] The association of Mahler, death, and Venice is expressed in the choice of Aschenbach's facial features and of his first name.

Physical resemblance is a slender basis for replacing so "inner" a character as Aschenbach with an artist in a different medium. Moreover, there are several important reasons for separating the real composer from the fictional writer. First is the gulf, already noted, between the sweep of Mahler's symphonies; their disparate elements, some of them "common"; the "formlessness" attributed to them not only by the critics of earlier decades but also by musically sophisticated concertgoers today; and the work of Aschenbach's maturity, work that emphasizes simplicity and purity of form, expunging all "common" words. Second, there is the obvious distinction of their habits of work: Aschenbach's daily routine, with its patient accumulation of small insights, was a luxury Mahler could not afford; his extensive responsibilities as conductor and music director left him only a few months in the summer in which he could devote himself, with enormous intensity, to composition. Then there are differences in antecedents and social background: Aschenbach's ancestors are austere and self-denying officials, in whose image he forges his own formidable discipline; Mahler came from an aspiring Jewish family in a provincial corner of Bohemia, a family for whom Gustav was the great hope, the child who had to cope with the difficulties of those of his siblings who survived into adulthood.[32] Aschenbach, we are told, was married quite young, and his domestic happiness was terminated by the early death of his wife. Instead of settling in one city, Mahler moved restlessly from place to place and job to job, having a number of romantic affairs with women but only marrying, quite late, the much younger and notably beautiful Alma Schindler, with whom he lived a tumultuous life that swung between rapture and despondency. Unlike Aschenbach, who has only distant relations with a married daughter, Mahler was deeply attached to his own two young girls.[33] There is no hint that he shared Aschenbach's fascination with pubescent male beauty.

All this means that if Aschenbach is to become a composer who resembles Mahler, some radical surgery must be done either on Aschenbach or on Mahler. If the characteristics Mann ascribes to his protagonist are retained, this composer may look like Mahler, but his music will not sound like Mahler's, his way of working will not be Mahler's, his family history and temperament will not be Mahler's, his sexual identity will not be Mahler's—if "Mahler" is to be so modified, the identification looks pointless. On the other hand, if Mahler, with some of his actual qualities, is to be the protagonist, then Aschenbach must diverge radically from the central figure of the novella: without the rigorous inherited discipline, without the striving for purity of form, without the homoerotic yearnings, can any of Mann's central concerns and themes remain?

Visconti's great insight was to recognize that something could be preserved. Common to Aschenbach and Mahler is a strong sense of their own finitude. Both are conscious of the shadows that have fallen across their lives from the very beginning.

## 3

The obituary chapter informs us that Aschenbach was a delicate child, educated at home because of worries about his health. The question, for his parents, his teachers, and himself, was not about his talent but rather about the ability of his constitution to enable the expression of that talent. Despite these worries about his own frailty, he has a strong desire to attain old age, for his image of complete artistry requires a response to all stages of human life.[34] It is easy to understand how his severe discipline could emerge from this predicament, how the commitment to husbanding scarce resources could be expressed in the self-denying routine, the withdrawal from social distractions, even from social relations, and in the daily dedication to duty. As each work is painstakingly crafted and completed, there arises the new desire to move on to the next, to repeat again or even surpass what has just been accomplished. Aschenbach's constantly renewed struggles may begin with the thought of creating masterpieces corresponding to the "Ages of Man," but they go beyond it. The writer presented to us in the novella recapitulates a central theme of Schopenhauer's pessimism: beyond each accomplishment looms a new challenge, "All striving arises out of a lack, out of discontent with the present circumstances, and is thus suffering; but no satisfaction lasts, being instead the starting point for a new striving."[35] The sense of frailty Aschenbach feels, the shadow that falls across his life, is the prospect of death's intervening before the work has been done—and that sense is intensified by the thought that the work must always be incomplete.

Part of what troubles Aschenbach, the possibility that the planned work will be interrupted, is vividly expressed by many writers, in famous sonnets by Milton and Keats, for example, although typically against the background of a belief, or at least a hope, that the projects envisaged might be completed—neither poet adds the pessimistic thought that striving is endless.[36] Like Aschenbach—and, I believe, like Mann—Mahler poses for himself, both in verbal reflections and in his music, the pessimistic challenge, seeing the incompleteness of achievement not merely as a contingent phenomenon (some are unlucky and fail to accomplish what they intend; others have enough time to realize their ends) but as a fundamental feature of human existence. Shadows fall across human life because death is *inevitably* premature, accomplishment *inevitably* incomplete, so that any human existence is a truncated form of its envisaged whole, a life deprived of meaning by the death that interrupts it. This shared anxiety about the possible negation of value provides a basis out of which Visconti's guiding insight could be realized. Mann's Aschenbach responds to it in a yearning for the apprehension and communication of pure beauty, an escape to and creative depiction of a Platonic realm—an endeavor whose possibility is bitterly repudiated in the anti-Socratic musings at the fountain.[37] If Aschenbach is to become a composer modeled on Mahler, aesthetic ideas about purity of form have to give way to a different set of attitudes, the impetus to affirm, despite human finitude, the enduring significance of life's joys and beauties, attitudes that could readily be attributed to Mahler-Aschenbach, understood in his decisions and actions, and heard in his music. Plainly, this would depart in many respects from the novella Mann wrote, and it would not give the central place to discipline, or the lure of beauty, or the eruption of homoerotic feelings. It would, however, elaborate themes in Mann's story that previous chapters have so far left undeveloped.

From early in his life, Mahler was familiar with death: his elder brother died before he was born; of his mother's fourteen children, eight (all boys) died early. Mahler's parents—and Mahler himself—may have regarded him as a "replacement" for the first born, Isidor, who was the victim of an accident when he was one.[38] Mahler confronted the possibility of his own death in the 1880s and 1890s (that is, during his twenties and thirties) and, more threateningly, in 1901. With great determination, he had resisted treating what he viewed as minor medical discomforts—migraines and hemorrhoids. His failure to seek care for his "subterranean troubles" led to a frightening episode on the night of February 24, 1901: Mahler suffered profuse bleeding. The doctors who were summoned eventually managed to staunch the flow but informed him that the hemorrhage could have been fatal and advised him to undergo surgery. Mahler was apparently convinced that he had been in serious danger and agreed to the treatment he had so long postponed.[39]

In 1907, shortly after the death of the beloved Putzi, Mahler himself was examined by a physician and learned that his heart had been damaged by childhood rheumatic fever. The local doctor (who had attended the child) had originally come to examine Alma, after she fainted (almost certainly from the stress of seeing her daughter's coffin), and Mahler volunteered himself for an examination in a curious attempt to provide some reassurance.

> Mahler wanted to cheer us up in our mournful room and said: "Look here, doctor, don't you want to examine me as well? My wife

is always worrying about my heart. She shall have some good news today. She needs it." The doctor examined him. He stood up and looked very serious. Mahler was lying on the sofa, Dr. Blumenthal had knelt down beside him, and said, almost cheerfully (like most doctors when they diagnose a fatal illness): "Well, your heart is certainly nothing to be proud of!" And this diagnosis was the beginning of the end for Mahler.[40]

Visconti shows a fictionalized version of the examination, in which the doctor speaks words close to those actually used: "There's no reason to be proud of a heart like that." Yet we should be wary of the conclusion Alma draws, that this was the "beginning of the end for Mahler." To be sure, Blumenthal's diagnosis inspired him to consult a Viennese specialist, and the composer was then advised to give up the strenuous outdoor physical activity he loved. Yet the damage to the valves of the heart, discovered by those who examined Mahler, did not make heart failure inevitable—it should not have been a death sentence. Valve damage from rheumatic fever in childhood predisposes the patient to bacterial endocarditis, which was incurable before the advent of antibiotics, but many of those with the predisposition avoid any such infection.[41]

Why, in the wake of his daughter's death and on the occasion of his wife's collapse, did Mahler make the bizarre proposal that Blumenthal should examine *him*? What had prompted Alma's worries about her husband's heart?[42] Surely there must have been prior conversations on the topic, but, however confident Mahler's devotion to exercise may have made him, it is hard to avoid suspicion that the supposedly reassuring gesture masks a deeper concern—that it was not just *Alma* who needed the "good news" but Mahler too. It is easy to envisage a film centered on a Mahler figure, a man haunted by death from his earliest years, who must repeatedly come to terms with his own mortality and whose anxieties are confirmed in the immediate aftermath of the searing loss of a beloved child.

In that summer of 1907 or possibly that fall, the bereaved composer read a book of poems written by Hans Bethge and loosely based on Chinese sources. The reading inspired him to begin a new work, and its eventual title paid tribute to his concerns about his own finitude. Had it been forthrightly labeled as a symphony—as it could easily have been, given that its predecessor had also deployed voices from the opening measures to the conclusion—*Das Lied von der Erde* would have been Mahler's ninth. Vividly conscious of the fact that Beethoven and Bruckner had both died after completing nine symphonies, Mahler attempted to cheat the fates by withdrawing from *Das Lied von der Erde* the symphonic designation.[43] The ploy failed. After *Das Lied*, he finished an "official" ninth symphony—but, early in 1911, while the tenth remained incomplete, he fell ill in New York. There was no cure for his bacterial endocarditis, and his wish to be buried beside Putzi prompted a decision to make the long trip back to Vienna. Shortly after May 18, a respectfully shocked world, including Thomas Mann, on holiday in Venice, learned of Gustav Mahler's death.

The fear of death, clear in Mahler and readily attributable to von Aschenbach, has nothing to do with the pains or agonies of dying or with concerns about what might come after. In Aschenbach's case, it cannot be the fear of the distress caused to loved ones, of the hole that will be left by one's departure, for, as Mann makes clear, his protagonist has no such intimate connections. For Mahler, in contrast, a wife and child would be left behind—yet by 1911, as he knew with intense sadness, Alma had been unfaithful to him. In the summer of 1910, at the Tobelbad spa, where she had gone for reasons of health, she had met the young German architect Walter Gropius, and a diverting acquaintance soon flamed into a passionate affair.[44] Mahler's last weeks were surely pervaded by a sense that his struggle to win Alma back was now pointless, by a recognition that for all the dedicated care of her nursing, her life and her love would soon be directed elsewhere. Perhaps he thought, during that tortuous journey home, of his remaining daughter growing up without him. Yet regret, concern, reproach, and the bitterness of personal defeat would surely have overlain a deeper anxiety, one pervading his life from childhood on, a sense of the vulnerability of his artistic strivings, whose priority he had made evident, before their marriage, in the division of family labor he had presented to Alma: his duty was to compose, hers to support—and if he demanded much, that was because he, and his work, had much to give.[45]

Like Aschenbach, Mahler had a conception of his life as centered on a sequence of works that would express his own intense reactions to his experiences at different stages of his life. Not only are his actual compositions marked by the threat of premature truncation, of the intervention of death before he had written enough, but also by serious doubt that there could ever be enough. Human finitude pervades the songs and symphonies—the sequence of compositions is permeated by the need to struggle against the negation that death, an *inevitably* premature death, will bring. They are rooted in a vivid awareness of the variety of life's joys but darkened by the fear that, because the joys are transitory and ephemeral, they are worthless. Mahler seeks, again and again, to convey the intensity and vitality he finds in nature, in love, in human relationships and bonds, while recognizing the shadows that fall across them, and he struggles to affirm the worth of sources of joy known to be transitory. The songs and symphonies hardly serve as exemplars of the aesthetic values that the obituary attributes to Aschenbach, but they grow organically out of a sense of finitude Aschenbach and Mahler share with Adrian Leverkühn, too.[46] Mann's late protagonist writes to his devoted friend, Zeitblom, deploring his "dog's existence," the vegetative state in which he can compose nothing, a state honor would require him to denounce.

> It would be impossible to occupy oneself with what has already been achieved, when one is in a condition of inability to do anything better. The past would only be bearable, if one were to feel one had gone beyond it, instead of having merely to admire it in the consciousness of present impotence.[47]

Schopenhauer's insatiable Will pervades Leverkühn's confession. It is latent as well in Aschenbach's disciplined pursuit of masterpiece after masterpiece and in Mahler's successive attempts to write "songs and symphonies of life and death."[48]

## 4

Much has been written about the "programs" claimed to be present in Mahler's works. Not only did the composer offer evocative titles for individual symphonies and movements of symphonies, but, in letters to and conversations with his friends, he expanded on these indications, sometimes even suggesting a "significance" for particular moments.[49]

An extreme position would suppose that these works were envisaged as tone poems (in the manner pioneered by previous composers, such as Liszt), that they were written from an outline dramatic narrative, and that they should be heard as unfolding that narrative. A polar opposite contends that the inconsistency of the explanations Mahler actually gave—and the diversity of his remarks about the value of such explanations—renders talk of programs entirely pointless. More plausible than either of these extremes is the view, articulated and defended in a variety of ways by Mahler scholars, that the composer offered explanations and literary or philosophical connections with the aim of guiding the ears of his potential listeners,[50] that his suggestions reflected, to quite different degrees, ideas and images that had been with him as he wrote, and that their significance for him and for his audiences is greater or less with respect to different works and different stages of his career.[51]

Although the final section of this chapter will reconsider the possibilities of cross-illumination among music, literature, and philosophy, my aim is neither to endorse any specific program for any Mahler work[52] nor to offer a developed thesis about the role of programs in the processes of composing them: I shall not seek a dramatic narrative for a particular symphony or try to fathom the significance of cowbells here or a drumbeat there. In suggesting that the songs and symphonies express a continued preoccupation with intense joys that are shadowed by the prospect of death, I intend something more abstract: an intellectual need to affirm what is transitory, accompanied by powerful emotions of exultation and sadness. Mahler pointed to this need in writing about his Second Symphony (and its "program"):

> I called the first movement *"Todtenfeier."* It may interest you to know that it is the hero of my D major symphony that I bear to his grave, and whose life I reflect, from a higher vantage point, in a clear mirror. Here too the question is asked: *What did you live for? Why did you suffer? Is it all only a vast terrifying joke?*—We *have* to answer these questions somehow if we are to go on living—indeed even if we are only to go on dying! The person in whose life this call has resounded, even if it was only once, must give an answer. And it is this answer I give in the last movement.[53]

The symphonies can be heard—perhaps almost always *are* heard—as struggles to reach a moment of affirmation.[54] For that moment to emerge, it must be preceded by a real sense of the poles of experience as they have been felt in the recent life of the composer; there must be darkness and sorrow, bitterness and defeat, ecstasy and wonder, whimsy and everyday happiness—that is, if you like, a *shared* "program."

The Second Symphony, the "Resurrection," shows this pattern extremely clearly. Its first movement, marked *"Todtenfeier"* (funeral rites), is unusually long and poses Mahler's preoccupying question. The force of the challenge is so great as to seem unanswerable—and Mahler famously had difficulties in going on. For over a year,[55] he was unsure whether this movement could be incorporated into a symphony or whether it would simply stand alone as a "tone poem." Even after he had completed the three middle movements, he faced the problem of finding an adequate counterpoint to the opening *"Todtenfeier."*[56] Hearing at a memorial service a setting of a poem by Klopstock, his "Resurrection Ode," Mahler discovered his ending.[57] The final movement opens stormily, recapitulating some of the anguish of the first, before the extraordinary moment when the chorus barely breathes—the marking is triple piano—the word *Auferstehen* (Resurrection).

Characteristically, Mahler did not simply set the words written by someone else but added his own text. The added words are commands to believe, to believe that one will not be entirely lost, that one's life has not been in vain, and the more agitated setting of these words makes it evident that Mahler has not entirely settled his own doubts. If this ending brings affirmation, it is not because of the reminder that we may hope for a literal resurrection, one assured by the truth of Christianity—that would be too simple for the struggle that continues to pervade both words and music, too easy for the recollection of the pain, still present as it is being transcended. In his accessible introduction to Mahler, the great musicologist Deryck Cooke raises the important question of whether a symphonic answer to the questions that haunted Mahler can speak to those who do not share the religious beliefs apparently presupposed:

> But for the many of us who cannot answer this challenge by invoking the Christian belief in immortality, what significance can there

be in the culmination of the symphony—the part which presents the ostensible "message" of the work?

Strangely enough, it does have great significance for us, since a hearing of it comes as a tremendous emotional experience. Yet the reason is clear. Music cannot express intellectual concepts, but only feelings; and what we all respond to is the feelings of faith and inspiration in the music, whether or not we are convinced by the concepts in the text which were the objects of these feelings. Mahler's affirmations are ultimately of faith and inspiration in life itself, whether they arose, as in the Second, Third and Eighth Symphonies from the religious beliefs he held at the time, or as in *The Song of the Earth* and the unfinished Tenth, from his realistic coming to terms with mortality when his religious beliefs failed him.[58]

There are many insights here. Cooke is entirely correct, I believe, in recognizing the impact of this finale on the many listeners who have no truck with any literal afterlife, and the last sentence quoted recognizes the multifaceted character of Mahler's attempts at affirmation. Cooke errs, however, in attributing to Mahler a belief in the literal truth of the words he set—for any such simple faith is at odds with the composer's own struggles, at odds with the depths plumbed in the earlier movements of the symphony (and recapitulated at moments in the finale), and hardly concordant with mundane facts about his life.

If Mahler believed in the literal truth of the Christian resurrection, the question raised by the *Todtenfeier* would have an easy answer—the memorial service for Bülow would hardly have been needed for its revelation. At that stage, he was not even nominally a Christian. Born into a Jewish family,[59] he found his career handicapped by his ethnic origins.[60] Although he occasionally claimed that he had converted to Christianity in 1891—three years before writing the Finale of the Second Symphony— he was baptized only in 1897. His reasons seem to have been purely pragmatic: his sights were set on the directorship of the Imperial and Royal Opera in Vienna, and there was no hope for a conductor, however talented, identified as a Jew.[61] Indeed, Mahler confessed to his friend Ludwig Karpath that he had converted out of "self-preservation" and that doing so "cost [him] a great deal."[62]

The biographical details are concordant with the more generalized spirituality, severed from any tie to Christian doctrine, the more abstract affirmation of life that can be heard in the Finale of the Second Symphony. Consolation comes in the slow crescendo of the chorus, from the first bare breath to its final declaration. This upward movement itself, not the doctrine of the words, reveals how the harshness and bitterness of the earlier music can provide elements out of which human voices can themselves rise to affirmation. Out of the arresting dissonances but organically connected with them comes a stately crescendo that makes its own resolve. Mahler borrowed from Klopstock not an eloquent expression of true and comforting doctrine but the possibility of a gesture. The gesture is not grounded in any prior and independent source of consolation—the religious truth that we shall all live again—but rather produces consolation through the fact that it can be made.

In similar fashion, *Kindertotenlieder* ends with a superficially religious promise. As with the Second Symphony, this poignant song cycle can be heard as constituted by two framing movements—the opening desolation of the terrible loss, the final fury of the storm and the singer's protest, resolving into the redemptive coda—separated by three movements that recall episodes from the children's lives.[63] Many hearers (and critics) would take the pattern to be omnipresent in Mahler's major works: a question posed or challenge made, episodic exploration, attempted resolution. To insist on that form, however, would be to lose sight of other important connections—*Kindertotenlieder* shows alternating patterns of darkness and light, as the bleak first movement gives way to illusory hopes, hopes dashed in the third song and revived in the fourth, while the fifth and last moves from despair to the closing consolation.[64] The children have been rescued by God and rest, as if in their mother's house (Mahler originally substituted *Schoss* [womb] for *Haus* [house], but it would have destroyed the rhyme scheme).[65] In the fifth and final song, the storm dies away, and the sun (hailed—bitterly—at the end of the opening movement) shines through as the music resolves into a major key and a radiant and serene coda.

Only a naive hearing could take this for literal truth. The vision of the children alive in heaven would be of a piece with the wistful yearnings that they are enduring parts of the cosmos, stars (Song 2), or the illusory hopes that there will be a reunion with them on the mountaintops

FIGURE 3.2. *Kindertotenlieder* 1: close.

(Song 4). The first and third songs show why such longings arise and how unrealistic they are. The sun will continue to rise, but the disturbing conclusion of the vocal line in Song 1, an upward interval of a tone and two repeated accented notes, makes plain how hard it is to affirm the "joyous light of the world" (*Freudenlicht der Welt*).[66] The long arching line of Song 3 (marked "*Schwer. Dumpf.*"—heavy, dull, muffled, hollow), repeated twice, brings out the range and depth of grief caused by knowledge that the dead little girl is irreplaceable. Yet from the tempestuous anguish of Song 5 emerges the possibility for the singer of living on, the possibility of accepting death. The fury abates, and the Christian allusions serve only as overtones for conjuring a resigned peace, an attitude more abstract than the faith that they are literally living somewhere else—among the stars, on the mountaintops, in a Christian heaven. As with the Second Symphony, the act of affirmation endorses itself.

Even a work that appears initially to be different in character reveals Mahler's preoccupation with the struggle for affirmation. From the opening sleigh bells to the evocation of a child's vision of heaven in the last movement, where the whimsical assignment of the saints to household duties is matched by the buoyancy of the lines and the sunny orchestration, the Fourth Symphony seems free of any serious engagement with the prospect of death. In the context of its predecessors and successors, I hear it differently, as taking an ironic stance to the earnest exhortation to faith that closes the Second. It is as if Mahler were distancing himself from his previous gestures of affirmation and from the evocations of shadows to which those gestures have responded, questioning whether the problem of finding value in admittedly transitory things might be mocked for its over-seriousness. The symphony can be heard as yet another way of dealing with the preoccupation so evident in earlier as well as later works. Instead of struggling toward affirmation, one can propose instead that such affirmation is entirely unnecessary and that the prior efforts have been unsatisfactory, even naive—faux naïveté exposes the credulity of judging that the "philosophical problem" must be taken seriously.[67]

This mode of wrestling with the preoccupation—through an attempt at ironic rejection of it—is, like the more direct attempts of its predecessors and successors, unstable. Mahler discovered that any way of fighting his way through to affirmation could only be temporary. Each of the major works brings a moment of resolution,[68] but, in its wake, there are new joys to be celebrated, new shadows cast upon them, and the task begins again, prompted by a different stage of life and a different fund of experiences. Like Mann's central figure, Mahler's life is centered on the production of a sequence of masterpieces whose composition will vindicate the value of his existence and whose central theme is the problem of vindicating value. The vindications of the past never seem adequate to the shadows that fall on the present, and even the effort to solve the problem once and for all by denying the need for vindication cannot succeed. The radiant parody of the invocation of heaven, an invocation as otiose as it is earnest, does not capture an ironic mood Mahler can maintain. After the Fourth comes another symphony, one whose first movement is marked, appropriately, "Funeral March."

5

According to a story, one good enough to be apocryphal, a Hollywood producer who attended Visconti's film was so impressed with the score that he wanted the name of "this Mahler guy's" agent. The producer's admiration was probably caused by the skilful repetition of one of Mahler's most beautiful—and now most familiar—themes,[69] the melody sounded by the first violins in the opening measures of the Adagietto, the fourth movement of the Fifth Symphony. This opening material is heard as the film begins, and, after several scenes in which no music accompanies the events displayed, parts of the Adagietto, all featuring the opening theme, often parts that intensify its emotional force, are played again and again. Because the Adagietto is heard in so many of the later scenes, it might appear that Visconti is overusing it, but this, in my judgment, is one of the film's major successes. The melody, with its sequence of initially ascending steps—two whole-tone steps, a repeated note on the first beat of the measure, resolving to the tonic a half-step higher, followed by an upward fourth, a descending half-tone, again a repeated note, and an incomplete resolution on the supertonic—conveys a sense of longing unfulfilled, making it brilliantly suited to the action, outer and inner, of the film and of the original novella.[70]

According to a famous (notorious?) piece of testimony offered by Mahler's friend, the conductor Willem Mengelberg, the Adagietto was a love letter sent by the composer during his whirlwind courtship of Alma. Mengelberg reports that "instead of a letter, he sent her this manuscript without further explanation. She understood and wrote back that he should come!!! Both have told me this!"[71] Yet if it was a love letter, it was a curious one, not simply in virtue of its being a "song without words" but also because of its musical resonances.

FIGURE 3.3. Mahler, Adagietto, opening theme.

[Musical notation]

**FIGURE 3.4A.** Opening of *Kindertotenlieder* 2.

[Musical notation]

**FIGURE 3.4B.** Opening of *Rückertlied*.

As Mahler scholars have noted, there are close affinities between the Adagietto and the themes of two other Mahler works: the second of the *Kindertotenlieder* and the most well known of the *Rückert-Lieder* ("Ich bin der Welt abhanden gekommen," "I have almost lost touch with the world").[72] Critical judgment often results from careful analysis of the score, attention to details of melodic line, shifts in key, harmonic structure, and the like. Before taking up the substantive issue of the affinities between the Adagietto and other works, it will be useful to recognize a different mode of considering (and writing about) music.

*Analytic* consideration of, and commentary on, music (or poetry, or painting) proceeds from a theoretical perspective to identify theoretically important elements in the structure of the work considered. Good theory supplies tools for understanding the forms present in different works, for appreciating connections among works, and for understanding the historical development of a genre. By contrast, *synthetic* consideration of music (or other arts) can be undertaken prior to the adoption of any theory, through the juxtaposition of different works that are taken to be importantly connected. The synthesis may be *internal* to an art form, or a genre, or even to an individual composer, in relating works of the same type—pieces of music, or, more narrowly, songs, or, even more narrowly, Mahler songs. Alternatively, the synthesis may be *external* in some respects: perhaps by relating a Mahler song to a Schubert *Lied* or to a Wagner opera, perhaps by relating a symphonic movement to a song, or, in the more radical case, by connecting music to poetry, to visual art, or to philosophy. The broader conception of philosophy defended above (section 2 of chapter 1), a conception this book attempts to exemplify, builds synthetic complexes that are radically external, suggesting affinities among works of art, music, and literature and philosophical themes, even juxtaposing quite diverse art forms to ideas from different philosophers.

To say that synthetic consideration or commentary is prior to theory is to suppose that some judgment about the connection can be made without delving into the structures recognized from any previously adopted theoretical perspective. Those judgments are reached by using our eyes and ears, by reflecting on the thoughts and feelings that arise in us. In principle, they are corrigible by theory, for, if we had reason to count a theoretical perspective as a valuable one, its delineation of a commonality where we had perceived none, or of marked differences where we had judged affinity, would rightly lead us to question our judgment— perhaps our seeing or hearing was too casual, our feeling too shallow, our thought confused or jejune. Ultimately, however, there is no basis for evaluating theory apart from the reactions underlying synthetic consideration and commentary: theoretical perspectives are assessed by their power to illuminate and deepen the synthetic connections reflectively endorsed, so that some significant fraction of them are vindicated and made comprehensible.[73] Synthetic commentary on music (or poetry, or painting) consists in proposing connections for reflection: it operates in the manner attributed to Nancy Cartwright (see section 2 of chapter 1)—"Consider this!"

Back now to the particular example of current concern: the affinities of the Adagietto to other musical works. Analysis of the scores of the Rückert song, of the second of the *Kindertotenlieder*, and of the Adagietto itself will disclose various shared features—perhaps most evidently the slow ascending sequences that lead to partially resolved suspensions—but prior to any such analysis, and to my mind more immediate and powerful, is the affinity felt by any attentive listener and, particularly, by anyone who has performed any of these works.[74] There is a common tenderness, a wistfulness, and, especially in the *Kindertotenlieder* song and the Adagietto, a sense of yearning. "*Ich bin der Welt abhanden gekommen*" differs, however, from the other two, in that the movement of longing reaches a conclusive resolution: the singer is at peace, and the peace is ultimately expressed in the final cadence, in serene renunciation of the world and the expression of tranquil love in song. "*Nun seh' ich wohl*," however, yearns for reunion with the lost children; its ascending phrases seem to reach for them, with gentle hope (the opening phrase, especially as repeated at "*Ihr wolltet mir*") or more desperately and tempestuously ("*was dir nur Augen*"). Instead of a convincing resolution, the longing ends in the singer's strange incomplete cadence, marked *subito piano*, on "*Sterne*" (descending, e-c-g), after which the orchestra repeats the first notes of the opening ("yearning") phrase, to a suspension only partially resolved. Desire falls short of its objective, reaching at most the illusion of fulfillment, and if the listener needed further confirmation of its failure, it is only necessary to hear the first measures of the movement—*Schwer, dumpf*—that follows.

The Adagietto shares this lack of resolution—indeed, there is not even the *illusion* of fulfillment. Mahler deploys the same musical material, again and again, intensifying it but never really developing it. In its entirety, the original from which Visconti drew, the fourth movement of the Fifth Symphony, is cyclic rather than directional.[75] (*Für Elise*, which Visconti's film has Tadzio sound out in Aschenbach's presence, might be heard as similarly cyclic, a simpler and more immature version of the Adagietto, the adolescent's counterpart to Aschenbach's dominant music). The opening theme, repeated so many times in the film score, yearns for a close it never attains, and in its intensified recapitulation it becomes the embodiment of desire (*Sehnsucht*) and thus a fitting accompaniment for Aschenbach's unsatisfied longings and for his directionless wanderings around Venice in pursuit of Tadzio.

Another musical connection deserves note. All three pieces—the *Rückert-Lied*, the second of the *Kindertotenlieder*, and the Adagietto—are offspring of *Tristan*. The longings they embody are there already in the opening measures of the Prelude and in the impassioned phrases that

FIGURE 3.5. *Kindertotenlieder* 2: two extracts.

convey the lovers' demand for a union of impossible completeness. Like the Rückert song, albeit on a vastly protracted scale, *Tristan* has a direction, a movement toward fulfillment and resolution, not in the peace of retreat from the world but in the close of the *Liebestod*—it would be an exaggeration to regard the music-drama as a five-hour search for orgasm eventually attained in death, but there is something to the idea.[76] Mahler was not shy about acknowledging his debt to Wagner: the Adagietto quotes the "gaze" motif from *Tristan*.[77] If the score was a "love letter to Alma," evocations of *Tristan*—like allusions to renunciation of the world—seem to veer in dangerous directions: to offer a love that can be satisfied only in death may not be the best way to woo. *Tristan*, however, eventually achieves its end, pressing toward a climax both musical and sexual, in the closing *Liebestod*. The Adagietto, an indefinitely orbiting counterpart to the music of Wagner's opera, reaches no such climax.

Yet the Adagietto is not simply the expression of sexual desire as yet unfulfilled but also an encapsulation of the life pattern common to both Aschenbach and Mahler, the constant striving for a vindicating expression that is never permanently realized. It is a musical embodiment of Schopenhauer's emphasis on the transience of accomplishment, the inevitable incompleteness of a life. You might make a fully coherent film out of this, a film in which Aschenbach is Mahler, with Mahler's sensibilities, and in which Mahler's music plays a central role. It could include flashbacks to earlier incidents in the composer's life, the diagnosis of heart trouble, the death of a daughter, the struggles to vindicate life's joys and beauties, despite their transitoriness (but it would *not* include the absurd and unnecessary exchanges between Alfred and his *Meister*). Aschenbach would come to Venice in need of rest and would have a new vision of beauty—one like others before it—which he would feel an urgent need to understand and to affirm. He would recognize that this beauty is ephemeral—Tadzio has imperfect teeth and a pale complexion—yet he would be fascinated by the thought of responding to him and to the ideal of human beauty he embodies. He would strive to be in Tadzio's presence and to find music adequate to the boy's effect on him. In losing Tadzio in the labyrinth of alleyways, in a city he knows to be permeated by disease and death, he would appreciate the hopelessness of his endeavor not just in this current version but in all those that have preceded it. In his collapse at the fountain, all the supposed resolutions in his compositions would sound hollow in his head, and he would be left only with the indefinitely protracted yearning of the Adagietto, a musical counterpoint to the anti-Socratic musings of the novella. He would die there in the rubbish-strewn piazza knowing that he had failed.

That imaginary film would set Mann's novella—*faithfully* set it— without its coda. There would be no counterpart to the scene on the beach, to Tadzio's mysterious walk into the sea and to Aschenbach's devoted but fatal gesture of pursuit. Instead, there would be a bleak finale, a confession of incompleteness, of failure, of defeat. Is it possible to find a different conclusion, to extend the associations with Mahler's music to match the mood of the ending on which Mann—after the difficulty acknowledged in his letter to Heinrich—eventually settled? Can we marry any Mahlerian music to Mann's closing scene—and thereby illuminate those last pregnant pages? For all its contrapuntal brilliance, the actual close of the Fifth Symphony will not do.[78] Its *Wunderhorn* exuberance is remote from the autumnal setting of the deserted beach, from Aschenbach's dizziness and premonitions of death, from Tadzio's transformation. A different work of Mahler's is more promising. The last scene of the novella begins with Aschenbach's discovery that the Poles are about to leave Venice, that he will be parted from Tadzio. Perhaps we should consider that scene in light of the great farewell song, the *Abschied Lied*, that Mahler wrote.

# 6

After the three heavy blows he experienced in 1907—besides the death of his beloved elder daughter and the diagnosis of his heart problem, he also lost his job at the Vienna Opera—Mahler slowly began to plan a new composition. Inspired by the poems he read in Hans Bethge's *Die chinesische Flöte* (The Chinese flute), he conceived a six-movement piece, one that could equally be considered an orchestral song-cycle or a symphony.[79] *Das Lied von der Erde* was born in grief and anxiety— despite Mahler's efforts to reassure his friends, the prospect of imminent death is apparent in the letters he wrote in the summer of 1908, the period in which he composed most, if not all, of *Das Lied*.[80] He described the new work to Bruno Walter as "the most personal thing I have done,"[81] and Walter endorsed the judgment:

... it is an "I-work," the likes of which Mahler had never created, not even in his First. . . . Every note he writes talks of himself only, every word which has been formulated a thousand years ago expresses only himself—*Das Lied von der Erde* is the most personal sound in Mahler's work, maybe in all of music . . . [82]

Like *Kindertotenlieder*, *Das Lied* is framed by an opening song, one that presents a deep challenge, and an answering finale, in this case an exceptionally long slow movement, *Der Abschied* (The farewell). For this last song, Mahler set in dialogue with one another two poems he found on facing pages of *Die chinesische Flöte*, one based on Mong-Kao-Jen entitled "Awaiting the Friend," and the other derived from Wang-Wei, with the title "The Departure of the Friend." Mahler made several changes to knit these poems together and, as with the finale to the Second Symphony, added lines of his own.

*Das Lied* expresses, as clearly as any of his earlier works, Mahler's preoccupation with the shadows that fall over life's joys. It is evident in the descending theme of the first movement, in which the voice plunges through an octave, singing *"Dunkel ist das Leben, ist der Tod"* ("Dark is life, dark is death"). That phrase, heard three times, each time at higher pitch, and the second time with an eerie chromatic change on the penultimate note, leaves no doubt that this movement is the *"Trinklied vom Jammer der Erde"* (Drinking song of the earth's *misery*).[83] Yet that is not the mood of its opening, with the apparent confidence of the fortissimo horn calls giving way to the tenor's accented ascending scale to a gleaming top F, marked *"mit voller Kraft"* (with full power).[84] The wine glows in the bowl, but before it is drunk, there must be a song, a song recognizing—and overcoming—the misery of the human condition. This is not the song of a drunkard (he will come later), for the wine has not yet been touched, and the singer's appraisal is sober. Yet its initial strength fades— the opening affirmation modulates to bitter defiance (the song of misery will resound in the soul's laughter) and then to troubled uncertainty in the anxious sighing phrases that describe the waste of the "garden of the soul," followed by a muted echo of the opening confidence. The verse closes with the first summation: Dark is life, dark is death.

Confidence is renewed in the second strophe, in which the words turn away from confrontation of the miseries of human existence, as if the singer is forcing a celebration that cannot easily be sustained if the facts are faced, offering an attempted tribute to the earth's gifts that ultimately has to confess the value of oblivion ("a full glass of wine, at the right time, is worth more than all the riches of this earth"). Once again, the refrain testifies to the darkness of life and death, its pain intensified by the higher pitch, with the chromatic shift at the end decisively undercutting the attempt at bravado.

Assertion has failed. The orchestral interlude, somber, tender, even wistful, sets the mood for the singer's quiet entry ("*p ma appassionato*"), as the text proclaims the eternity of the earth, its annual renewal. Yet the moment of quiet acceptance is only the setting for an anguished protest against human finitude—our physical home is reborn each year, but *we* are granted not even a century to delight in the decaying trash of the earth. Bethge's text already suggests the agitated pace at which the thoughts succeed one another: the half-formulated complaint is that we are given only a short span to enjoy the pleasures of our physical world, but before that idea has been enunciated, those pleasures themselves have been devalued—ephemeral as they are, they can only be corruptible and worthless. Mahler's chromaticisms and the leaps that punctuate the descending passages in the vocal part intensify the sense of desperation. They prepare for a wild parody of the opening attempt at affirmation—the horns return to their once-confident motif, as the trumpets play an ominous descending scale, and the voice leaps in pungent chromaticisms, punctuated by cross-rhythms: our predicament is that of an ape, crouched in the moonlight in a graveyard, his howling cacophony piercing through the sweet aroma of life.

*Now*, at this moment of full recognition, complete understanding of our miserable condition, now is the time for drink. The wildness of the music—in orchestra and in voice—gives way to the opening phrase, with the whole-tone steps replaced by half-tones (compressed? diminished?), in the only affirmation left. The wine must be emptied to the dregs. For the third time—this time quietly, meditatively, with resignation—the singer testifies to the darkness of life and death. At his final word—"*Tod*" (death)—there is a sudden fortissimo, perhaps to acknowledge the victory of mortality. The orchestra returns to the strong horn calls of the opening—as if we could now understand what they really meant, how empty they really were.

As insightful commentators have recognized, philosophical concerns and ideas are at play here, and the pertinent philosophers are Schopenhauer and Nietzsche.[85] The problem of human finitude permeates the *Trinklied*, challenging composer, performers, and listeners to affirm the possibility of value in human life, given its transience. The song opens with an attempt at affirmation, a projected response to what is characterized very early as sadness or grief ("*Kummer*" is more elevated, less abject than "*Jammer*," wretchedness, misery). The persona envisaged is Nietzschean: the will is to assert itself, to find genuine joy, the limitations are to be overcome. The gestures prove, however, to be empty—the would-be transcendence of mortality is exposed as debased misery, the howling of a tormented ape. Nor is Schopenhauer's solution, the abnegation of the will, sustainable, for the closing refrain cannot preserve the mood of resignation—the triumph of death must be bitterly acknowledged, and the protest is renewed, the will impotently tries to reassert itself, in the closing orchestral measures.

The challenge is to be taken up, *creatively* taken up, in the long finale—*Das Lied* is not simply an exercise in giving musical expression to ideas available in existing works of philosophy *but a musical search for a new, superior, philosophical possibility*.[86] Before we can come to the *Abschied*, however, the challenge is deepened, and some materials for answering it are assembled. This is the philosophical work of the middle movements.

Any tendency to protest that the predicament presented in the opening song is overstated and histrionic, the affirmation demanded overblown and unnecessary, is immediately diffused by the melancholy of the second movement, *Der Einsame im Herbst* (The lonely one in autumn).[87] The sighs of the winds, first oboe, then flute and clarinet, lead to the sad phrases with which the singer describes the beauties of the declining world—the frost on the grass, the drooping blossoms, the faded lotus leaves. Weariness is in words and music, and the extinguishing of the lamp prepares for sleep. With great intensity (*innig*), the singer yearns for rest, for revival, for healing, and her voice expands in an arc of passionate sorrow (comparable to the long phrase that ends the strophes of the third of the *Kindertotenlieder*), an invocation to the "sun of love" (*die Sonne der Liebe*) to shine once again and to dry up her bitter tears. That vocal line is an elegy for love lost, for the transience of the deepest emotional connections to others, sounded from the faded aftermath, with the glittering jewels of the autumnal dawn, the withered blossoms, reminders of what has been and what will never come again. Loneliness is all the more melancholy, even less easy to bear, because of the memories of the moments of relief—*inevitably evanescent* relief—in companionship, friendship, love.

Those moments of relief are brought into the present in the next two songs. The third movement, marked "*Behaglich heiter*" ("agreeably cheerful") appears to offer a change of mood. Elegantly clad young people sit in a porcelain pavilion, built in the middle of a pond and reached by a bridge of jade. They are friends who drink tea together, who chat, who write verses. Tenor and orchestra combine to offer a happy, even perky, depiction of their comfortable existence—until the tempo slackens, the dynamic grows softer, and there is a key change to the relative minor. The tenor sings of the stillness of the pool, and the curious "mirroring" of the pavilion in the water. As the tempo reverts to the opening, it appears that the original cheerful mood will be recaptured, but the scuttering movements of the high winds, accompanied by the sustained high tones of the violins lead to a quizzical ending: the "music evaporates" as if it were "a transparent mirage."[88] The singer's apparently happy line sets the words "All standing on its head" ("*Alles auf dem Kopfe stehend*") as if there were no difference between the friends on the island and their watery reflection. The serene moment may be illusory, the porcelain is easily shattered, the tea drinking and the gossip—the song ends on "*trinken, plaudern*"—will pass without significant trace.

A similar sense of *transient* joy is heard in the following song. Young girls gather lotus blossoms on the river bank. Their beauty, like that of the tea-drinking friends, is mirrored in the shining water—this is the moment of their most intense loveliness. Suddenly the idyll is interrupted by a counterpart to their physical perfection. The orchestra summons (brilliantly) the exuberance and energy of young men on horseback, who burst onto the scene, and one of the horses tramples the grass and the flowers. The youths ride off, and peace returns: the beautiful girls are again reflected in the calm waters, but the male presence has been felt. The song closes with two long, ambiguously tender vocal lines that sing of "the loveliest of the maidens," who sends a glance of tender longing after the disruptive rider—the dark warmth of her eyes expresses the arousal of her heart. A passing moment of unfulfilled longing, a moment of beauty and tenderness—something perhaps to be remembered in the autumnal loneliness to come, when the flowers and the beauty have faded.

The fifth song, *Der Trunkene im Frühling* (The drunkard in spring), might easily appear to belie the concerns I have been emphasizing, its cheeky cheerfulness (it is marked *"keck"*) denying any more serious intent—it can even seem out of place in the entire work. Thomas Mann, possibly in an unreceptive mood, once heard the movement as undercutting the value not only of *Das Lied* but of Mahler's music: "I was very tired and only endured with difficulty the piece that followed, *Das Lied von der Erde*, with the feeling that, at bottom, I can't stand Mahler. *"Ein Vöglein singt im Walde"* [sic; "A little bird sings in the woods"], with solo violin, how should I set that against the oppression of brutal tyrants?"[89] Yet two features of the fifth song connect it to the challenge of the first: where the opening movement surveyed the human predicament as a prelude to drink, the evocation of the drunkard shows us what the attempt at solution—or evasion—amounts to; more subtly, the singer's final exhortation *"Lass mich betrunken sein!"* ("Let me be drunk!"), set to an awkward chromatic line, with the flourishes in the orchestra that bring the movement to its close, conjure the mood of the initial affirmation—in effect, we have been returned to the starting point, reminded that the challenge remains unanswered.

A closer look at the three parts of the drunkard's song reinforces this conclusion. Life is dismissed as illusory (recalling the identification of reality and its reflection in the tenor's previous song, *"Von der Jugend"*), so that there is no compulsion to face its cares, and the singer finds oblivion in drink. In the second section, however, life intrudes on his sleep. Nature, renewed in the springtime, awakens him, yet this too seems a dream. For a moment, there beckons the possibility of immersing himself in *that* dream, of responding to the song of the laughing bird and of renewing a fully human life on and with the reborn earth. The mysterious quality of the orchestral setting (in the measures after [6]), serene in itself yet seeming to issue demands on the human singer or listener, is punctuated by the *natural* gaiety of the bird. Just as the opening song separated human existence from the permanence of the earth and

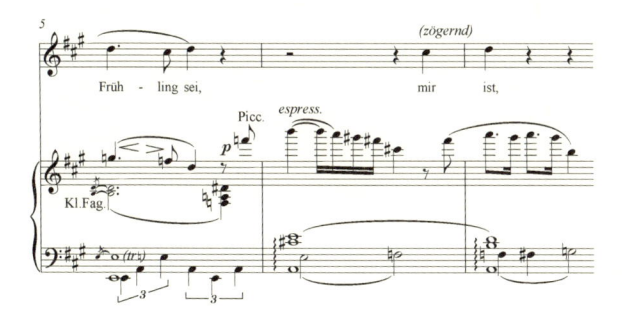

FIGURE 3.6. *Das Lied von der Erde*: extract from movement 5.

its springtime renewal—counterposing the image of the howling ape—so now the drunkard turns away from the invitation to return to life. Orchestra and singer take up the mood of the opening, the tenor vowing to drink until the moon shines—the moon that earlier illuminated the ape in the graveyard. The profound muted challenge of the middle section[90]—as disquieting as it is inviting—reveals the shallows of the drunkard's cheerfulness, the inadequacy of his evasions. By the end of the fifth movement we have come full circle. The problem of vindicating human existence has been intensified, not answered or bypassed.

So we come to the farewell. The final movement begins with a text that announces parting: the sun sets behind the mountains;[91] the main musical motifs are wistful but gently insistent, no less regretful than the outcry of the first movement, but muted and restrained. It is as though we are to look back, as the end of day—or of life—nears, on the elements that have formed part of it, the types of experience made vivid in the middle movements. The mood is calmer, tinged with melancholy. The river is no longer a place where beautiful girls gather flowers; instead it sings harmoniously of rest and sleep. The birds no longer chirp to awaken the drunkard to the springtime but perch, tired, on the branches. The cry of the lonely one of Song 2 is temporarily held in check, reduced to a sigh that the friend will come to share the beauty—the fading beauty—of the evening. Then the restraint is broken, and the voice swells in a line that is both celebration and lament for the world "eternally drunken with loving and living" (*"ewigen Liebens-Lebens-trunk'ne Welt,"* words Mahler added to Bethge's translation).

The resonances of earlier movements resound in this finale, but they do so with overtones of consolation. The evening shadows bring a welcome cool, the moon no longer shines harshly on the graveyard but hangs "like a silver vessel" (*Silberbarke*) in the sky, the wind that bent the stems of the flowers (Song 2) is now more gentle—though the mood is autumnal, anticipating death or the "falling asleep" of the earth—the vocal and orchestral lines are serene rather than agitated, accepting instead of protesting. Desire, the insatiable restlessness of Will, is to cease, to lapse into dreams, dreams not induced by the artifice of drink but part of the earth's natural rhythms, the rhythms of its breath (*"Die Erde atmet voll von Ruh' und Schlaf. Alle Sehnsucht will nun träumen . . ."*).

As the earth falls asleep, the orchestral texture simplifies: the singer, accompanied by flute and a pedal in the double bass, reflects on the chill of the evening. She waits—as the lonely one of the second song waited—for the arrival of a friend. This expected arrival is no longer for any renewal of love: where the second movement yearned for the "sun of love" to shine again, the finale has been clear, from the singer's first words on the sun's departure—it is to be a final farewell. The friend—in one guise, Death, but in another the compressed personification of all the singer has loved—is eagerly anticipated, so that there may be a last shared moment of joy, joy in the beauty of the evening. Protest is not entirely over, for anger surges momentarily in a cry of reproach: the singer has been left "so long alone." Now, however, she has the resources to calm herself, as the orchestral accompaniment (winds, harps, and strings) prepares for her voice to sing in celebration of the beauties she

FIGURE 3.7. *Das Lied von der Erde*: extract from movement 6.

perceives. Instead of the passionate outcry for love to return and for its sun to dry her bitter tears, she concludes this section with a line of elegiac adoration and affirmation, marked by emphatic cross-rhythms: "O Schönheit, o ewigen Liebens, Lebenstrunk'ne Welt!", a farewell tribute (made in full consciousness that this is a moment of parting) to a world not artificially intoxicated but naturally overflowing with life and love.[92]

To end there would have been to affirm without providing any hint about how the affirmation is to be sustained or to be vindicated. A lesser composer—or a less *philosophical* composer—might have settled for that, but Mahler interpolates at this point an orchestral interlude based on themes that have previously been suited to the singer's mood—reflective, serious, yet quietly affirmative as it has been—but now developing them to renew the challenge of the opening song. The singer's line is echoed in the first violins before a quickening of the tempo introduces a short section (in A minor) that begins to unsettle phrases previously heard as peaceful. This intermezzo introduces far more intense development of several familiar motifs, in the section marked *Schwer* (heavy), running from [38] to [48] in the score, reminding us of the initial challenge, the anguish it expressed, anguish heard in more muted ways in the intervening movements. A counterpart to the opening juxtaposition of the beauties of the earth and the recognition of human finitude, symbolized in the cacophonous howling of the ape, the insistent phrases in horns and bassoons at the climax (around [47] in the score) deny the possibility of any *easy* affirmation.

After the climax of the orchestral interlude, there is a rapid reduction of the orchestral forces and a diminuendo, so that the voice reenters accompanied only by tamtam and a bass note held in the low strings. Mahler switches at this point to Bethge's version of the Wang-Wei text, immediately amended so that the original first person gives way to the third person (an important modification if the identification with the voice of the first poem is to be preserved). The long-awaited friend—to be understood, I suggest, both as Death and as the personification of all the voice has held most dear—arrives. In this encounter, the friend holds out the cup of farewell—the drink needed at *this* moment—asking why his comrade (the leave-taker whose perspective the singer has offered) must depart.[93] Before the reply is given, Mahler sounds again in the orchestra an insistent theme from the orchestral interlude, first *forte* and then *piano*—as if the challenge must now be faced.[94]

The vocal reply, accompanied at first by winds, horns, harps, and strings, almost entirely *piano* or *pianissimo*, is marked "very gentle and full of expression" (*"sehr weich und ausdrucksvoll"*). The singer offers a concise summary of a human life, a life conceived as past: in this world, my fortunes were not good. The protagonist will leave to wander in the mountains, to find rest for her lonely heart. Against orchestral phrases heard restfully in the opening sections of the movement, given an anguished intensity in the interlude, and now restored to a consoling tenderness, the singer sees herself as going to her home (a line Mahler interpolates into Bethge's derivation from Wang-Wei). She will no longer roam far and will quietly await her final hour.[95]

The orchestra prepares for an answer to the confessed harshness of human life and to the finitude of our existence with an extraordinary passage: there is an enormous reduction in tempo, winds give way to strings (with harps persisting), and the dynamic and tempo markings are emphasized: "*Langsam! ppp! Ohne Steigerung. NB*" ("Slow! Extremely soft! Without crescendo. NB"). In a soaring phrase of long-held notes, with great expressiveness, the voice sings words with which Mahler completely rewrote Bethge's closing pair of lines. Instead of:

| *Die Erde ist die gleiche überall* | The earth is the same everywhere |
| *Und ewig, ewig sind die weisse . . . Wolken* | And the white clouds endure forever, forever . . . |

Mahler sets a poetic development of the thoughts that (presumably) attracted him to this poem:

| *Die liebe Erde allüberall* | The lovely earth all over |
| *Blüht auf im Lenz und grünt auf neu* | Blooms in the spring and grows green anew |
| *Allüberall und ewig blauen licht die Fernen,* | Everywhere, and the distance forever shines blue, |
| *Ewig, ewig . . .* | Forever, forever . . . |

The setting of these lines goes beyond the leave-taker's apparent confession of resignation, the avowal that the heart will be quiet and await the last departure: the voice swells again, not this time in lament (as in the arching outburst of the last line of the second song) but with a sweeping serenity that dies down and away in a two-note phrase (*Ewig*), sung seven times,[96] expressing complete acceptance. The movement closes not in defeat or even in sorrow but with a quiet solemnity in which protest and regret have been transcended.

Of the many commentaries on this remarkable passage, none strikes me as more insightful than that offered by Benjamin Britten:

**FIGURE 3.8.** *Das Lied von der Erde*: extract from movement 6.

It has the beauty of loneliness & of pain: of strength & freedom. The beauty of disappointment & never-satisfied love. The cruel beauty of nature, and everlasting beauty of monotony.

...And there is nothing morbid about it...a serenity literally supernatural. I cannot understand it—it passes over me like a tidal wave—and that matters not a jot either, because it goes on forever, even if it is never performed again—that final chord is printed on the atmosphere.[97]

In the immediate context of the farewell song, it is as though the leave-taker can look back, in the fading light, at a world on which the shadows are encroaching and accept it as permanently beautiful and worthwhile.

If it should still seem fanciful to understand this ending as the response to a challenge issued in the first movement, it is only necessary to note

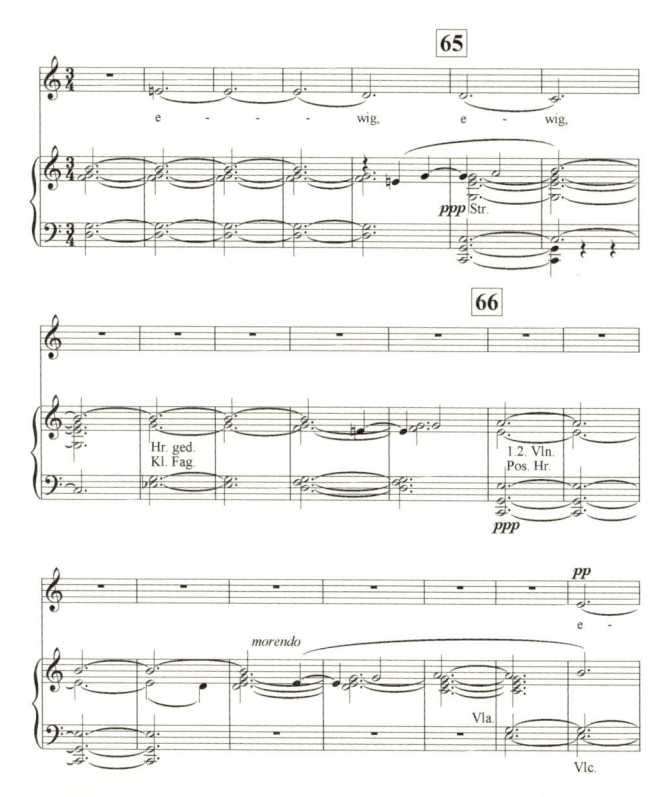

FIGURE 3.9. *Continued on next page*

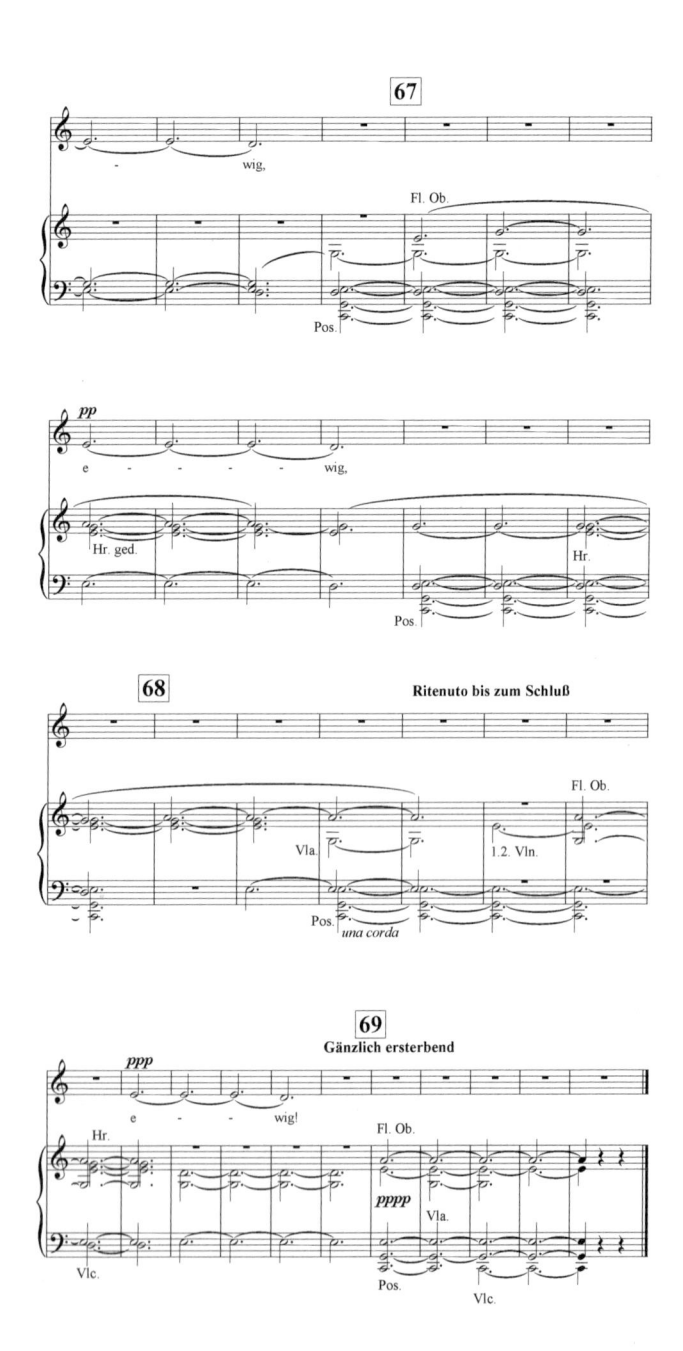

**FIGURE 3.9.** *Das Lied von der Erde*: closing measures.

that Mahler's added words echo the first line of the verse that precedes the passionate outcry against human finitude. In the opening song, just before introducing the image of the ape, Mahler amends Bethge's words in a way that connects the initial despair and the final affirmation. In Bethge's version: *"Das Firmament bleibt ewig, und die Erde / Wird lange feststehn auf den alten Füssen"* ("The heavens endure forever, and the earth / Will long stand fast on its old foundations"); Mahler replaces this with *"Das Firmament bleibt ewig, und die Erde / Wird lange feststehn und aufblühn im Lenz"* ("The heavens endure forever, and the earth / Will long stand fast and blossom again in spring"). In the first movement, there is a contrast between this renewal of the earth and the brevity of human life ("But you, man, how long do you live?"), an anguished protest. In the finale, the leave-taker comes to the closing moment of serenity, restores the connection between the life that is ending and the indefinitely renewed earth, a connection denied as the ape in the graveyard is separated from the enduring heavens and the blossoming spring, a connection rejected in the drunkard's response to the laughing bird—all that is condensed into those fading, consoling repetitions of *"Ewig"* and into that chord "printed on the atmosphere."

Nietzsche and Schopenhauer, philosophers who echo in Mahler's thoughts as they do in Mann's, might offer explanations. For one, it is a matter of finding a way to affirm life despite its finitude (the preoccupation I have attributed to Mahler); for the other, it is a matter of abnegating the will, perhaps expressed in the "quiet heart" that "awaits its hour." Yet already, in the opening movement of *Das Lied*, these possibilities were considered and found wanting. The initial attempt at Nietzschean affirmation founders on the apprehension of a finite human subject, detached from the enduring earth, a miserable caricature of life howling at the moon. The closing refrain, with its acknowledgment of the darkness of our condition, cannot sustain Schopenhauer's ideal state of silencing the will—the *fortissimo* on the final word, *"Tod,"* announces the revival of resentful anger, the protest against the triumph of death, and the closing orchestral measures renew, vainly, the striving to affirm.

The interior movements only deepen the sense that the celebrated philosophical answers are inadequate. The lonely one of Song 2 anticipates a mood that will be completed in the finale, singing with intensity of the coming rest (in the measures after [13], *"Ich komm' zu dir, traute*

FIGURE 3.10. *Das Lied von der Erde*: close of movement 1.

*Ruhestätte"*), but her mood cannot be maintained: the desire for life and love breaks out again in the closing lines. The apparently quiet pleasures of the beautiful young people of Song 3 are fragile, evanescent, even trivial (tea drinking, chatter), no more significant than their reflections in the water of the pool—these satisfactions constitute no basis on which a vindication of life's joys could be constructed. Similarly, the romantic yearnings aroused in Song 4, even the beauty of the girls and the exuberant energy of the careless boys, are all transitory—they fade as the flowers do in autumn and are not renewed. Nor is it possible to seize the drink proffered in the opening song, to turn away completely from life into a world of artificial illusions, for spring breaks in on the drunkard's sleep, offering its invitation and posing its demands. To venture back into life would raise all the unsolved problems, but, as the close of the fifth movement makes evident, to turn back to oblivion is no more than evasive bluster.

How, then, are matters different in the finale? What has made it possible for the singer to depart with anything more than what the previous movements have accomplished? I suggest that the acceptance of the conclusion, the serenity Britten rightly heard but wrongly categorized as supernatural, is achieved by finding a sense of connection. That possibility was already hinted at in the opening movement, in the lovely paean to the renewal of the earth (beginning just before [31], *"Das Firmament bleibt ewig"*), but it was immediately withdrawn through the sundering of humanity from the rest of nature (*"Du aber, Mensch"*—"But you, o man"). The connections between ourselves and others are indeed transient, whatever impact we have on the cosmos or on the history of our own species will eventually wither into nothingness, yet that does not prevent human beings and human actions from being part of an enduring project—but not an infinite project, for the planet will eventually cease to support life, the sun will ultimately burn out. Our lives can connect us to something larger than our individual selves—and that is enough to lend them worth.

The singer's closing lines point to the possibility of this connection and to its genuine worth. She will die; her individual existence will cease. That can be viewed, stably viewed, as a homecoming, and in its prospect the heart can remain still, quiet, and accepting. For beyond her own life will be the renewal of the earth, people who will love and work together as she has loved and worked, achieving, as she has achieved, hard-won and ephemeral ends. Beyond the human community the earth itself will be reborn, with its laughing birds and springtime blossoms, and with the blue of the far horizons. All that will continue, not forever, but indefinitely, and she can affirm her own part in the history of the whole with those final words—"*Ewig, ewig*"—and with the chord "printed on the atmosphere."

Religious people may propose that for this to be convincing there must be a mind with a plan behind the entire show, giving it point and direction. In an important and suggestive essay, the eminent philosopher Thomas Nagel defends the centrality—to human life and to philosophy— of understanding the connection between our individual existences and some larger whole.[98] Nagel maintains that the question cannot simply be rejected: "the question 'What am I doing here?' . . . doesn't go away when science replaces religion."[99] In my judgment, he is completely right about the enduring hold of the question, although too generous in thinking religion could provide any adequate answer to it. Trouble does not merely lie in the fact that there is almost certainly no transcendent being with a Great Plan for the Universe.[100] Even if there were, how could our being part of that Great Plan lend significance to what we do? Why would the mere fact that it expressed the will of some vaster, perhaps incomprehensible, being give our lives point and worth?[101]

Mahler's own response to the central philosophical question lies in the close of *Das Lied*, in the words he wrote and the vocal and orchestral lines he composed for them. Listeners who know something of his philosophical reading and philosophical tastes may be tempted to venture a translation of his answer into discursive prose, to attribute to him a religious (or quasi-religious) resolution of the problem. Mahler scholars recognize the composer's interest in the animistic ("panpsychic") worldview of Gustav Theodor Fechner and see that view as inspiration for aspects of several of Mahler's works.[102] Of particular relevance is the proposal that the closing lines of *Der Abschied* embody Fechner's odd cosmology (in which souls infuse all parts of the cosmos, from stones to plants and animals, to human beings and higher forms of existence).[103] Were this perspective forced on us, the problem posed by Cooke in relation to the Second Symphony would arise in a more extreme form: Fechner's radical animism enjoys rather less currency than the Christian doctrine of the resurrection.[104] Yet the importation of Fechner into the closing moments of *Das Lied* arises, I believe, solely from the yearning for a discursive statement of Mahler's intended solution to the problem. The power of the music—and the power of the answer expressed in the music—is grounded in something far more apprehensible than metaphysical speculation. Just as Schopenhauer's deep questions about the possibility of worthwhile human lives do not grip us because we accept his philosophical system—and, in particular, his refiguring of Kant's noumena as insatiable Will—but continue to challenge us, as they once challenged Wagner and Mahler and Mann, because of well-grounded reflections on the character of our existence, so too the answer offered by the *Abschied-Lied* is rooted in familiar and elementary features of our lives. The leave-taker has lived and loved, her joys and successes are transient, her life will have an effect for a while, its actions traceable in the enduring, indefinitely renewed, world from which she departs, but, like the ripples caused by a stone thrown into a pool, the impact will eventually, perhaps even quite soon, diminish to nothing. The connections, transitory as they are, are real, not to be argued away or to be embedded in conjectures about the ensoulment of everything. *The philosophical question asks whether those connections are enough. Mahler's singer affirms that they are—or, to be more exact, that they can be, that finitude is no obstacle to value—and the power of the answer lies in its moving listeners to a corresponding affirmation.*

Mahler's finale for *Das Lied* is a philosophical contribution, one that goes beyond Nietzsche and Schopenhauer (not to mention Fechner). The temptation to attempt a verbal translation is understandable—but it ought to be resisted. Instead, we should allow the music to show what cannot be directly stated. In the closing section, I shall try to defend this perspective against skeptical objections.

First, however, we should return to Aschenbach, for whose death we are now finally prepared.

## 7

We may seem to have wandered some way from Mann's novella and from Visconti's film. Yet the analytic exploration of *Das Lied von der*

*Erde* was no irrelevant excursion but rather important preparation for reading or seeing the ending. The coda—Aschenbach's last visit to the lido—should be understood with the themes of the last section echoing in our ears. To continue the fantasy of a film that would fuse Mahler and Aschenbach, the music for the close of that film should be the final measures of *Der Abschied*, heard with the rest of *Das Lied* in the background.

The two-page coda to Mann's novella begins with the suffering Aschenbach apparently beyond the bitterness of his anti-Socratic ruminations at the fountain. His "half-physical" indisposition leads him to begin his day rather later than usual, and, on his way to the lido, he learns of the imminent departure of the Polish family. He responds with a revival of his old discipline, taking up, for the last time, his station on the "inhospitable" beach, where an autumnal atmosphere reigns. He is, perhaps, "*der Einsame im Herbst,*" the singer of the second movement of *Das Lied*, one who hopes that the "sun of love" will shine on him again.[105] It does not. Instead, what greets him is an undisciplined children's game, unsupervised by the adults who are occupied with their packing. The game ends in a provocation and the ensuing wrestling match between Tadzio and Jaschu. The beautiful youth is defeated, but the struggle continues past the moment of conventional victory, as Jaschu takes his revenge for past subservience, perhaps for past humiliations. Tadzio's face is thrust into the sand, his body jerks impotently in efforts to unseat his tormentor—it is the overthrow and defeat of beauty. Drawn into the conflict, Aschenbach readies himself to intervene, but at that moment Tadzio is released, and he walks into the sea.

All this could be part of the film in which the composer Mahler-Aschenbach, weak of heart and sick at heart, makes a slow way to his place on the beach, accompanied by themes from the second movement of *Das Lied*. Serious strain is visible in his face as he looks on at the boys' struggle, hearing the music with which the tenor sings of the howling ape. A version of Vere, but one afflicted with a serious cardiac ailment, he looks on as Claggart prepares to destroy Billy, to smash "Beauty."

It might end there, too, with the strain too much. Aschenbach-Mahler might collapse back into his chair, the *Meister-Erzieher*, the one who apprehends and communicates higher beauty, extinguished by the extinction of beauty's embodiment—for Jaschu's vengeance might go

FIGURE 3.11. Tadzio on the sandbar, one of the final images from Visconti's film. This frame captures the autumnal character of the deserted beach, with the unattended camera (specified in Mann's description). Tadzio has not yet turned to beckon to Aschenbach.

too far, leaving Tadzio breathless, lifeless on the sand, uniting him with Aschenbach in death. But that is not the end. Instead, the boy walks into the sea (the "infinite sea"?), wandering on the sandbar: separated from his companions and from the spectator, he gazes into the misty distance. There he is transformed.

He looks back, as if inviting Aschenbach to follow, and the writer returns the gaze, *as at first*. The sea, into which Aschenbach is summoned is the counterpart of the enduring earth of which Mahler's leavetaker sings, the seasonal rhythms of the one corresponding to the tidal motions of the other. We have come to the finale of *Das Lied*, to that extraordinary moment of hushed mystery before the voice breaks out in its final confession of appreciation and affirmation, of gratitude and love, of the acceptance of human life and human death.

Some of these ideas and feelings have already been prepared earlier in the novella. Aschenbach has conceived the sea as a resting place before, in the thoughts of a comforting death as he sat in the mysterious gondola[106] and, most explicitly, in a rare earlier moment of contentment at the lido.[107] In chapter 3, we were told of his love for the sea, how it answered to the desire for rest of the overwrought artist, how in being undivided, without measure, and eternal it stood in opposition to his strivings, promising the respite of nothingness, of nonexistence. For a moment, he could even think of this promise of rest as the fulfillment of his vocation: "To rest in what is perfect (ideal, complete in itself) is the longing of those who strive for what is excellent, and is not nothingness itself a form of perfection?"[108] At this moment, the figure of Tadzio crosses his vision of the sea—the boy intersects the blurred horizon, just as he will in his final pose. Aschenbach's thoughts are redirected: he returns from the momentary desire for rest to the life of insatiable strivings, to the attempt to capture evanescent beauty.

As Mahler and his leave-taker look on the mountains—and on the indistinct blue of the horizon—so Aschenbach looks on the sea. So, too, did his creator. An essay written in 1909 ("Sweet sleep!") endorses the fictional writer's seaside ruminations:

> The sea! The infinite![109] My love for the sea, whose vast simplicity I have always preferred to the demanding multiplicity of the mountains, is coeval with my love for sleep, and I am well aware of the common root of both predilections. I have in myself many elements of Indian thought, a large dose of a heavy and immoveable desire for that form or formlessness of what is complete, what is often called "Nirvana" or "Nothingness," and, although I am an artist, I harbor a very nonartistic inclination to the eternal (*zum Ewigen*), which expresses itself in a dislike of division and measurement. What speaks against it, believe me, is self-critique and discipline, is, to use the most serious word, morality . . . [110]

Aschenbach is recalled to his duty by the arrival of Tadzio not simply because of the boy's beauty but because beauty is an occasion for the renewal of discipline, for the revival of "the will for the artistic work."[111] There comes a moment, however, when the call to discipline is rightly refused, when (as the essay on Schopenhauer puts it) someone can find, in his death, "life, the liberation from the fetters of his tired individuality."[112] Mann is referring to the death of Thomas Buddenbrook, who has struggled bravely and with intelligence to play a role for which he was ill-suited—but the point is fully general. Even for a writer, a distinguished and much-admired writer, there is a moment at which the call for more striving can be—*should be*—refused, when the desire for dissolution, for a final union with the "vast simplicity" of the cosmos becomes acceptable and compelling. That moment is prefigured in Aschenbach's musings on his first morning at the beach—but he is not yet ready to declare "I have done enough."

The vision of the coda is different: Tadzio does not call him to a further exercise of discipline, a further celebration of beauty (beauty has, after all, just been defeated), but enters the sea—and is transfigured. From the embodiment of transitory beauty, he metamorphoses into something that will endure as long as the sea, an emissary of death, not hostile and threatening as others have been, but kindly, with the promise of that rest for which the tired artist had previously yearned. He is the friend of *Der Abschied*, the bringer of the farewell cup. He is also Hermes: the ambiguous god who so fascinated Mann, Zeus's messenger, but also the protector of thieves, patron of subtle arts, diplomat, and trickster— now manifested to Aschenbach as the bearer of souls (*Psychagog*) to the realms of the dead.[113] It seems to Aschenbach as if the boy-Hermes is beckoning to him, with a smile, and he "makes as if to follow." Indeed, he does follow Hermes—knowingly and willingly—to death.

The imaginary film would end here, with a sinking back into the beachside chair, a softening of the facial features into an accepting smile, accompanied by the closing measures of *Das Lied*. Perhaps these final moments would be punctuated by scenes of newspaper headlines announcing Mahler-Aschenbach's death, of sad admirers slowly turning the pages of their copies of his books, scenes reminding us of the "respectfully shocked" world that hears of his demise. Those interpolated scenes would present Aschenbach's links to the world that endures beyond him—but the last connection would be to the gently smiling boy on the sandbar and the sea stretching indefinitely behind him, before a closing shot of the composer's face, serene and at rest, as the final chord of *Das Lied* fades into silence.

The conceit of a film about Mahler-Aschenbach, a film attempting to be faithful to Mann's novella, has been used to suggest a reading of the coda, of the ending toward which Mann struggled. Taking Aschenbach-as-Mahler seriously provides ways of giving substance to the interpretation and (I hope) ways of making it plausible, but the essence can be summarized without relying on the conceit or on the identification. At the end of *Death in Venice*, Aschenbach can accept the end of his strivings. His heart, worn out by his years of steadfast discipline, of dutiful service, is taxed beyond its powers by the threat to what he has tried to apprehend and to express—beauty is almost overcome before him. Aware of his finitude, of his inability permanently to cherish and protect what has been most important to him, he can nonetheless recognize himself as having lived and loved, as having struggled and created. He can see himself as connected with the enduring world he must now leave. He is not deceived: the connection is affirmed in the novella's closing lines, in the shocked respect with which news of his death is greeted.

Aschenbach has been gripped with a thought of his life as made worthwhile through the constant striving to affirm it, his efforts always shadowed by the prospect of a premature truncation. The pressure to move on from one work to the next, to struggle for new evocations of transient beauty and affirmations of their worth, is central to who he is—the mind must beat on, as he walks in Munich during that oppressive spring day, and it must revive itself when his reflections on the sea are interrupted by Tadzio's presence on the beach. At the end, however, he and Tadzio are both changed, and he can accept the incompleteness of his work and his life. He can simultaneously hold the ideal of an indefinitely extending sequence of accomplishments, whose realization would permanently embody the value central to his life, and accept the fact that his successes are only partial. His attitude is a mixture of affirmation and abnegation, the one grounded in recognition of what he has done and its reverberations in an enduring world, the other based on knowing that his work is incomplete and that the echoes he leaves will eventually diminish into silence.

The philosophical attitude on death toward which Mann works and that (on this reading) he assigns to his protagonist develops further a theme emphasized in one of Schopenhauer's many explanations of the abnegation of the will:

> Since a human being is nature itself, and indeed is nature in the highest degree of self-consciousness, nature being only the objectified will to live, so any person who has grasped this perspective and remains true to it may certainly and rightfully console himself for his own death and the death of his friend by looking back on the enduring life of nature, which he himself is.[114]

Mann frees this thought from the dubious metaphysics, replacing the derivative claim that we are identical with the world that endures beyond us with the proposal that we are linked to it, connected in virtue of what we do, what we give or create. Our admittedly finite strivings are neither worthless (as Schopenhauer judges them) nor charged with some task of transcendent affirmation (which Nietzsche yearns to accomplish) but, at least potentially, capable of forging that connection to a larger whole, in the consciousness of which we can serenely accept our own passing. If we are fortunate, these strivings are enough.

The attitude commended in this way is, however, hard to sustain, requiring as it does two distinct judgments that pull in opposite directions. For, on the one hand, the continued affirmation of life, expressed in the desire to strive for further connections to a world that will endure after those efforts cease, demands that the tasks at hand be perceived as important, while, on the other hand, the acceptance of life for what it has been and what it has accomplished presupposes a kind of *completeness* in what has already been done. Reconciling this tension is logically possible—you can see your connection to the larger universe as *adequate* but wish to *enrich* it further—but any such assessment is psychologically vulnerable to doubts about the value of what has been accomplished. Little wonder, then, that writers and musicians whose *works* sometimes present this attitude cannot always *live* by it.[115]

To read the coda in this way is not mere fancy, even though the text of the novella does not *compel* it: like Hermes, Mann is a master of ambiguity.[116] The perspective attributed to Aschenbach emerges, more fully formed, in the late masterpiece Visconti, insightfully if inchoately, uses as a foil. Toward the end of *Doktor Faustus*, Leverkühn's father and his father-counterpart, Max Schweigestill—the *paterfamilias* on the farm that so resembles Adrian's childhood home, the farm on which he has chosen to live—die almost simultaneously. The journey back to his birthplace for Jonathan Leverkühn's funeral would be too long, but, despite illness and against medical advice, Adrian attends the corresponding local ceremony for Schweigestill. Accompanied by the devoted Zeitblom, he returns from the service to be greeted by the familiar pungent smell of the dead man's pipe. "'That endures,' said Adrian. 'Quite a while, perhaps as long as the house stands. It lingers on in Buchel [Leverkühn's childhood home] too. The period of our lingering afterwards, perhaps a little shorter or a little longer, that is what is called immortality.'"[117] The ordinary unpretentious endurance of Max Schweigestill, his continued connection with a world he has left, is symbolized in, although not restricted to, the odor of the tobacco, impregnated in the walls and woodwork of the house in which he has passed his entire life.

Mann takes up the thought again in Zeitblom's description of Leverkühn's final work, *The Lamentation of Dr. Faustus*, a cantata the composer attempts to introduce to a small audience of friends at a soirée that precipitates his collapse. Zeitblom's analysis is simultaneously a presentation of Leverkühn's interpretation of Faust's closing hours and an expression of the meaning of the composer's own dissolution and death. Like Leverkühn, Faust brings his friends together. They share the farewell cup, and, like Mahler's leave-taker, Faust insists on his departure. The cantata concludes with a passage for orchestra alone, music that penetrates the depths of despair, quite without comfort or redemption. Yet out of this terrible lament grows hope.

> It would be the hope beyond hopelessness, the transcendence of despair—not the betrayal of it, but the miracle that goes beyond faith. Hear the close, listen to it with me! One group of instruments after the other drops out, and what remains, with which the work dies away, is the high g of a cello, the last word, the last suspended sound, in a pianissimo fermata, slowly fading. Then there is nothing more. Silence and night. But the note that continues to hang and pulsate in the silence, the note that is no more, for which only the soul listens, and which was once the expression of sorrow, is no longer that but changes its meaning, and endures like a light in the darkness.[118]

Leverkühn's music, Aschenbach's writings, Mann's novels and stories, Mahler's songs and symphonies, all are summed up in that fading high note on the cello, enduring after it has ceased, as Max Schweigestill's pipe smoke endures. Endeavors may be unfinished, aspirations unsatisfied, accomplishments transitory or incomplete. It may matter, nevertheless, that they *have been*.

## 8

But what of us, we who are not Aschenbach nor Leverkühn nor Mahler nor Britten nor Mann? We too have projects, plans on a far smaller scale, that are indefinitely extensible into the future, and we live, too, with the certainty that they will remain incomplete, with the knowledge also that they, and we, have sometimes, perhaps often, failed. What bearing can Mann's novella, or Britten's opera, or Mahler's *Das Lied* have on *our* situations or on *our* assessment of them? What significance can the reflections in which I have engaged have for thought about ordinary lives and the ordinary deaths that will terminate them?

These questions come in two parts. First is a general worry, one that surfaced already in the second section of chapter 1, about the possibility that literature or music, or would-be philosophical commentary on literature and music, could inform serious thought about the worth of *any* human life, whether a form of ordinary human existence, an actual life of rare creative achievement, or the fictitious life of some idealized protagonist. Second is the doubt that the exploration of literature and music, or at least those literary and musical works that have been the focus of previous sections, has any significance for addressing philosophical questions, including the "central philosophical problem," as they arise in connection with lives whose horizons are more limited, whose projects are more mundane. These concerns deserve a more thorough and extensive answer than I have hitherto attempted, and I shall close by trying to address them. Because the first is the more fundamental and sweeping, and because my efforts to meet it will supply resources for approaching the second, I shall begin by amplifying my defense of the possibility of philosophy that shows what cannot be stated in other, more "respectable," ways.

A useful starting point is Zeitblom's urgent entreaty to listen to the close of his friend's final composition (not, of course, a serious possibility for the readers of Mann's novel, since the score of the *Lamentation* has not been provided).[119] Zeitblom is doing what I attempted in the sixth section of this chapter, where I recommended listening to *Das Lied von der Erde* — and, indeed, listening in a very particular way. To foster the intended mode of listening, both of us must point to features of the focal works: we must prepare the listener for experiences and reflections we hope will ensue. For the point of our urgings is to bring our readers to a previously unanticipated perspective, a different Gestalt on life and on the factors that make a difference to its mattering. We envisage a process in which people are brought to see or hear or think or feel in novel ways, so that questions that had been viewed as unanswerable admit of solution. The source of skepticism about the philosophical import of works of art lies in a conviction that a process of this kind could not have any serious standing, that judgments formed in this way would not be trustworthy, that feelings so produced would be baseless. However our own inclinations lead us to read a novella, to listen to a song-cycle, or to view a painting or film, however we are guided (manipulated?) by the pointers others supply in their exhortations to reading or hearing or viewing, it would be irresponsible to change our minds on any matter of importance.

To come to terms with the roots of skepticism, it will be necessary to have some understanding of the kinds of psychological changes that (intense) experience of works of art might engender, at least an outline[120] of the processes that occur, so that we have a sense of their character and of the depths to which they might reach. Before attempting a sketch, however, it is worth recognizing explicitly an apparent consequence of skepticism. Effectively, the skeptic conceives the contributions that works of art make to our lives in terms of their episodic effects: they give us passing pleasure or relieve us from boredom or induce a momentary sense of uplift we find agreeable—they are on a par with the baser satisfactions obtained from a glass of beer or a game of skittles, differing, if at all, only in intensity.[121] Any lasting effect on people's lives, a shifted perspective on themselves and their prior plans and aims, for example, would simply be gratuitous and unwarranted. To conceive the experience of art in this reduced way rubs roughly against the sensibilities of devoted art lovers—but friction can only *motivate* an attempt to respond to the skeptic; it cannot *constitute* an effective answer.

In reading a work of fiction or a poem or in listening to a piece of music,[122] we pass through a sequence of psychological states partly shaped by our antecedent judgments, conceptions, and emotions and partly the product of our apprehension of the words or the sounds. We imagine the actions and situations described in words; we identify the emotions and moods expressed in the music.[123] The occurrence of these states sets up connections with other parts of our psychological lives, recalling past judgments or emotions, sometimes modifying our established ways of conceiving and evaluating. The result is what I shall call a *synthetic complex*, whose elements may be radically disparate: memories of our own experiences, images from earlier perceptions or encounters with other works of art, judgments previously endorsed or rejected, emotions now excited by different objects, or even emotions of types we have not previously felt. The power of some works of literature and music to build synthetic complexes accounts for their enduring hold on us — as we return to them, again and again, the synthetic complexes they generate grow and change, perhaps expanding into areas of our psychological lives that were initially quite remote from their influence, so that we come to think of the pertinent works as inexhaustible.

The formation of synthetic complexes, when they persist as stable parts of our thinking and feeling, can revise our conceptions and judgments. Of particular concern are *endorsements* and *rejections*, judgments in which a subject concludes that some state of affairs is tolerable or to be resisted, or in which she takes a scenario as a serious possibility for herself, a goal to be worthy of pursuit, a course of action she has hitherto viewed as necessary to be trivial and dispensable (these are prominent examples among a wide range). Prior endorsements or rejections are evoked by reading or listening; they are brought into the synthetic complex generated, and they may be reinforced by it, found to align themselves with the judgments and emotions now made or felt,[124] or, conversely, they may jar with the present contents of consciousness. In the latter case, the experience of the work of art may lead to the embedding of a *stable* synthetic complex produced by *discarding* the endorsement or rejection previously made.

In section 2 of chapter 1, Dickens's *Bleak House*, and specifically its depiction of the plight of Jo, the crossing sweeper, was used to illustrate this possibility. That simple example can now be considered more carefully. Some of Dickens's Victorian readers, and some contemporary readers who think of the urban poor either as responsible for their own condition or as properly served by the "market forces" of a free society, might come to the novel with judgments starkly incompatible with the images and emotions evoked by the descriptions of Tom-all-alone's.

Reading may lead them to endorse emotions of outrage and to discard their prior judgments of the wise providence of unfettered capitalism. Skeptics question the propriety of allowing a work of *fiction* to displace the older attitudes, and we can now see that the root question concerns the *relations* between the recently induced synthetic complex and the broader corpus of the subject's psychological attitudes. Were the reader to have compelling arguments for the earlier endorsement of economic "freedom," it would be irresponsible to embed the synthetic complex unless it could meet and overcome those arguments. If, on the other hand, the original enthusiasm for capitalism was simply taken over from an unquestioned tradition, and if the reader recognizes that unthinking acceptance of that tradition is manifested in the callous disregard for the poor, prominent in some of the voices sounded in the novel,[125] the change of heart is not so evidently irresponsible.

More on this, shortly. First, however, it is important to see the respects in which this particular illustration is so simple. In the "Deaths in Venice" considered in this chapter and its predecessors, many different types of human predicament and human possibility are at issue. Mann's novella and Mahler's *Das Lied* induce in reader and hearer a diversity of types of image, emotion, and judgment, and a serious engagement with these works involves apprehending the structures of theme and mood embodied in words or music—one should understand the relations between Aschenbach's musings on the sea on his first morning at the beach and the perceptions of his final moments, recognize the kinship between the soulful cry that ends the song of *"Der Einsame in Herbst"* and the soaring affirmations of the finale. Whether or not I have done it well, there is philosophical work, the work of Dewey's "liaison officer,"[126] to be done in helping others build synthetic complexes the philosopher judges to be valuable. Those complexes can range, as mine have done, over an author's corpus of writings, over the writings of other authors as well, and into different genres. The focusing of music on philosophical issues may be achieved through attention to the ways in which words are set—indeed, vocal settings can serve as a bridge by means of which a sensitive hearer can approach music without words, broadening further the possibilities for the growing synthetic complex: *Kindertotenlieder* and *Das Lied* may help us trace philosophical themes in those Mahler symphonies where the human voice is absent.[127]

Back now to the skeptic's complaint, first in the form in which it arises for relatively simple examples and then for the more intricate cases. The imagined reader of *Bleak House* may undergo a change of mind because of a feeling of new insight into the conditions of urban life: "I had never realized that the poor live in such squalor," he may say. If that is the source of the new reaction, the skeptic has a serious point. Dickens's great novel should not be treated as a source in empirical sociology—it can be the provocation to investigate the facts about how poor people live in cities, but it cannot rightly substitute for any such investigation. Encounters with works of art can thus lead people to inquire into matters they had previously taken for granted, playing a role in *discovery* but having no force as *justification*.[128] Yet that is not the only possibility for the reader. Perhaps the impact of *Bleak House* leads him to view familiar phenomena in a different way, to understand that in situations he knows to be widespread, options he had assumed to exist may not be available, to see his casual assumption that those options—"the deserving poor can always escape through hard work"—are the uncomprehending, comfortable platitudes voiced by those who do not think seriously about the facts, to feel resentment toward the voices in the novel that dismiss problems of poverty, and *to see himself as one of those who has spoken in this way*. The synthetic complex built here contains images our reader finds worthy of protest, a recognition that he himself has not protested similar things about which he has long known, and that his deafness to the need for protest has been the product of his casually endorsing a tradition that is both well regarded and personally comfortable. If this is the pattern of his change of heart, then it is far less obvious that further evidence is needed or what that evidence might be.

Skeptics may respond by contending that the conclusion just reached depends on the simplicity of the example, or, more ambitiously, that the simplicity of the example allows ideas about responsible judgment to be easily distorted. An illustration that moves in the direction of the issues addressed by Mann and Mahler will enable the skeptical concern to be forcefully expressed. Imagine a listener who attends a performance of Mahler's Second Symphony, who is swept up by its finale into fervent acceptance of the truth of Christianity—or, to take a more extreme example, a previously unconvinced reader of Fechner who finds a performance of the finale of *Das Lied von der Erde* so compelling that she becomes a passionate convert to panpsychism. What differentiates her from the reader of *Bleak House* who changes his mind about the rightness of unfettered capitalism? The tugging of the heartstrings, the *Schwärmerei*, may seem acceptable in the Dickensian case, and some may even tolerate it when the outcome is affirmation of the resurrection, but when the encounter with art has generated a conviction that the inorganic world is full of souls, something seems to have gone badly wrong.

The leap into panpsychism is so plainly premature that it is difficult to envisage anyone making it, yet, as with the imagined reading of *Bleak House*, it is not entirely obvious how someone tempted toward animism might engage in further inquiry. If she were genuinely provoked to the metaphysical possibility, where would she seek evidence? The obvious answer is that nothing more is needed to quash the thought of pervasive ensoulment: contemporary listeners (and probably their modern predecessors too) share a picture of the world and its contents that understands inorganic matter and organisms, even sentient and sapient ones, without recourse to souls, and commitment to that picture would make it gratuitous to invoke mysterious entities in response to some momentarily urgent metaphysical need.[129] The real import of this fanciful case consists in exposing an important condition on the formation of synthetic complexes. Responsible building of such complexes should be *reflectively stable*: that is, as the reader or listener ponders the connections she makes in light of the full range of her antecedent attitudes and commitments, she should discover that the complex is sustainable. The reader of *Bleak House* jettisons some old convictions, but the synthetic complex that displaces them accords with quite general and fundamental commitments to avoid wishful thinking and to suspend judgment about what has been casually taken for granted, once it is clear that it can be called into question. The newly hatched panpsychist either abandons commitments of this kind in response to a momentary inclination or, if she never had them, stands in need of reeducation.

The first grade of reflective stability comes in admitting only those synthetic complexes that achieve the best overall fit with prior attitudes and commitments.[130] The simplest case of the requirement debars the adoption of attitudes that presuppose something the subject has conclusive reasons to deny: as when a work of literature or music inspires endorsements that only make sense on the assumption of beings whose existence would be at odds with a mass of evidence. Sometimes higher grades of reflective stability can be in order. In modifying our attitudes we should not simply be content to assess the fit of potential changes with the perspectives we currently have but also to explore the ideas and commitments of our fellows—we try to acquaint ourselves with the best of what is known and thought and felt. Endorsements and rejections are sometimes rightly held hostage to other people's verdicts. As we saw at the end of chapter 2 (sections 8 and 9), Thomas Mann's decision to endorse a particular identity and a specific mode of life as valuable cannot be divorced from the effects of that decision on others. Any approach to the ethical life that views ethical judgments as justified in virtue of the ability to defend them in a particular type of conversation[131] will take the possibility of that defense to be a condition on the formation of synthetic complexes.

Some will suppose that justification only accrues to judgments of questions of fact and that the standards of justification are (broadly) scientific. Others will adopt a three-tier picture: most basic are the matters of fact we justify through undertaking the inquiries we label "scientific"; although these constrain our ethical judgments, the latter are also subject to further conditions, through the introduction of other people's perspectives. Finally, there are ultimate endorsements about values, and these are required to be consistent with the facts and the ethical considerations (and perhaps subject to yet more conditions). The second of these views is an important advance on the first, but it overlooks the interpenetration of the levels it tries to separate. Significant ethical discussion cannot be divorced from consideration of what matters in human life; nor can factual inquiry, even rigorous scientific inquiry, be detached from the values we properly endorse.[132] *If* our encounters with art and literature warrant us in endorsing or rejecting particular claims about what is valuable, the sort of justification they provide is not "second rate" or "tacked on" but interwoven with the searches for evidence we view as our paradigms of rigor.

Finally, we are prepared to address skeptical concerns, as they arise with respect to the philosophical themes I have taken to be *shown* in the works that have been the focus of this book. Both Mann and Mahler, as I have read and heard them, address a fundamental challenge they find in Schopenhauer and Nietzsche. Human finitude undercuts the worth of what we are and do: our strivings are endless, our accomplishments ephemeral, our lives incomplete. We should either recognize the futility of our actions (abnegating the will) or find some way to transcend the run of common humanity (in some act of self-affirmation). To this challenge Mann's coda and Mahler's *Abschied Lied* have been taken to *show* the possibility of value in the connection with something that endures beyond the individual self. The novella and the *Lied* evoke a synthetic complex into which readers and listeners can absorb their experiences and integrate them with the endorsement of finite human worth.

The complex achieves the first level of reflective stability. The facts are agreed on: a human life ceases with bodily death, the effects of any life on human society and the broader world will dissipate into nothingness, and human society, sentient life, and our planet will eventually be no more. All that can be embedded into the complex of thoughts and feelings induced by the closing pages of *Death in Venice* or the final moments of *Das Lied von der Erde* without any displacement from equilibrium; those facts simply do not bear on the sense that the life with finite connection matters. Nor does a broader search for facts about nature introduce trouble. Hence, if reflective stability is to be threatened it must occur through a potential clash of human perspectives. Endorsing the value of the connected life must be seen as something that could not be sustained in an ideal conversation with one's fellows. There are *versions* of the endorsement that would succumb in this way: the connections that matter might be viewed as lying in the apprehension and communication of beauty, in the realization of an aesthetic ideal that rode roughshod over the lives of others — that question arose sharply and uneasily with respect to Mann's own attempt at self-endorsement (see section 8 of chapter 2). The endorsement itself, however, is by no means committed to any such version: although it may be a constraint on its articulation that the possibility of connected lives for others be honored, the endorsement survives the skeptical challenge.

Yet there is a last important doubt: don't the actual careers of the creators on whose works I have drawn, Thomas Mann and Gustav Mahler, belie the thought of a reflectively stable synthetic complex evoked by *Der Tod in Venedig* or *Das Lied von der Erde*? Even if Mahler achieved an answer to the challenge of finitude, a challenge pervading not only *Das Lied* but his earlier songs and symphonies as well, he was apparently forced to renew his struggles—there followed a (numbered) Ninth Symphony and an incomplete Tenth. Mann's disciplined efforts would extend for more than forty years beyond the writing of *Death in Venice*, punctuated by bitter self-doubt and the late desolation of wondering if he should have died after completing *Doktor Faustus*.[133] The case of Mahler might be handled by special pleading. His Ninth Symphony can be heard as extending the farewell of *Das Lied*, as a sequence of *Abschied-Lieder* without words, while the Tenth responds to the very different disturbances introduced into Mahler's last years by Alma's infidelity.[134] Mann, however, clearly worried about the same questions for decades—witness his tactless confession to Katia on their thirty-third wedding anniversary that he would not choose to relive his life.[135] His preoccupation reflects, I believe, his own conception of the Artist-*Erzieher*, compelled to submit endorsements of the value of a human life—of his own life—to continued question, to place himself upon trial again and again.[136] The true Artist-*Erzieher* seeks an extreme standard of reflective stability, one in which the most basic endorsements are embedded in synthetic complexes again and again and scrutinized from perspective after perspective.[137] We return to the division of labor envisaged in section 1 of chapter 2, in which the role of the artist is to explore and secure the values by which others live—live less reflectively and more lightheartedly: Mann (and perhaps Mahler too) becomes Tonio Kröger, making the worthwhile life safe for Hans Hansen and Ingeborg Holm.

So we return to the second and more obvious version of the question with which this section began: What is the significance for the many whose lives are patterned along other lines, who are dedicated to pursuits that are less self-lacerating? If the lives of more than a few exceptional individuals attain genuine worth, they do so not in virtue of some large effect that lingers for decades, perhaps even centuries, celebrated in our collective memory, but because of differences felt only by a few and only for a short period of time. As Leverkühn says, apropos of Max Schweigestill's pipe smoke, "immortality" is a period sometimes a little shorter, sometimes a little longer—but, relatively soon, most of us will have perished as though we had never been. Nevertheless, the connections we make with those who survive us are real: we rear, guide, teach, produce, or preserve parts of the physical or social environments in which those who come after us live—Schweigestill maintains the farm his father passed on to him and bequeaths it in turn to his son. The connections that matter most are those that enrich the lives of those we love, the shared projects we undertake with them, the contributions to family, to community, or to some lasting structure that our descendants will enjoy—for a longer or shorter while.

If the fundamental challenge to the possibility of worth in admittedly finite human lives is turned back—if, for example, Mahler and Mann show us that it is answerable—a natural proposal is that *some* human lives obtain worth through creating or fostering the possibility of worthwhile lives for others.[138] Value is a matter of having enough of the right sort of impact on others—where the vague phrase, "right sort of impact," is understood in terms of positive effects on those others having the opportunities to find their own projects, to shape their own lives in ways that connect them to yet further people (and the equally indefinite "enough" is to be pondered later). This proposal faces an obvious skeptical objection: if the value of your life depends on your contributions to the lives of others, specifically on your aiding them to achieve something worthwhile, and if the value of their lives accrues from what they do to promote the worthwhile lives of yet further people, then a regress looms—at some point, it seems, there must be something *intrinsically* valuable, a terminal accomplishment that can confer worth on everything that contributed to it. The objection misses something crucial that Mahler and Mann show us: value lies in the relationship itself. If what you do sets up conditions that help enable others to act in similar ways, ways of their own choosing, that suffices for the generation of value.[139]

Aschenbach, I have suggested, is a philosophical abstraction, a special case, and that is precisely because the human connections, the substance out of which the overwhelming majority of worthwhile lives are constructed, have been entirely removed. His impact on the broader human world is thoroughly reduced—it is not clear whether he has had any intimate exchange with anyone during recent years or even during the past two decades—and channeled through his painfully crafted writings. His "immortality" will come through what Diotima claimed were the best sort of "offspring," and perhaps she would be right to think that the period of his lingering on will be somewhat longer than the average. Because of his detachment, our assessment of the worth of his life need not probe the sacrifices demanded from others by his rigorous discipline—the complications that arise in the life of his creator are of no concern. We can focus on the works that result from his strivings, and, unless we are in the grip of some misguided prejudice against "the Apollonian," unless we endorse the jejune complaints about "pure form" Visconti assigns to his "Alfred," there is no reason to doubt that Aschenbach has achieved enough.

A world without Aschenbachs would be a lesser place, for the human totality of connections—ordinary connections through fostering of family, friends, community—would lack the reflective dimension embodied in Aschenbach (and Schopenhauer and Nietzsche and Mahler and Mann): it would simply be a world of the "lightly living."[140] There is value in the division of labor we actually have, in which some[141] great artists lay themselves bare, again and again, in efforts to contest and vindicate a sense of human worth. Recognition of this division of labor and its significance can, however, inspire an unfortunate form of elitism, prominent from Diotima and Plato to the present, one that restricts value either by insisting on great achievements, or on self-consciousness about the sources of value, or on both. We gravitate too easily to the mood of Stephen Dedalus at the end of *A Portrait of the Artist as a Young Man*, aspiring to fly very high.

Joyce brought his apparent hero down in a painful landing, replacing him with Mr Bloom, a man whose written contributions—advertising copy—are the most ephemeral of productions. Yet Bloom's connections to the lives of others and to the environment through which he moves are manifold and sympathetic—his life, in process, incomplete, untidy as it is, has a chance of proving worthwhile. In this he is distinguished from almost all of those with whom he is connected: the lives of Joyce's Dubliners—and of *Dubliners*—are overwhelmingly cramped and empty. Elitism, to which *Ulysses* and *Finnegans Wake* are powerful antidotes, seduces us into supposing that this confinement is inevitable for those who belong to "the herd."

Not simply the possibility of valuable human lives but the *distribution* of such lives should be a matter of reflective concern. In a world with enough resources to relieve all members of our species from the confinement of possibilities produced by a daily struggle for survival, a world that might transcend the "puerile and insignificant" condition in which humanity has spent most of its history,[142] opportunities for worthwhile human lives, lives that make value-conferring connections in their individual, freely chosen ways, might be far more widely distributed than they are. *Death in Venice* can be read as a protest against *particular* ways in which lives are throttled and distorted: Britten's setting of the novella is an eloquent outcry against the *social* causes of truncated lives. Beyond the horizons of story or opera, however, lie questions about the possibility of extending the opportunities for valuable lives more broadly—successors to the issues that preoccupied Dickens in his simpler but nonetheless important ventures in philosophical showing.

So, finally, to the predicament of those of us who live well enough to reflect on our existence, who have time to read Mann and to listen to Britten and Mahler, whose disturbances of the universe will not be large but felt through everyday actions that affect those around us. Assuming the *possibility* that worth may accrue through links to a world that endures beyond us, primarily and paradigmatically through our constructive effects on the lives of others, there are still questions to be addressed. Are those connections of the right sort, broad enough to avoid the charge that we have been parochial? Are they sufficient in the differences they make? These are serious matters for our reflection, issues to be resolved through probes and tests similar to those that surfaced in evaluating the stability of synthetic complexes. Because the distribution of valuable lives ought to concern all of us, we should scrutinize our opportunities for ameliorating the imbalances of that distribution, imagining how those who do not enjoy our advantages might view our efforts. Recognition of the possibility that our contributions may fall short, both on the scale at which we make them and in the intensity of their effects, may—perhaps *should*—nag at us, as the thought of the insufficiency of what has so far been achieved gnaws at Aschenbach and Mahler and Mann.

There is no algorithm for resolving these questions. Our projects, however rich and deep, are inevitably incomplete and almost always marred by our errors and lapses. Philosophy in a discursive mode may offer pointers, gestures of the kinds I have made in recent paragraphs, identifying the contours of the problem, but it cannot supply sharp instruments to cut through to an unambiguous decision. In the end, as we ponder the question "Have I done enough?", each of us faces, on a smaller scale, the challenge that has dominated this chapter: how to find a reflectively stable synthetic complex. We may yearn for a satisfying response, a criterion offered in precise language, by philosophers of preternatural wisdom. The gestures of abstract philosophy may indeed orient our eyes and ears and minds, but, in the end, we may find answers we can live with and by not in any refinements of analysis but by hearing and reading, attentively and repeatedly, synthetically and philosophically, the works of great artists—creative geniuses like Benjamin Britten, Gustav Mahler, and Thomas Mann.

# NOTES

## 1. DISCIPLINE

1. For some early reactions (and Mann's own attitude toward them), see *HarpM* 1:316 and *dMM* 2:1314ff. Heinrich Detering provides an excellent account of the first reviews of *Königliche Hoheit* and the puzzles about how to read it in *GKFA* 5.2:156–193. Mann's frustrations with the critical discussion are evident in a 1910 letter to Ernst Bertram, where he writes: "After the overflow of stupidity and wrongly directed subtlety that I have had to submit to in connection with my last book, I was so gripped by your analysis that I could hardly hold back my tears" (*Briefe* 1:81). The frustration continued throughout his lifetime.

2. Perhaps a better translation for this title would be "Spirit and Art" or "Mind and Art," but since Aschenbach's monograph isn't available for our inspection, it is impossible to tell.

3. It is arguable, I believe, that he never entirely overcame these difficulties and that the final version—with its abrupt "conclusion"—testifies to the problem of sustaining on the scale of a novel the brilliant lightness of touch Mann could achieve in individual episodes.

4. *dMM* 2:1478 notes that two generations of critics have already been at work and that a third is already under way. Even with the relative abatement of interest

in Mann (largely concomitant with increased attention to other twentieth-century German writers), it would now be appropriate to talk of four or five generations of studies.

5. Mann's aspirations to count as a *Dichter* (literally a "poet" but, functionally, an elite "man of letters") rather than as a mere "writer" are plain from the opening lines of his most extended effort at poetry (the *Gesang vom Kindchen*, written during his apparent discovery of parental love after the birth of his third daughter, and fifth child, the longtime favorite, Elisabeth [Medi]). The ambition to measure himself with Goethe is as central to Mann's literary life as is the similar preoccupation with Shakespeare to Joyce. In both instances, the fruits of the ambition were the most poetic prose fiction in the respective languages (the verse is minor at best). Mann's diaries, which record his extensive reading, show very little interest in poetry: apart from Goethe and Shakespeare, Platen is the outstanding exception. For discussion of Mann's longing for "*Dichter* status," see *HarpM* 1:194–196.

In Mann's usage, "*Schriftsteller*" is a generic term, covering both those great writers who count as *Dichter* and the lesser figures whose status is merely that of *Literat* (a title that might accrue from mere industry without genius or be the result of dilettantism). Both in the *Gesang vom Kindchen* and in his early essay on the social position of the writer in Germany ("*Die gesellschaftliche Stellung des Schriftstellers in Deutschland,*" *Essays* 1:119–123), Mann wants to make a claim for the credentials of prose to achieve the highest literary levels—so that he and Nietzsche could qualify as *Dichter*. (I am grateful to Mark Anderson for pressing me on this point.)

6. This is not to slight the great achievement of *Buddenbrooks* in particular but simply to note that, from *Death in Venice* on, Mann is able to present complicated thoughts and judgments more economically than in his first novel, where the treatment is often naturalistic and the ironies relatively straightforward. The great novels of his maturity—*Der Zauberberg, Joseph und seine Brüder*, and *Doktor Faustus*—have an extraordinary density and would have been impossible without the evolution of Mann's style. Interestingly, in support of his lifelong judgment that *Königliche Hoheit* was slighted and misunderstood, the second novel can be read as moving toward the mature style.

7. For an illuminating discussion of the achievement of ambivalence in *Zauberberg*, particularly in the portrait of Hans Castorp, see Alexander Nehamas, *The Art of Living* (Berkeley: University of California Press), chap. 1. Nehamas's subtle reading could, I believe, be extended to interpretations of Settembrini, Naphta, and Peeperkorn, as well as Zeitblom and Leverkühn, and through them to Mann's long engagement with the Enlightenment and the nineteenth-century reaction to it—but this is work for another occasion.

8. *Essays* (1926–1933) 3:202; also in *UMS* 125 and (in English) *K* 109.
9. *Essays* 3:202–203; *UMS* 125; I have slightly amended the translation from *K* 109.
10. *Essays* 3:203; *UMS* 125; *K* 109 translates the phrase somewhat differently.
11. Lieutenant Bilse had published in 1903 a roman à clef about events in his garrison. Mann was evidently offended at being included in a genre whose paradigm was so low budget a work and took some pains to emphasize the long history of fictionalization of actual people and events. *Essays* (1893–1918) 1:39–40. The book under prosecution in Lübeck was Johannes Dose's *Der Muttersohn*; Dose was eventually acquitted (for details, see *dMM* 2:1110ff.).
12. *Essays* 1:41.
13. *Essays* 1:42, 45.
14. *Essays* 1:42, 46, 47, 49.
15. *Essays* 3:203; *UMS* 126.
16. In several places, Mann refers to *Der Tod in Venedig* as a "tragedy" (see, for example, *Essays* 3:203). Yet his characterizations of it are so various and, in the case of his correspondence, seemingly correlated with the views and sympathies of those to whom he is writing that it is hard to rely on the shifting judgments. Six months after the novella was published, he wrote a letter to his brother Heinrich, permeated by a sense of difficulty and defeat even deeper than that he had attributed to Aschenbach: he doubts his ability to respond to the "poverty of the age"—even though the sense of that poverty lies heavily upon him. His brother, he claims, is spiritually better attuned for writing in such times; he himself should "probably never have become a writer." There follows a bitter characterization of his previous work: "*Buddenbrooks* was merely a bourgeois novel, inappropriate for the twentieth century. *Tonio Kröger* was tearfully sentimental, *Königliche Hoheit* vain, *Tod in Venedig* half-formed and false. These are the final recognitions and the comfort for the hour of death" (*THBW* 166–167).
17. In the same letter, Mann claims that his entire interest is in decline (*Verfall*) and that this prevents him from concerning himself with "progress" (*THBW* 166).
18. *Essays* 1:121. The distinction Mann draws in this passage is orthogonal to issues of quality and thus contributes to his case for claiming that prose works are capable of attaining the highest levels of literary achievement.
19. *Essays* 1:121.
20. Although I have translated "*Bürger*" as "citizen" and shall continue to do so, it has to be acknowledged that there is no English term that fully captures Mann's usage. Not every citizen is a *Bürger*, for having a right to that designation presupposes a certain social status and a certain moral worth. The principal

figures of the Hanseatic port depicted in *Buddenbrooks* are definitely *Bürger*, but many of those who serve them and work for them are not. The *Bürger* are the "solid citizens," those who contribute to the economic and social health of the town, uphold its institutions, and exemplify and defend its moral fabric. Stealing a phrase from Ibsen, we might call them the "pillars of the community." These overtones should be heard in my future references.

21. Outsider status might be the effect of having attitudes or inclinations at odds with those conventionally approved, for example, being attracted to members of your own sex. Chapter 2 will explore the relationship between Aschenbach's romantic proclivities and his claims to figure simultaneously as artist and citizen.

22. For Tobias Mindernickel, see "Tobias Mindernickel" (*GKFA* 8.1:181–192); Piepgott Lobsam, "*Der Weg zum Friedhof*" (*GKFA* 8.1:211–221); Paolo Hofmann, "*Der Wille zum Glück*" (*GKFA* 8.1:50–70); Friedemann, "*Der kleine Herr Friedemann*" (*GKFA* 8.1:87–119); Detlef Spinell, "Tristan" (*GKFA* 8.1:319–371); Schiller "*Schwere Stunde*" (*GKFA* 8.1:419–428).

23. *Buddenbrooks*, part 10, section 5 (*GKFA* 1.1:708–730). For readers of *Ulysses*, it is interesting to compare Tom's situation with the offer made to Bloom in "Circe," when Boylan generously allows him to "apply himself to the keyhole" so that he can watch his wife's adultery: it is not clear which predicament is the more agonizing.

24. *WWV* 1:§52; *WWV* 2:§59.

25. See the final sentence of *Buddenbrooks*, part 8, section 7 (*GKFA* 1.1:576).

26. For the passages alluded to here, see *GKFA* 8.1:271, 272, 273–274. The comparison between the artist and the castrato is prominent in the notes for *Tonio Kröger* (*GKFA* 8.2:208, 210).

27. Mann clearly intended *Krull* as another ironic and comic exploration of the separation of the artist from bourgeois society. After his near-arrest during a visit to Lübeck (the basis for the similar incident in *Tonio Kröger*), he began to ponder the similarities between artists and confidence men (*dMM* 1:550–551). The connection is made very clearly in the early scene in *Krull*, in which the protagonist and his father visit the actor Müller-Rosé in his dressing room (book 1, chap. 5).

28. *GKFA* 8.1:317, 318.

29. Tonio's version, however, might well have lacked some of the ironic insights of the real thing.

30. The disillusionment of young Felix Krull when he sees the pimples on Müller-Rosé's back exemplifies what Mann—and Tonio!—regard as the result of going behind the scenes and viewing the artist as he is.

31. *GKFA* 8.1:508.

32. *GKFA* 8.1:501. Aschenbach is fifty-three and was awarded the "noble particle" on his fiftieth birthday. The opening words of the sentence, which give both his original name and the elevated version, can be read as tacitly asking which designation is more suitable. Interpreted in this way, Mann raises, in the first six words of the novella, the question of whether his protagonist deserves the honor he has received—whether he is "the real thing."

33. The nearest anticipation of this elaboration of the artist-bourgeois and outsider themes is in the pregnant story "*Schwere Stunde*," in which Schiller faces Aschenbach's initial predicament (his writing will not go forward). Like Aschenbach, he allows himself the opportunity of a break (compare *GKFA* 8.1:420, 506). Aschenbach shares his high ambition, and both are committed to the moral seriousness of high art. Yet Schiller overcomes—it is only a "heavy hour." There is one interesting and important difference between the stories. Aschenbach's ambitions are not associated with any definite rival; for Schiller, however, as for Mann, there looms the presence of the man in Weimar, the standard against which writing in German must be judged. Ironically, by the time of *Death in Venice*, Mann had toyed with the thought of a story about an infatuation of the aged Goethe—and, much later, in *Lotte in Weimar*, he would come to direct terms with that looming presence.

34. As we shall see, there are echoes of the *Symposium* and, particularly, of the *Phaedrus*, which Mann evidently read with considerable care. The preparatory notes quote extensively from these dialogues: *GKFA* 8.2:478–482.

35. The essay on Schopenhauer was written in 1938 (*Essays* [1933–1938], 4:253–303); in 1924, Mann wrote a short speech in honor of Nietzsche's eightieth birthday (*Essays* [1919–1925]), 2:236–240), and in 1947 he fulfilled a long-considered intention and wrote an extensive essay on Nietzsche (*GKFA* 19.1:185–226; *Essays* 6:56–92). As the entries in Mann's diaries reveal, he reread both authors extensively throughout his lifetime. As we might expect, in the period leading up to the writing of "Schopenhauer," he read widely in Schopenhauer's writings (May 17, 18, 23, December 20, 1937; January 24, February 6, 1938 [*TB* {1937–1939} 62, 65, 144, 164, 172]). He also returned to Schopenhauer at times when his writing was apparently focused elsewhere; for example, January 1, 1920; April 17, 1936; January 29, 31, 1940; November 15, 1944; June 24, 1950; October 3, 1953 (*TB* [1918–1921] 357; *TB* [1935–1936] 292; *TB* [1940–1943] 17–18; *TB* [1944–1946] 123; *TB* [1949–1950] 204; *TB* [1953–1955] 123). References to reading Nietzsche are even more common, often admiring, but sometimes sardonic (December 21, 1946; *TB* [1946–1948] 75; "Read in *Ecce homo*. A lot of embarrassing, paralytic nonsense, but decisive for prose in German"). Of course, we have no diary records of Mann's daily reading for the period before 1918 or that between 1921 and 1933, since he burned the pertinent *Tagebücher*.

36. *Briefe* (1948–1955) 3:248; the letter was written on March 13, 1952.

37. *Essays* (1933–1938) 4:281.

38. *Essays* (1926–1933) 3:189–190. Unlike his twenty-year-old self, the mature Mann is well able to distinguish between enthusiastic uplift and a more restrained and probing engagement with Schopenhauer's ideas. In my view, that distinction was already available to him when he wrote *Buddenbrooks*, so that the portrait of Tom's reading is not intended to reveal any sensitivity to Schopenhauer's complex ideas but simply the power of a voice that speaks to a man in great distress. Tom—like his creator—is an autodidact reading at a turbulent time.

39. *GKFA* 13.1:79; *BU* 91. Mann's attention to the details of his surroundings introduces a beautiful irony. For, in Schopenhauer's own discussion of the occasions on which the subject achieves some understanding of the world as it is, the world as will, the division of appearance into individual objects dissolves—"As soon as knowledge, the world as representation, is canceled, nothing remains except pure will, pure impulse" (*WWV* 1:234)—and hence, someone who achieved this state would be unaware of the ordinary circumstances in which it occurred. I suspect Mann intended to signal the overheated state of the callow reader and thereby to separate, as he does in the sketch of 1930, the "passionate-mystical" reading from the more "properly philosophical." The thought of this as a unique reading experience is preserved in the later autobiographical sketch. Indeed, Mann uses almost the same words.

40. *Essays* 4:285.

41. In 1925, Mann wrote a discussion entitled "Marriage in Transition," in which he took stock of "the metaphysical experience that prepared Thomas Buddenbrook for death," writing of the freeing from the individual (the dissolution envisaged by Schopenhauer) and the willingness to accept death. Tom and Aschenbach are both viewed as fugitives from the discipline of life and its ethical constraints, intoxicated into passionate acceptance of death—a standpoint Mann claims to have "understood from time to time with one part of my being" (*Essays* 2:275).

42. See, for example, T. J. Reed, Death in Venice: *Making and Unmaking a Master* (New York: Twayne, 1994); Hermann Kurzke, *Thomas Mann: Epoche—Werk—Wirkung* (München: Beck, 1997); Martina Hoffmann, *Thomas Manns Der Tod in Venedig* (Frankfurt: Peter Lang, 1995). Manfried Dierks offers a more extensive range of Nietzsche influences in chapter 1 of his *Studien zu Mythos und Psychologie bei Thomas Mann*, 2nd ed. (Frankfurt: Klostermann, 2003), but still emphasizes the role of *The Birth of Tragedy*. In downplaying that role in my subsequent discussions, I aim not so much to criticize the work of these excellent scholars (from whom I have learned much) as to liberate our

approach to Mann's novella from a prevalent perspective—and thereby to open up alternative ways of reading it.

43. During the writing of *Doktor Faustus*, Mann was often occupied in reading Nietzsche or works about him. In the period between April 10 and April 16, 1944, he took up the posthumous writings (*Der Wille zur Macht*), reading them together with *Human, All Too Human* (TB [1944–1946] 43–45). He returned to the *Nachlass* on January 7, 1945 (TB [1944–1946] 147). The inspiration drawn from Nietzsche in the 1910 essay on the "pure (absolute) writer" (see n. 19 and accompanying text) is from *Die Fröhliche Wissenschaft*. We do not know exactly what he read in his youth (before the encounter with Schopenhauer). Perhaps it included *The Birth of Tragedy*, but the autobiographical sketch of 1930 offers contrary indications.

44. *Essays* 3:187–188. It seems highly doubtful to me that reading *The Birth of Tragedy* would have generated that influence, for apart from the *Versuch einer Selbstkritik* it has none of the stylistic features that would make Mann, especially the young Mann, hail Nietzsche as decisive for German prose. The writings from *Human, All Too Human* on are a very different matter. In the late essay on Nietzsche, Mann cites *Jenseits von Gut und Böse* and *Zur Genealogie der Moral* as the highpoints of Nietzsche's achievement (*Essays* 6:63).

45. *Essays* 3:188. Again, these are hardly words likely to be inspired by reading *The Birth of Tragedy*—and, if they are accurate, they suggest that Mann would not have taken over, uncritically, the distinctions and theses of that book. The attacks on Christianity, especially the most pointed ones, come much later in Nietzsche's career, as do the attack on Wagner and the "revaluation of values." Mann's own late assessment of *The Birth of Tragedy* takes up the perspective of the later anti-Wagner foreword: Mann refers to Nietzsche's first work as a "prelude" to his philosophy, written in a mood of romantic enthusiasm quite foreign to his mature tone (GKFA 19.1:198; *Essays* 6:68).

46. *Essays* 3:188–189. As Mann goes on to say, to read in that way would be an embarrassment.

47. GKFA 13.1:92–93; BU 103.

48. For an admirable example of an approach of this sort, see Reed, "The Art of Ambivalence," in *Making and Unmaking*.

49. See, for example, "The Art of Ambivalence" (in Reed) or Dierks, "Untersuchungen zum *Tod in Venedig*," in *Studien zu Mythos und Psychologie*.

50. See Robert Pinsky, trans., *The Inferno of Dante* (New York: Farrar, Straus, and Giroux, 1994), 113, 115; the crucial passages in the *Commedia* (printed on the facing pages of Pinsky's edition) are 11:79ff. and 101ff. The Aristotelian principles of organization are already introduced, although not yet attributed to "the Philosopher," much earlier in the canto; see 11:22ff.

51. The review was originally published in *Galaxy* in March 1873. It is fully reprinted at http://www.complete-review.com/quarterly/vol3/issue2/jameshmm.htm.

52. See, for one clear example, book 1, chap. 62.

53. I draw the distinction from Wittgenstein's *Tractatus*. For further elaboration of it, see below.

54. Hermann Broch pursues this novelistic strategy (to my mind with great skill and success) in his trilogy *Die Schlafwandler* (Frankfurt: Suhrkamp [Taschenbuch], 1994). I am indebted to Bence Nanay, for convincing me that similar things could be said on behalf of Musil, and to Jeremy Adler for some illuminating conversations about James.

55. Both *La nausée* and *Huis clos* contain many passages that, however exciting philosophically, are mechanical as fiction—characters are simply used as mouthpieces for ideas.

56. Broch, *Die Schlafwandler*, 719.

57. The particular case of Mahler will be examined in chapter 3.

58. My list reflects my own idiosyncratic tastes, and surely others would offer different exemplars. I should note explicitly that, although I used Dante to introduce the second level of philosophical involvement, the *Commedia* can also be viewed as exploring philosophical questions bequeathed by the philosophico-theological tradition, in ways parallel to those followed by the post-Enlightenment figures in my catalogue. A similar claim could be made for Milton.

Is philosophical illumination found only on the highest peaks of the world's literature and music? I think not. If a literary or musical work is to succeed in philosophical showing, it must surely exhibit genuine understanding and intelligence—in James's terms, it must have "brain"—but that is entirely compatible with its falling short of the very high standards set by the writers and composers in my (perhaps idiosyncratic) canon. Good, but lesser, works of fiction are worth appreciating for their philosophical suggestiveness: Mark Twain's *Huckleberry Finn*, Lewis Carroll's *Alice* books, many of Iris Murdoch's novels, Pascal Mercier's *Perlmanns Schweigen*. Even though my focus in this book is on one of the masters of German prose and one of the greatest late romantic composers, it should not be concluded that philosophy by showing occurs only in such rarefied regions of the cultural landscape. For Twain, see Jonathan Bennett's superb essay "The Conscience of Huckleberry Finn," *Philosophy* 49 (1974): 123–134. The *Alice* books are not only full of local puzzles that have intrigued philosophical logicians but also invite reflection on what life in a world bereft of any apparent order would be like. Murdoch's double career as philosopher and novelist has inspired a few courageous interpreters to look for philosophical themes in her fiction, despite Murdoch's own—famous—claim that philosophy

1. DISCIPLINE   201

and literature are entirely different and separate. See, for example, her interview with Bryan Magee: http://www.youtube.com/watch?v=m47A0AmqxQE. My last example, almost certainly unknown to most English readers, is a taut and suspenseful novel—almost a piece of crime fiction—at whose center lies a complex of questions about aging, failure, and honesty, questions with filiations to those that occupy Mann in *Death in Venice*.

59. This contrast is emphasized by Murdoch in the interview cited in the previous note.

60. Antonio Damasio has defended a view of this type in several works from *Descartes' Error* (New York: Putnam, 1994) on. For my purposes, it is not necessary to adopt the details of Damasio's specific views—or any of the positions held by the neuroscientists and cognitive psychologists who have been influenced by him. The point is, rather, that everyday changes of belief, accompanied or promoted by emotional responses, can no longer be dismissed as regrettable lapses.

61. The weak answer to this question, enough for my purposes, would allow some examples of genuine philosophical thought to involve imagination and emotion as essential constituents. Those who accept a position like that defended by Damasio (ibid.), in which "cold" cognition is a pathology, will favor the strong answer, according to which the popular model of philosophical thought (a sequence of pure belief states) is a myth.

62. Plainly, my imagined skeptic has very definite tastes, since the strictures would eliminate some of the greatest philosophical stylists, including Plato, Hume, Schopenhauer, Nietzsche, William James, (the later) Wittgenstein, and Russell.

63. The point is fundamental to the pragmatist tradition, expressed forcefully in Peirce's early essays. It is encapsulated in the image offered by Neurath, in a passage made famous by Quine, who chose it as the epigraph for *Word and Object* (Cambridge, Mass..: MIT Press, 1960): "Wie Schiffer sind wir, die ihr Schiff auf offener See umbauen müssen, ohne es jemals in einem Dock zerlegen und aus besten Bestandteilen neu errichten zu können" (*Über Protokolsätze*).

64. Moira Gatens has written in illuminating ways about the ability of fiction to cause a mode of vivid imagination that is philosophically fruitful. See her brilliant essay "The Art and Philosophy of George Eliot," *Philosophy and Literature* 33 (2009): 73–90, to which I am much indebted. In suggesting that the arousal of the imagination should be combined with further reflection and discussion, I allude to an approach to ethical method I articulate and defend in chapter 9 of *The Ethical Project* (Cambridge, Mass.: Harvard University Press, 2011). Gatens's work and my own can be seen as elaborating Dewey's insight that "the arts, those of converse and the literary arts which are the enhanced continuations of social converse, have been the means by which goods are brought home to

human perception." John Dewey, *Experience and Nature*, vol. 1 of *John Dewey: The Later Works* (Carbondale, Ill.: Southern Illinois University Press, 1981), 322.

65. I follow Bernard Williams's judgment about the centrality to philosophy of this question, expressed in the opening pages of his *Ethics and the Limits of Philosophy* (Cambridge, Mass.: Harvard University Press, 1985).

66. In particular John Stuart Mill, who develops the thought that the worthwhile life must be fashioned and freely chosen by the person who lives it. For discussion, see my essay "Mill, Education, and the Good Life," in *John Stuart Mill and the Art of Living*, ed. Ben Eggleston (New York: Oxford University Press, 2010). From a very different starting point, Kant arrives at a related appreciation of the need for autonomous choice, and similar ideas were articulated by Wilhelm von Humboldt (from whom Mill explicitly drew).

67. Mann's philosophical development moves through the sequence of works given in the first section of this chapter, from *"Der Wille zum Glück"* and *"Der kleine Herr Friedemann"* through *Buddenbrooks* and *Tonio Kröger* to *Der Tod in Venedig*. As I shall hope to show, the novella is particularly rich. Yet even more philosophically insightful work was to come, in *Zauberberg*, *Joseph*, and *Faustus*. I hope the present discussion will prepare the way for a future attempt to make that apparent.

68. Whether Mann ever read either *Ulysses* or *Finnegans Wake* carefully enough to appreciate their kindred interest in philosophical issues about what makes lives worthwhile must be a matter of speculation. Diary entries reveal that he read in Levin's early introduction to Joyce (February 21, 1942; *TB* [1940–1943] 396), possibly prompted by Joyce's recent death, that he knew enough about Joyce's prose to recognize that they shared a penchant for parody (September 19, 1943; *TB* [1940–1943] 627), that he knew enough about "Finnigans Wake" [sic] to worry that it might be the work of genius of the times and that his own work might seem stale and traditional by comparison (August 5, 1944; *TB* [1944–1946] 85), and that he was happy to find himself included (with Henry James, Proust, and Joyce) among the four greatest writers of the age (October 29, 1945; *TB* [1944–1946] 270).

69. *Essays* 4:43.

70. *Essays* 4:46–50. The view of Wagner as uninfluenced by Schopenhauer, to which Mann objects (46) is now fully corrected by an articulated account of *Tristan*. See Roger Scruton's admirable *Death-Devoted Heart* (New York: Oxford University Press, 2004). Of course, the influence of Tristan (and the "Tristan chord") on the young Mann was profound—as Frau Klöterjahn's performance of the piano transcription clearly testifies (*GKFA* 8.1:350ff.). I suspect that Mann's youthful preoccupation with *Tristan* as paradigm for Wagner's works lies behind his judgment of Wagner as the artistic fulfillment of

Schopenhauer—in the interpretation I develop below in the text, Wagner, like Mann himself, can be granted more philosophical independence.

71. WWV 1, book 4, particularly §§56, 59, 61.

72. For the "Schopenhauer ending," see Stewart Spencer and Barry Millington, *Wagner's Ring of the Nibelung: A Companion* (New York: Thames and Hudson, 1993), 363.

73. For extensive defense of the interpretation I offer here, see Philip Kitcher and Richard Schacht, *Finding an Ending: Reflections on Wagner's Ring* (New York: Oxford University Press, 2004).

74. *King Lear* 5.3.291; the line is spoken by Kent, Cordelia's closest male counterpart.

75. Nietzsche's characterization of Wagner as a great "miniaturist" (*The Case of Wagner* §7; NW 6:28) seems initially absurd, one of the provocative paradoxes for which he is famous (and for which Mann celebrated him). There are many moments in the *Ring* that bear Nietzsche out—but the simple phrase Brünnhilde sings in farewell to her father is one of the most moving.

76. Mann was plainly fascinated with the *Ring* from his youth—witness the story "*Wälsungenblut*"—but as he grew older it became ever more central to his (critical) appreciation of Wagner. In 1944, he wrote in his diary that "the triad-world of the *Ring* is my musical home," despite which he confessed his continuing fascination with the Tristan chord (played on the piano). A few months later he recorded that he had been "gripped" by some parts of Tristan; the contrast recurs in September 1945: "The union of voices and orchestral music at the end of *Götterdämmerung* is far more successful than the *Liebestod*, where one would prefer to have the orchestra alone" (*TB* [1944–1946] 106, 232, 256; see also the praise of the "epic-mythical" sound of *Rheingold*, *TB* [1946–1948] 112, and Erika's judgment on the close of *Rheingold*—"That delights you," *TB* [1946–1948] 280). In 1949, he returned to *Tristan*, with "deepest admiration," responding especially to the drama of act 1 (*TB* [1949–1950] 104, 108).

77. James Joyce, *A Portrait of the Artist as a Young Man* (London: Penguin, 1992), 276.

78. At the close of the "Nausicaa" and "Ithaca" episodes. On Sandymount strand, where Bloom has been a keen observer—unlike Stephen (in "Proteus"), whose perceptions are overloaded with his own literary and philosophical preconceptions ("signatures" he imports to try to find meaning in his experiences)—Bloom dozes off, turning from Gerty MacDowell back to Molly. That turn is echoed in the last exchanges of the "Ithaca" catechism.

79. I defend this approach to *Finnegans Wake* in my *Joyce's Kaleidoscope: An Invitation to Finnegans Wake* (New York: Oxford University Press, 2007).

80. See, in particular, the exchange between Stephen and his (dead) mother in "Circe," which I take to play a role parallel to that of Bloom's closing vision of his (dead) son Rudy.

81. *Portrait*, 158.

82. *Ulysses* ("Calypso").

83. *Ulysses* ("Ithaca").

84. *Finnegans Wake* 113:13.

85. Particularly evident in the closing pages and, particularly, in ALP's penultimate one-word sentence—"Given!"—in which she declares that her husband has kept his promise (to give her "the keys to [her] heart"). See *Finnegans Wake* 628:15, 626:30–31. For a far more extensive explanation and defense of this interpretation of the *Wake*, see my *Joyce's Kaleidoscope*.

86. *Essays* 4:285. Mann might be read as anticipating Harold Bloom's notion of "strong misreadings" in *The Anxiety of Influence* (New York: Oxford University Press, 1973) and generalizing it to philosophy.

87. *Essays* 4:285.

88. Although I shall focus on *Death and Venice* and its precursors, the concern plainly persists through the great works of Mann's maturity: *Zauberberg*, *Joseph*, and *Doktor Faustus*. Those novels deserve far more extensive treatment than I can offer here.

89. As, most prominently, in *Joseph*, *Das Gesetz*, and *Der Erwählte*.

90. I have heard many presentations by colleagues and friends who have done this for the visual arts and for music: I think particularly of talks by Michael Fried and Robert Harrist, by Alfred Brendel, Elaine Sissman, and Carol Plantamura. As chapter 3 will consider at greater length, the critical illumination can proceed by explaining the technique through which particular effects are achieved (analytic mode) or by making connections between aspects of the artwork and other phenomena, including different artistic creations (synthetic mode). My treatment will primarily be synthetic in character.

91. As already remarked, this sort of philosophical work has a distinguished history in the French and German intellectual traditions. In recent decades, thanks to pioneering essays by Stanley Cavell (see, in particular, "The Avoidance of Love," in *Must We Mean What We Say?* [New York: Scribners, 1969]), it has flourished in Anglophone philosophy. Important work has been done by Alexander Nehamas, Robert Pippin, Joshua Landy, Martha Nussbaum, Candace Vogler, and Moira Gatens.

92. Dewey, *Experience and Nature*, 306.

93. This characterization occurs in a letter to Hedwig Fischer, the wife of Mann's publisher, in a letter of October 1913, in which he expresses his wish to avoid the charge of "optimism," leveled at *Königliche Hoheit*. Perhaps we

should be cautious about the views expressed in this letter, since, as Peter de Mendelssohn notes, Mann was worried that Hedwig Fischer might have reservations about a book in which "*Knabenliebe*" (love of boys) played so central a role (*dMM* 2:1479).

94. A point well made by David Luke in the introduction to his translation of the novella: *L* xli.

95. Many writers choose "Apollinian" as the adjectival form of "Apollo"; I see no reason to modify the third vowel.

96. As later discussions will make clear, I am not rejecting the idea of Nietzsche's influence on Mann's novella but merely opposing a particular—very popular—way of understanding that influence.

97. For a reading close to that I have outlined, see Martina Hoffman, *Thomas Manns Der Tod in Venedig: Eine Entwicklungsgeschichte im Spiegel philosophischer Konzeptionen* (Frankfurt: Peter Lang, 1995), esp. 78–92. T. J. Reed (*Reed*, esp. 154–155), Manfred Dierks ("*Untersuchungen zum* Tod in Venedig"), and André von Growicka ("Myth Plus Psychology," trans. in *K* 115–130) all offer more complex versions of the role of *The Birth of Tragedy*, and its celebrated dichotomy between the Apollonian and the Dionysian, in *Death in Venice*. Given the many insights of these distinguished commentators, it may seem folly to suggest, as I shall, that the importance of this particular Nietzschean work has been overrated.

98. As Reed lucidly points out (*Reed* 149).

99. Reed's title for his chapter on *Death in Venice*, "The Art of Ambivalence," is entirely apt.

100. *GKFA* 8.1:588; *LP* 72, *K* 60, *L* 260, *H* 135–136.

101. *GKFA* 8.1:567–586, *passim*; *LP* 56–70, *K* 47–59, *L* 245–259, *H* 104–133. To achieve naturalness, the English translators often place the identifying adjective elsewhere: thus, instead of the somewhat awkward "So the confused one knew and wanted nothing more" (that would remain close to the German phrase; *GKFA* 8.1:567), they offer "It came at last to this that his frenzy left him capacity for nothing else" (*LP* 56), "Entangled and besotted as he was, he no longer wished for anything else" (*K* 47), "So it was that in his state of distraction he could no longer think of anything or want anything except" (*L* 245), and "Thus the addled traveler could no longer think or care about anything but" (*H* 104). Only Heim captures the designating phrase used as substitutes for name ("Aschenbach") or pronoun ("he").

102. As Reed points out (*Reed* 163).

103. Dorrit Cohn, "The Second Author of *Death in Venice*," trans. and repr. from Cohn's *Probleme der Moderne* (Tübingen: Niemeyer, 1983) in *K* 178–195. Cohn's excellent and sensitive discussion raises the issue whether the second

narrator is to be identified with part of Aschenbach's own psyche. If that is so, it is a voice Aschenbach—like Mann—can sometimes regard with ironic detachment. One of the stylistic advances of *Death in Venice* is Mann's skill in developing various distinct modes of narrative presentation and weaving them together. That occurs quite evidently in the "Greek idyll" section of the novella (chapter 4) and in Aschenbach's Socratic ruminations. The more important separation, however, recognized by Cohn, lies in the differentiation of ethical points of view, in juxtaposing a voice that issues the judgments of conventional piety (the voice of the ancestors) with another that refrains from moralizing. In his later fiction, particularly in *Joseph und seine Brüder*, Mann was to elaborate the separation of narrative voices with extraordinary subtlety, distinguishing high religious style from critical religious discourse, sometimes treating both with irony, setting quasi-historical narrative beside a critical perspective on historical evidence, in ways that provoke readers to ponder the stability of judgments parts of the tetralogy appear to take for granted. The embryonic form of this complexity is already in the earlier novella.

104. The point holds, even if Apollonian art is unstable, a "camp of war" needing constant defense—and thus offers a "severe form of education, suitable for battle" (NW 1:41). If there is a single passage *The Birth of Tragedy* that might have affected *Death in Venice*, this would be my candidate. For, as we shall see below, the idea of military discipline is central to the portrait of Aschenbach.

105. NW 1:37.

106. NW 1:61–62.

107. The kinship with Schopenhauer on art as disclosing reality through some kind of apprehension of the will and the concomitant breakdown of individuation runs through the early sections of *The Birth of Tragedy*. For the praise of Homer, see NW 1:60; the German text involves a nice play on *anschaulich* and *anschauen*.

108. Since we lack any example of Aschenbach's prose, it is impossible to tell how significant an Apollonian artist he is—and it may seem (or be) absurd to compare his readers to the vast numbers who have heard or read the *Iliad* or the *Odyssey*. The point, however, is that we cannot take the characterization of Aschenbach as an Apollonian writer as a sign of his artistic failure (and, moreover, if we take the finely contrived style of *Death in Venice* as an evocation of Aschenbach's own writing, he would deserve high praise for his artistry). To use Nietzsche's own metaphor, there can be great monuments on either side of the gulf that divides epic from tragedy—even if those on one side reach up toward the clouds of illusion and those on the other are founded in reality.

109. It would be very hard to argue rigorously that Aschenbach's passionate interest in Tadzio fits into the metaphysics of *The Birth of Tragedy*, that it

accords with an apprehension of reality as pure will (or anything similar). In practice, the commentary on *Death in Venice* tends to assimilate Nietzsche's complex distinction between the Apollonian and the Dionysian to something like the simple contrast between intellectual detachment and raw emotion. For a novella about the subversion of detachment by the eruption of violent emotion, Mann would hardly have needed Nietzsche.

110. Of course, this may not be the one Mann used in the years leading up to his writing *Death in Venice*, and his notations in it may have been made at times during which he was occupied with different projects: material on Schopenhauer or Wagner or the late essay devoted to Nietzsche, for example.

111. Despite the numerous citations of Nietzsche in Mann's published writings, his letters, and his diaries, the principal reference to *The Birth of Tragedy* of which I am aware comes from the late essay in which Nietzsche's first work is characterized as a "prelude" (*Vorspiel*) to his philosophy (GKFA 19.1:198; *Essays* 6:68).

112. The most radical version of this hypothesis would suppose that he never read *The Birth of Tragedy* with any great care. To accept that version would require some explanation of the allusions to Dionysos in the novella (perhaps through citation of Nietzsche in some secondary source or simply through reading Euripides?). For the present purposes, I am content with the more modest claim of the text.

113. *Essays* 3:188–189.

114. *Essays* 3:189. It should be noted, however, that, as the judgment about the disastrous impact on German thought indicates, Mann wrote this passage at a time when particular aspects of Nietzsche's prose would have jarring resonances for opponents of the Nazis. Perhaps he would not have made exactly the same assessment in 1912. Nevertheless, the approach to reading Nietzsche is akin to that offered in the *Betrachtungen*—the artist who will be for Nietzsche what Wagner was for Schopenhauer must develop a special form of irony (GKFA 13.1:93).

115. A feature of Mann's reading habits is also revealed by the entries in the diaries. Especially when he takes up works with significant intellectual content (as in the cases of Goethe, Schopenhauer, or Nietzsche), Mann frequently records that he read "in" the pertinent volume. The examples are too numerous to list completely, but typical are entries for August 21, 1942: "After the (bad) lunch, in *Human, All Too Human* (TB [1940–1943] 465); and April 4, 1948—"In the evening, in *The World as Will and Representation* in connection with part of a conversation with [Bruno] Walter" (TB [1946–1948] 269). That is an approach to reading well suited to Nietzsche's later works, with their sequence of pithy aphorisms, but not to *The Birth of Tragedy*.

116. These will be considered more extensively in chapter 2.

117. In some editions, but by no means all, the coda is set off from the previous text (the quasi-Socratic speech) by inserting a blank line. Thus the Fischer Taschenbuch (*Schwere Stunde und andere Erzählungen* [Frankfurt: Fischer, 1991], 264) and the Luke and Koelb translations mark the break (*L* 261, *K* 61); GKFA 8.1:589 does not, and neither do the Lowe-Porter or Heim translations (*LP* 73, *H* 138). It should be noted, also, that Lowe-Porter does not number the chapters, separating them only by blank lines. Thus for her a line break would mark a new chapter — which Mann clearly did not intend. Reed's edition of the German text for English readers inserts the break. My own reading favors the demarcation, on the grounds of a significant shift in style, narration, and mood.

118. Chapter 3 will attempt a more extensive analysis of this coda.

119. As I shall suggest in chapter 3, this may be a further ambivalence of the novella. Most readers take it for granted that cholera is the cause of Aschenbach's death.

120. Aschenbach's position is clearly that of Mann's other outsiders, perhaps most notably Detlef, the protagonist of "*Die Hungernden*." We learn very early that Aschenbach had never known the careless easy-going attitude of youth — instead, he is vividly compared to a tightly clenched fist. GKFA 8.1:509; *LP* 9, *L* 201, *K* 8, *H* 13.

121. William James, *Varieties of Religious Experience* (Harmondsworth: Penguin, 1982), lecture 5.

122. James, *Varieties of Religious Experience*, 141–142.

123. Plato *Republic* 4.420b; *PW* 95.

124. Famously, the education of the philosopher-guardians culminates in recognition of the Form of the Good. The process is dramatized in Plato's myth of the cave.

125. Plato *Phaedrus* 247 d–e; *PW* 525.

126. Plato *Phaedrus* 250b, d–e; *PW* 527–528.

127. The most extended treatment of this theme is given in the *Symposium* (another dialogue on which Mann drew for *Death in Venice*); Plato *Symposium* 208e–209e (*PW* 491–492), citation 209d.

128. Nietzsche, unlike Schopenhauer, would allow for the possibility of a solution but would insist on the extraordinary difficulty (if not impossibility) of either formulating it or realizing it at the present stage of human culture.

129. For Schopenhauer's respect for Plato, see WWV 1, book 3, §31, where Plato and Kant are hailed as the two greatest Western philosophers (WWV 1, 1:222). The recognition of the Form (or Idea) is liberated from the causal connections of our experience through the power of a work of art, so that we partially break free from the world of appearance and grasp reality (§34; WWV

1, 1:233, 234, 239). Schopenhauer's account of how this works depends on his "correction" of Kant and his intricate aesthetic theory.

130. Schopenhauer supposes that Will is objectified not only in animals but also in other organic things and in inanimate nature. He views the laws of nature as expressions of a particular type of objectification of the will—in the regularities of the development of plants, in the laws of magnetism and gravitation, for example (WWV 1, book 2, §21; 1:154). Complex organisms are composed of entities at many different levels and thus subject to the pull of Will in many different directions (§27; 1:196–197).

131. The demands are issued in the preface to the first edition and often repeated thereafter; see WWV 1:8, 9. It is important to recognize the extent of what Schopenhauer asks for: the first volume (WWV 1) is a sequential argument for the pessimistic conclusion; the second (WWV 2) consists of a series of chapters providing commentary on aspects of WWV 1, keyed to specific chapters and sections; the second volume concludes with an appendix reviewing the problems Schopenhauer finds in Kant's views. The reader has to go through all of this material twice and also to read an earlier essay ("On the Fourfold Root of the Principle of Sufficient Reason"). There are good reasons to think Wagner followed Schopenhauer's instructions. Whether Mann did is far less certain.

132. See *Essays* 4:282. The chapter on death is WWV 2, §41.

133. *Essays* 1:17.

134. One reason for the lack of contemporary philosophical interest in Schopenhauer is that reading him carefully requires some sympathy with and knowledge of Kant's brilliant and difficult ideas—and also a willingness to entertain the ideas of a wide-ranging and original critic. Kantians are often irritated by the presumption of "correcting" their favorite thinker.

135. Schopenhauer is unusually well-informed about Indian thought and is wide ranging in his artistic and literary references (in marked contrast to Kant, of whom he quite reasonably remarks that art was foreign to him and "according to all appearances, he had little sensibility for beauty" [WWV 1, 2:645]; Kant is excused on the grounds that he probably had scant opportunity to see a significant work of art!). In addition, Schopenhauer shows a surprisingly broad knowledge of contemporary developments in science and medicine (see, for example, WWV 1, 1:179), his preference for Goethe over Newton on light and colors notwithstanding. Schopenhauer begins his attack on the abuses of Kant's ideas by his philosophical descendants with a critique of Fichte, the author of "the most senseless, and because of that alone, the most boring book" (WWV 1, 1:65). Other post-Kantians, particularly Hegel, originator of the "windbag philosophy," come in for even more scathing treatment.

136. *Essays* 4:287.

137. See WWV 1, book 2, §27 (esp. 1:197–204); and WWV 1, book 4, §54 (esp. 2:348–358).

138. Thomas Mann, *Briefe an Otto Grautoff und Ida Boy-Ed* (Frankfurt: Fischer, 1975), 30.

139. Diary entries of February 28, 1947; April 1, 1947; and November 17 1948. *TB* (1946–1948) 102, 110, 306.

140. As his marginalia and underlinings show, Mann read Nietzsche's "*Schopenhauer als Erzieher*" with enormous attention and interest. He probably viewed that essay as the same sort of productively passionate critique displayed in the polemics against Wagner, operating partly in reaction against Schopenhauer's conception of the best possibility for human life and partly in accordance with the constraints Schopenhauer had imposed.

141. A possible exception to this claim might be generated from recalling the most famous sentence of *The Birth of Tragedy*, the twice-occurring "It is only as an aesthetic phenomenon that life is justified" (§§ 5, 24; NW 1:47, 152). Nietzsche would later mock his own positive assertion (see, for example, the "Attempt at Self-Criticism"; NW 1:17).

142. Nietzsche's many-sided works allow quite different critical perspectives and have thus acquired a rich and varied philosophical literature discussing them. The reading I introduce here and develop in later sections and chapters is intended to conform to the interests and attitudes I have ascribed to Mann. For alternative versions, from which I have learned much, see Alexander Nehamas, *Nietzsche: Life as Literature* (Cambridge, Mass.: Harvard University Press, 1985); Bernard Reginster, *The Affirmation of Life* (Cambridge, Mass.: Harvard University Press, 2008); John Richardson, *Nietzsche's System* (New York: Oxford University Press, 1996); and Richard Schacht, *Nietzsche* (London: Routledge, 1983).

143. GKFA 13.1:87 (*BU* 98).

144. Diary entry of April 7, 1948 (*TB* [1946–1948] 246).

145. This concern continues in Mann's later fiction with an explicit juxtaposing of general philosophical views with the lives of characters who espouse (and imperfectly embody) those views: it permeates Mann's weighing of Enlightenment and counter-Enlightenment claims in *Zauberberg* and *Doktor Faustus*.

146. As Mann had recognized from early on: witness a letter to Grautoff (November 8, 1896), in which he praises a poem Grautoff had written as expressing more intensely the theme of "*Der kleine Herr Friedmann*"—the desire for "neutral Nirvana and peace" and the dissolution through sexuality (*Briefe Grautoff-Boy-Ed*, 79).

147. Reed cites Mann's preparatory notes to suggest a sympathetic reading of Aschenbach's asceticism (which he links to his own version of the Platonic themes in the novella) and suggests that the final version moves to a harsher judgment (*Reed* 160). On the account I shall offer, the positive evaluation of Aschenbach's asceticism remains present and should be considered in reaction to Nietzsche's classic discussion of the ascetic ideal.

148. Lowe-Porter opts for "hold fast" (*LP* 9), Luke favors "stay the course" (*L* 201), Koelb chooses "endure" (*K* 8), and Heim picks "persevere" (*H* 14).

149. Diary entry of February 19, 1938; *TB* (1937–1939) 179–180. At the evening meal, the couple apparently discussed their anniversary. Mann records his horror and confusion about his life (the life they had shared): "I said, I would not want to repeat it, the painful had too much dominated. I fear I may have caused K. [Katia] pain. Such judgments about life, one's own life, that is, however, identical with oneself (for I am my life), make no sense."

150. The idea that one should be able to affirm one's own life by declaring one's willingness to repeat it is presented by Schopenhauer (*WWV* 1, book 4; 2:358, 405). Famously, Nietzsche takes it up; see, for example, §341 of *Die Fröhliche Wissenschaft*, *NW* 3:570.

151. As Reed rightly points out, the theme of the breakdown of discipline produced by passion would have been sounded by the story Mann had previously envisaged, of the infatuation of the aged Goethe for a teenage girl (*Reed* 153).

152. *GKFA* 8.1:512–513; *LP* 12–13, *L* 203–204, *K* 10–11, *H* 18–20.

153. Why is she never named? Perhaps because the description used to identify her does so through her ornaments—of which Tadzio is the supreme example.

154. *GKFA* 8.1:581; *LP* 66, *L* 255, *K* 55, *H* 124.

155. *GKFA* 8.1:581; *LP* 66, *L* 255, *K* 56, *H* 125.

156. As already remarked, Luke correctly diagnoses this as the moment of Aschenbach's moral breakdown (*L* xli).

157. The dream is presaged by the image that flashes into Aschenbach's consciousness as he considers warning the lady of the pearls. As he envisages his return—to Munich, and to the bourgeois values he has defended—he sees again the mortuary chapel before which he had made his decision to journey to the south. That decision was accompanied by a vision of untamed growth, of seductive and undisciplined lushness, that prefigures the rites of the later dream.

158. In a letter from 1915, Mann explains that he had originally thought to embed some of the major preoccupations that were to be taken up in *Der Tod in Venedig* in a story focused on "Goethe's last love," exploring the infatuation felt by the septuagenarian for a teenage girl—it was to have been an "evil, beautiful,

grotesque, unnerving" story (*Briefe* 1:123). Mann went on to suggest the possibility that he might return to this material, but, by the time he felt ready to take on Goethe, his approach was quite different (and, to my mind, more subtle). For discussion of the vacillations of 1911, see *dMM* 2:141814–20.

159. Wilde's trial, condemnation, and subsequent suffering were sufficiently well known to make those with homosexual leanings extremely cautious. The response to *Death in Venice* shows how skillful Mann was in negotiating the presentation of desires he felt in himself. This aspect of the novella will come into prominence in the next chapter. "Somdomite" is, of course, the malapropism introduced by the Marquess of Queensberry in his challenge to Wilde.

160. *Briefe* 1:90. The letter is from July 1911.

161. Here I am in complete agreement with Reed, who describes it as "almost an obituary" (*Reed* 146).

162. As we shall see in the next chapter, Britten's opera uses this image to great effect, an achievement both of the libretto and the obsessive phrase the composer uses to set the words.

163. Reed supposes that chapter 2 was written late and inserted into the previously completed draft (*Reed* 170). I see no compelling reasons either to accept or reject this hypothesis. Mann might have recognized very early that he would need a clear account of the state from which Aschenbach falls—or that might have come to him only as he worked out the details of the end of the novella. The considerations given in the text incline me to think that the placement of the chapter is compositionally well considered and not simply a matter of interposing some needed material where it won't break the flow.

164. As the surviving journals tell us, on June 20, 1944, Mann "began with the destruction of old diaries" (*TB* [1944–1946] 68). More detail about the process comes from an entry almost a year later. According to the later entry, diaries were burned on May 21, 1945: after his customary tea, Mann took the records of his early life out to an oven in his garden in Pacific Palisades. "Afterwards old diaries destroyed, the execution of a long-adopted plan. Burnt in the oven outside" (*TB* [1944–1946] 208). The surviving diary from the beginning of his exile (early 1933) makes Mann's original decision very clear. The old diaries, which had always been carefully locked away, had been left behind in Munich, and Mann was very anxious that they not be read by the Nazis (who would, presumably, have used his amorous confessions for propaganda purposes). On April 7, 1933, his diary confesses "new worries because of my old diaries," and the next day he formulates a plan to send the key to his son, Golo, so that the diaries may be packed up and sent on to him (*TB* [1933–1934] 40). The plan misfired, and the suitcase containing the diaries was confiscated, causing further alarm: the diary entry for April 30 contains an unusual reference to physical contact with

1. DISCIPLINE    213

his wife, Katia: "K and I sat much of the time hand in hand. She understands to some extent my fear on account of the contents of the suitcase" (*TB* [1933–1934] 66). May 2 brings some relief, in the form of news that the suitcase has arrived in Switzerland; on May 19, the suitcase was delivered to him, with the contents apparently intact, although going through them caused great anxiety. On May 20, he writes: "Today, after breakfast I continued with the unpacking, examination, and repacking of the contents of the suitcase. The wrapping paper seemed untouched, but the case was not locked, as it had doubtless been when it was sent off, and the contents, which could in any event have been rearranged by the transport, gives at least the impression of having been gone through" (*TB* [1933–1934] 88, 89). On May 21, 1933, Mann was in low spirits, and perhaps he formulated on that day his plan to destroy the early diaries—carrying it out on the twelfth anniversary of his decision?

165. For some representative entries, see May 27, 1920 (*TB* [1918–1921] 440); June 29, 30, 1936 (*TB* [1935–1936] 323); April 7, 1938 (*TB* [1937–1939] 204); June 10, 1940 (*TB* [1940–1943] 94); February 2, 1946 (*TB* [1944–1946] 305); August 11, 1951; December 12–15, 1951 (*TB* [1951–1952] 90, 146–149); April 7, 1953 (*TB* [1953–1955] 46).

166. November 14, 1944 (*TB* [1944–1946] 123).

167. November 15, 16, 1944 (*TB* [1944–1946] 123, 124).

168. "Even without sleep I shall write": diary entry of October 7, 1946 (*TB* [1946–1948] 49).

169. The pose of the figure suggests Hermes, an important motif in this novella and throughout Mann's fiction. The features, especially the red eyelashes, link the stranger to other characters who play the role of adversary or tempter: for example, Esau (in volume 1 of *Joseph*) and the devil who appears to Adrian Leverkühn (*Doktor Faustus*).

170. Reed takes discipline to be an all-or-nothing affair, remarking that "Aschenbach's creative discipline is essentially broken at the very outset" (*Reed* 171). I see, instead, a gradual process. Hence, the decision to travel south is only the beginning.

171. *GKFA* 8.1:597–598, 509; *LP* 8–9, *L* 200–201, *K* 7–8, *H* 11–13.

172. Letter to Samuel Fischer of August 22, 1914 (shortly after the outbreak of the war!), translated at *K* 94.

173. *GKFA* 8.1:515–516; *LP* 15, *L* 206, *K* 12, *H* 23.

174. Compare *GKFA* 8.1:504, 583–584. *LP* 5–6, 68; *L* 197, 257; *K* 5, 57; *H* 6, 128–129.

175. *GKFA* 8.1:519, 517. *LP* 17–18, 16; *L* 209, 207; *K* 15, 13; *H* 29–30, 26.

176. *GKFA* 8.1:519, 517; *LP* 22–23, *L* 213–214, *K* 19, *H* 39–40.

177. *GKFA* 8.1:529–530; *LP* 25, *L* 216, *K* 21, *H* 45.

178. GKFA 8.1:532–533; LP 27–28, L 218, K 23, H 49.

179. GKFA 8.1:538, 508. LP 32, 9; L 222, 200–201; K 27, 8; H 13, 57. I have followed the three most reliable translators (Luke, Koelb, and Heim) in rendering *Wertzeichen* as "postage stamps," but I suspect Mann used this word rather than the more common *Briefmarken* to hint at the thought that the letters are "marks of worth"—so that Lowe-Porter's translation, "tributes," even though not literal, captures an important connotation.

180. See, for a few among many examples, October 21, 1933 (*TB* [1933–1934] 229); July 14, 1938 (*TB* [1937–1939] 255); November 12, 1948 (*TB* [1946–1948] 329); September 27, 1949 (*TB* [1949–1950] 104); October 29, 1952 (*TB* [1951–1952] 291).

181. GKFA 8.1:540; LP 34, L 224, K 28, H 61.

182. GKFA 8.1:546; LP 38, L 228, K 32, H 69. For obvious stylistic reasons, none of the translations to which I have referred switches from past to present in translating this paragraph. Interestingly, the original English translation—Lowe-Porter's—does not even translate *"Er will es und will es nicht."*

183. *"Denn die Schönheit, mein Phaidros, nur sie, ist liebenswürdig und sichtbar zugleich"* (GKFA 8.1:555); Rudolf Kassner's translation of the *Phaedrus* gives: "Nur die Schönheit ist zugleich sichtbar und liebenswürdig, beides" (*Gastmahl/Phaidros/Phaidon* [reprinted in the series of *Diederichs Taschenausgaben*] 108).

184. During his stay in Venice, Mann wrote a short piece on a question posed by a Viennese newspaper—*"Auseinandersetzung mit Wagner."* The original manuscript was apparently written on the stationery of the Hôtel des Bains (*Essays* 1:150–153, 361).

185. As we shall see in the next chapter, Britten appreciates the importance of this pivotal moment.

186. "Schopenhauer, as psychologist of the will, is the father of all modern treatment of the mind"; *Essays* 4:301. Schopenhauer's discussions of the sexual drive as important objectifications of Will and his repeated remarks to the effect that Will is either unsatisfied or satiated and bored trade on the ordinary conception of the will as a psychological phenomenon.

187. For the metaphysical account, see *WWV* 1, book 2, §27, esp. 1:196, 197. Mann's fullest interpretation of the internal conflict is given in the 1938 essay "Schopenhauer"; *Essays* 4:298, 299.

188. *WWV* 1, book 4, §57; 2:392. See also 390.

189. *WWV* I, book 4, §55; 2:368.

190. *WWV* I, book 4, §§ 66, 68; esp. 2:461, 463–464, 470–471.

191. GKFA 8.1:519, 536. LP 17, 30–31; L 208, 221; K 14–15, 26; H 28–29, 53–55.

192. *Zur Genealogie der Moral* 3.5; NW 5:344.

193. GKFA 8.1:513; LP 13, L 204, K 11, H 20.

1. DISCIPLINE    215

194. Citations to Nietzsche: *Genealogie* 3.5, 3.7; NW 5:345, 351. Citation to Mann: GKFA 8.1:506.
195. This is to take on the role but to disagree with Nietzsche about the disease. *Genealogie* 3.15–17; NW 5:372–382.
196. *Genealogie* 3.18; NW 5:382.
197. Mann writes of Aschenbach's turn away from "knowledge," which I gloss as "scientific knowledge," particularly of human motives and conduct; GKFA 8.1:513; LP 12–13, L 204, K 10–11, H 19–20. Nietzsche's discussion of the fourth form of the ascetic ideal is *Genealogie* 3.23–28, NW 5:396–412; see also section 344 of *Die Fröhliche Wissenschaft* (from which *Genealogie* 3.24 quotes), NW 3:574–577. For James's image, see note 122.
198. GKFA 1.1:11.
199. GKFA 1.1:624.
200. GKFA 10.1:735.
201. GKFA 10.1:733.
202. GKFA 10.1:736–737. The reference to "*Ecce Homo*" alludes not only to the passion of Christ but also to the title of Nietzsche's book, published shortly before his own collapse. Leverkühn's contraction of syphilis, his breakdown, and long final state of helplessness are, of course, modeled on Nietzsche.
203. Whatever we make of the dialogue between Leverkühn and the devil (*Doktor Faustus*, chap. 25) or the self-conscious decision to risk contracting syphilis (together with the consequent failures to obtain treatment), it seems impossible to resist the connection between the infection, the creativity, and the eventual collapse. To assess Leverkühn's life, these must be taken as an organic whole—that is the minimal point of the title.
204. For Zeitblom, Adrian Leverkühn is the central figure in his existence, one whose claims override any made by his profession as a teacher or by his family (even by his "good Helene"). Readers might be tempted to think Zeitblom's own life obtains whatever value it has through his efforts to preserve Leverkühn's artistic legacy—but that would be to overlook his moral standing in resisting Nazism and the possibility that his life's worth is grounded quite differently than he takes it to be. Even by Mann's standards, *Doktor Faustus* thrives on ambivalence and irony, and any serious interpretation must come to terms with its complex attempt to do justice both to the Enlightenment and the nineteenth-century reaction against it.
205. The style of the obituary chapter subtly prepares the way for conclusions about the limitations of Aschenbach's artistry. If you imagine that the author of this chapter is the moralizing "second narrator" (see note 103) who exults moralistically at Aschenbach's collapse at the fountain, it is easy to read the

praise lavished in chapter 2 as hollow—a setting-up of the protagonist for the fall to come later.

206. GKFA 8.1:94; *L* 3.
207. GKFA 8.1:111, 112; *L* 8.
208. GKFA 8.1:118; *L* 27.
209. GKFA 8.1:111; *L* 8.
210. This claim will be elaborated and defended in the next chapter.
211. Again, see Nehamas, *The Art of Living*, chap. 1.
212. GKFA 5.1:751, 815.
213. GKFA 5.1:629.
214. GKFA 8.1:592; *LP* 74, *L* 263, *K* 62, *H* 141.
215. In 1964, Wladyslaw Moes, a Polish baron, informed the Polish translator of *Death in Venice* that he had been the original for Tadzio. Apparently, Jaschu was also based on a real boy, the son of a friend of Moes's mother (*L* xxxiv).
216. GKFA 8.1:556; *LP* 46–47, *L* 236, *K* 39, *H* 86.

## 2. BEAUTY

1. Henrik Ibsen, *Pillars of the Community*, trans. Samuel Adamson (London: Penguin, 2005), act 1; the biblical reference is *Matthew* 23:27 (authorized [King James] version).
2. A maxim Aschenbach rejects in his turn away from "sympathy with the abyss": GKFA 8.1:513; *LP* 13, *L* 204, *K* 11, *H* 20.
3. GKFA 8.1:312, 313; *L* 188.
4. GKFA 8.1:311; *L* 186.
5. GKFA 8.1:550, 551; *LP* 47–48, *L* 231–232, *K* 35, *H* 77–78.
6. *Symposium* 189d–193d; *PW* 473–476.
7. *Briefe* 1:160.
8. *Essays* 1:42, 46, 47, 49. Cited in section 1 of chapter 1.
9. GKFA 8.1:243, 317; *L* 135, 191.
10. *Birth of Tragedy* §§5, 24. Nietzsche apparently thought the sentence good enough to warrant repeating it; *NW* 1:47, 152.
11. Here I am in agreement with Reed (*Reed* 156ff.). Plato and Plutarch offer Mann a complex of ideas on which he can draw to explore the problems of reconciling the role of the artist with that of the citizen. Fundamental to this complex, as we shall see, is the Platonic link between beauty and virtue. A significant feature of the Platonic tradition—although not of Plutarch's discussion—is the elevated character of homosexual love. My discussion will develop these points rather differently from the ways in which Reed does.

12. That tradition runs from Plato through Rousseau and Mill to Dewey. The three later thinkers all view the arts, including literature, as playing a fundamental role in exploring and communicating the values, receptivity to which is the goal of education, properly conceived. Standard conceptions of the history of philosophy focus on different lineages, but it is interesting to think how philosophy—and education in philosophy—would look if the Plato-Rousseau-Mill-Dewey tradition were taken as central.

13. John Dewey, *Democracy and Education*, vol. 9 of *John Dewey: The Middle Works* Volume 9 (Carbondale, Ill.: University of Southern Illinois Press, 1985), 338 (italics in original).

14. See, for a representative passage, John Dewey, *Experience and Nature*, vol. 1 of *John Dewey: The Later Works* (Carbondale, Ill.: University of Southern Illinois Press, 1985), 304–305.

15. The copy in the Zürich archive is marked with frequent underlinings and marginal annotations, particularly exclamation points.

16. *Schopenhauer als Erzieher* §I; NW 1:339.

17. *Schopenhauer als Erzieher* §I; NW 1:340.

18. *Schopenhauer als Erzieher* §I; NW 1:341. Mann notates this passage in the margin of his copy with an exclamation mark.

19. *Schopenhauer als Erzieher* §IV; NW 1:365. Again, Mann marks this passage with a marginal line, adding a word I was unable to decipher. The theme is elaborated at length on other pages Mann also annotated: for example, in §VI NW 1:384 (almost the entirety of which is marked by marginal lines) and in §VII NW 1:409 (decorated with a line and two exclamation marks in the margin).

20. "A professional scholar can never be a philosopher: for even Kant couldn't bring it off, but remained to the end, despite the innate pressures of his genius, a philosopher only in embryo." *Schopenhauer als Erzieher* §VII; NW 1:409.

21. In his early years, Mann seems to have adopted at least part of this conception of the role in application to himself, since he writes of the conditions under which a writer can be "of real service" (*Essays* 1:49).

22. *Schopenhauer als Erzieher* §I; NW 1:341.

23. *Schopenhauer als Erzieher* §III; NW 1:350.

24. GKFA 8.1:515; LP 14, L 205, K 12, H 22.

25. *Notizbuch* 2:112–113; cited in *HarpM* 1:195 and more fully in *dMM* 1:818.

26. *Schopenhauer als Erzieher* §IV; NW 1:370–371. Mann marked this passage with a marginal line. Goethe's late romance would thus have served as an apt alternative to the case of Aschenbach. Two decades later, Mann was ready for a different ironic treatment in *Lotte in Weimar*, where Goethe serves as absent but focal object for the early chapters and then as a disconcertingly intimate presence.

27. *GKFA* 4.1:191–199.

28. *GKFA* 8.1:562; *LP* 51, *L* 240, *K* 43, *H* 95. On my reading, this sentence poses severe translational problems, and it is unsurprising that translators gloss it in very different ways. *Sinnlich* might be the relatively chaste "sensible" or "sensory" or "of the senses," but Mann allows for the possibility that the beauty in question is "sensuous" or even "sensual" (and permits us to wonder which connotations might be present in Aschenbach's own awareness, as well as which pertain to the boy's beauty). Nor can one avoid the issue, as Koelb and Heim both attempt to do, by opting for "physical beauty," since, given the Platonic resonances that dominate the discussions of beauty, the range of types of beauty that can be sensed ought to be wider than the physical: we should recall the sentence from the *Phaedrus* Aschenbach has quoted and the further gloss that beauty is the only denizen of the world of transcendent forms our senses can perceive (*GKFA* 8.1:555; *LP* 45, *L* 235, *K* 38, *H* 84).

29. Aschenbach's attitude may be expressed in a much-cited passage from Mann's late essay on Chekhov, written in 1954 (the year before his death). "And yet one writes, tells stories, presents the truth and thus delights a needy world, in the dim hope, almost in the faith, that truth and beautiful form will have the effect of freeing the soul, and thus be able to prepare the world for a better, more beautiful, more spiritually elevated life" (*Essays* 6:279–280; see also 269–270). Like Mann himself, Aschenbach seems moved by constant self-criticism and thus sympathetic to Chekhov's dictum, "Dissatisfaction with oneself forms a basic element of every real talent." (*Essays* 6:279).

30. *GKFA* 8.1:534; *LP* 29, *L* 219, *K* 24, *H* 51. The last three translate Mann's *Phäake* as "Phaeacian," but Lowe-Porter opts for "Phaeax." The Phaeacians lived on the island of Scheria, Odysseus's last stopping place before arriving in Ithaca: the mythological associations suggest people who live well, in grace and luxury (which would fit with Aschenbach's thought that the boy is used to ease). Phaeax was a Greek orator, apparently not very successful—hence, unless I misunderstand her, Lowe-Porter's choice seems obscurely motivated. Aschenbach's epithet has another interesting resonance. Shipwrecked on the beach, Odysseus observes Nausicaa, the beautiful daughter of the King of the Phaeacians, and, with her aid, he is equipped to make the final stage of his journey. Tadzio is a beauty, observed on the lido—and Aschenbach may inchoately hope that the boy will help him achieve his official goal of representing beauty (although Tadzio's principal role may be to assist him in undergoing the final journey—Tadzio as Hermes, bearer of souls).

31. ". . . and to you, Critobulus, I would say, 'Go abroad for a year: so long a time will it take to heal you of this wound.'" Xenophon *Memorabilia of Socrates*, trans. H. G. Dakyns, available online at Project Gutenberg. See *GKFA* 8.1:539; *LP* 33, *L* 223, *K* 27–28, *H* 59.

32. *GKFA* 8.1:554; *LP* 44–45, *L* 234, *K* 37, *H* 82–83. Surprisingly, Luke, normally the most faithful of translators, renders *"menschlicher Jugend"* as "of young men." This is to anticipate a stage of thought Aschenbach has not yet reached. Like other translators, I preserve gender neutrality.

33. Schopenhauer sharply dissents: WWV 1 §40; 1:266. As we shall discover, Schopenhauer's grounds for disagreement, rooted in his concerns about the sexual drive, are crucial to the dialectic behind Mann's presentation of Aschenbach.

34. In his classic monograph, Kenneth Dover makes this point very clearly: see his *Greek Homosexuality* (New York: MJF, 1989), 162.

35. *Phaedrus* 244–257b; *PW* 522–533.

36. Plutarch, *Selected Essays*, trans. Moses Hadas (New York: Mentor, 1957), 15. Unlike Plato, Plutarch offers a dialogue in which the relative merits of homosexual and heterosexual love are seriously debated—and, in closing, he leaves his readers with the claim that heterosexual love seems more likely to endure.

37. Plato *Symposium* 207; *PW* 490.

38. Plutarch, *Selected Essays*, 15.

39. Plato *Symposium* 219d; *PW* 501.

40. Mann carefully preserved the diaries from 1918 to 1921 and from 1933 to 1955, stipulating that they should not be opened before the twentieth anniversary of his death. (His diary records this decision, first proposing a period of twenty-five years after his death and later settling for an interval of twenty years. *TB* [1951–1952] 18, 223.) His provision thus allowed for the possibility that his wife and his children might have the opportunity to read them—indeed, Katia Mann survived until 1980 (after the publication date of the first volumes). The diary passages about future publication do not register any concern about how his wife or children would react to what they might read.

41. See, for only a few of a very large number of instances, *TB* (1918–1921) 118, 235, 379, 387; *TB* (1933–1934) 397, 405; *TB* (1935–1936) 58, 369, 381; *TB* (1937–1939) 181; *TB* (1940–1943) 304, 316, 339; *TB* (1944–1946), 40, 260; *TB* (1946–1948) 263; *TB* (1949–1950) 207. This linguistic tendency was evident even after the publication of the first volume of the diaries: it was noted by the critic Marcel Reich-Ranicki in his review (reprinted in Reich-Ranicki, *Thomas Mann und die Seinen*, 53). Occasionally, *hübsch* is applied to women—see, for example, *TB* (1935–1936) 128.

42. Visiting Nordwijk in August 1947, Mann expressed his joy in returning after eight years. Seated on his balcony, looking over the sea, he surveyed the scene: "The Dutch type mostly not attractive. From a distance a few images to capture the attention." The next day repeats the complaint: "Nothing for the eye to love (*Augenliebe*—eye candy?) in the vicinity, indifferent humanity." After a few days, he confesses his boredom. *TB* (1946–1948) 145, 146.

43. For prominent examples, see *TB* (1933–1934) 296 (January 24, 1934), *TB* (1935–1936) 177 (September 21, 1935), *TB* (1940–1943) 395–396 (February

20, 1942), *TB* (1944–1946) 215–216 (June 15, 1945), *TB* (1946–1948) 129–135, *TB* (1949–1950) 207–221. Even more explicit and extensive is the romance of the summer of 1950, when, on a visit to Switzerland, Mann was greatly taken with the charms of a young waiter, Franz Westermaier: see *TB* (1949–1950) 205–259 *passim*; these pages contain some interesting passages about his family's reactions to his evidently besotted state. I shall explore Mann's sexuality at greater length in section 4.

44. Frederick's sexual inclinations are unclear, but many of his contemporaries, as well as later scholars, have supposed that they were primarily directed toward men. Those suppositions rest on his early intimacy with one of his father's pages, on the apparently sexless character of his marriage, and on his public celebrations of male friendship (as, for example, in the "Platonic" temple he had erected at Sans-Souci). Frederick would surely have been an outstanding subject for anyone with the complex sexual orientation assigned to Aschenbach—or felt by Mann himself.

45. *PT* 1:67; *PTM* 61.

46. *PT* 1:140–141; *PTM* 65. *PT* 1:415; *PTM* 72–73; *PT* 1:449; *PTM* 75. See also *PT* 403, 407, 459–460, 500, 503; not reproduced in *PTM*.

47. *PT* 2:325; *PTM* 127.

48. *THBW* 429.

49. *Essays* 3:126–133, 247.

50. *TB* (1933–1934) 335.

51. For the poem, to which I'll return, see *PL* 47. It is quoted in *Essays* 3:126–133, 246–247.

52. *PTM* 24.

53. It seems very probable that he had read the Plutarch dialogue, given his acknowledgment of having overlooked the homosexual references in Plutarch when he was young (*PT* 1:141; *PTM* 65).

54. *PT* 1:60, 64; *PTM* 52, 56.

55. *PT* 1:67; *PTM* 61. It is worth noting that, by the time Platen came to endorse this ancient view, women were already proving themselves in the ambient cultural world, so that his reiteration of the classical argument involves either blindness or self-deception. The classical justification would have been even less available to Thomas Mann, for whom female cultural achievements would have been even more impossible to ignore. Nevertheless, despite Mann's knowledge of Katia Pringsheim's unusual intellectual accomplishments (her ability in mathematics and physics, for example), and despite his celebration of them in *Königliche Hoheit* (where Imma Spoelmann guides the prince's studies in mathematical economics), he took it for granted that his wife's role was to support his own endeavors. See section 8.

56. *PT* 1:90; *PTM* 64.
57. *PT* 1:141; *PTM* 65.
58. *PT* 1:457; see also the reaction to La Rochefoucauld's less rosy view of friendship, *PT* 1:403 (these passages are not in *PTM*).
59. *PT* 1:700–701; *PTM* 92–93.
60. *PT* 1:838; *PTM* 102.
61. *PT* 1:838; not in *PTM*.
62. *PT* 1:781; *PTM* 101.
63. *PT* 1:838–839; not in *PTM*.
64. The same word, *Abgrund*, occurs in both their meditations (*PT* 1:838; *GKFA* 8.1:589).
65. Platen writes: "Reading and eternal reading! It almost seems I only live to read, or even that I do not live but merely read" (*PT* 2:104; *PTM* 114).
66. *PL* 43.
67. *PL* 47.
68. *Essays* 2 (1919–1925) 272. Plainly, in Mann's consciousness, Platen's short poem resonated in Wagner's *Tristan*, itself embodying ideas from Schopenhauer (akin to those expressed by Platen). The complex web of connections was reinforced by the knowledge that Wagner had written the great duet of act 2 of *Tristan* (in which Tristan and Isolde yearn for the abolition of their separate selves) in Venice, a city that had figured significantly in Platen's own liberation. It was also the city in which Wagner himself would die.
69. See, for example, *PT* 2:187–188; not in *PTM*.
70. *PT* 2:928; *PTM* 216. Platen surely enjoyed the beach for reasons similar to those that moved Mann.
71. Plato *Phaedrus* 250d; *PW* 528.
72. *PT* 2:179; not in *PTM*. See also the entry for February 5, 1819 (*PT* 2:203).
73. Entry of June 8, 1819; *PT* 2:281 (not in *PTM*). This part of the diary is in French, a language Platen used with his mother and in which, at various periods of his life, he records his thoughts and feelings in his diary. (He also writes in other languages—for instance, in Portuguese, when he is studying that language.) I have no general theory of why German gives way to French (or to other tongues).
74. Entry of June 9, 1819; *PT* 2:283 (not in *PTM*).
75. Entry of June 9, 1819; *PT* 2:284 (not in *PTM*).
76. Entry of June 24, 1819; *PT* 2:288 (not in *PTM*).
77. *PT* 2:314; not in *PTM*.
78. *PT* 2: 313; not in *PTM*.
79. Recall Mann's letter to Grautoff, discussed in chapter 1 (n. 138 and accompanying text).

80. *PT* 1:683–684; *PTM* 90.

81. Entries of June 6 and June 18, 1816; *PT* 1:537, 538; the latter appears in *PTM* 82.

82. *Schopenhauer als Erzieher* §I; *NW* 1:341.

83. *PT* 1:838; *PTM* 102.

84. *GKFA* 8.1:509; *LP* 9, *L* 201, *K* 8, *H* 14.

85. She manages to leave her room at the beginning of chapter 3 and conducts the next series of "interviews" in one of the hotel's public rooms.

86. *LIW* 281–282.

87. Later in Goethe's reverie is an interesting passage on the androgynous nature of the artist: "It's no accident that I resemble the doughty woman. I am my bronzed grandmother in the form of a man, I am womb and seed, androgynous art, determinable by everything and anything, but determined by myself, enriching what the world receives" (*LIW* 298–299).

88. The exception is Jaschu, whose individuality is subsumed in his relationship to Tadzio.

89. Unusually, Katia Pringsheim pursued studies in mathematics and physics at the university level. One of the reasons for her hesitation in accepting Mann's proposal was her unwillingness to give up this part of her intellectual life. See *dMM* 1:924, *HarpM* 1:233, *KMM* 19, 28–29.

90. *GKFA* 4.1:51, 50.

91. *GKFA* 4.1:313.

92. *GKFA* 4.1:293.

93. *GKFA* 4.1:370.

94. *GKFA* 4.1:395. See also *GKFA* 4.1:364.

95. *GKFA* 4.1:399.

96. As chapter 1 explained, the diaries, to which Mann confided his feelings and longings, records kept for years in a cabinet to which he alone had the key, were left in Munich when he began the journey that would turn into years of exile. After it was clear that he could not return to Munich, and after the plan for his second son, Golo, to collect the diaries and forward them had gone awry, Mann was clearly extremely anxious and disturbed. See chapter 1 n. 164 and accompanying text.

97. *KMM* 77–78.

98. *TB* (1918–1921) 470.

99. *TB* (1918–1921) 470.

100. *TB* (1918–1921) 453. The passage cited is preceded by the words "Rencontre with [*mit*] K." followed by an ellipsis. The editor (Peter de Mendelssohn) omitted a more explicit description of what happened on this evening. On a visit to the Thomas Mann Archiv in Zürich, I was able to consult the original

and thus to confirm that there was difficulty in consummating intercourse. I am grateful to Katrin Benedig and her colleagues in Zürich for their help in deciphering Mann's handwriting.

101. *TB* (1918–1921) 517.

102. For Katia's reassuring touch when the diaries seemed to have been confiscated, see *TB* (1933–1934) 66. For some of the many occasions on which he sought nocturnal comfort from her, see *TB* (1918–1921) 523 (May 27, 1921), *TB* (1937–1939) 168 (January 30, 31, 1938), *TB* (1946–1948) 230 (March 1, 1948), *TB* (1951–1952) 237 (July 6, 1952), *TB* (1953–1955) 299 (December 22, 1954).

103. The most extensive confession of his homoerotic impulses comes in the summer of 1950, in the diary entries recording his attraction to "Franzl" Westermaier (*TB* [1949–1950] 205–259).

104. *TB* (1933–1934) 397–398.

105. *TB* (1946–1948) 318 (October 22, 1948).

106. *TB* (1946–1948) 262, 263, 264, 265; the final vision was apparently some compensation for a walk abbreviated by the demands of work and correspondence.

107. *TB* (1933–1934) 296.

108. *TB* (1933–1934) 297.

109. *TB* (1933–1934) 411. As in the earlier entry, Mann describes the relationship with Klaus Heuser as a "life-validating consummation."

110. *TB* (1940–1943) 395–396.

111. Platen's diaries also contain a similar expression of joy in having loved—even though he cannot claim to have *been* loved: *PT* 2:167; *PTM* 121.

112. *Essays 2* (1919–1925) 277.

113. Klaus Mann, *Tagebücher* (1933), 129; cited in *HarpM* 1:710. The passage continues by suggesting that, in contrast to his father, Klaus has not repressed his sexual drives but has lived them out to the full. Instead of thinking of passion and "intoxication"—even intoxication at the prospect of death—as seduction, Klaus claims to view it as an intensification (heightening—*Steigerung*) of life.

114. *KMM* 21.

115. For the contrast between the diaries' treatment of Katia (whose name her husband wrote as "Katja") and the attention to haircuts, coffee consumption, and other similar mundane features of Mann's life, see Reich-Ranicki, *Thomas Mann und die Seinen*, 63 (from a discussion review, centered on the *TB* [1937–1939], a review originally published in 1981).

116. *TB* (1933–1934) 140. Identifying the marriage in this way seems initially to inflate Mann's sexual interest in his wife—Jaakob's love for Rahel might appear to have a strong sexual focus, one at odds with the incompleteness of Mann's attraction to Katia. Yet there are aspects of the treatment of the relationship in

*Joseph* that point differently: the depth of Jaakob's love for Rahel is most often expressed in the moments at which he comforts her, both in their long period of waiting and in the years of her infertility. By contrast, on the night of his first wedding, when the body that stimulates his sexual energy is that of Lea—a wonderful bed companion—the lovemaking is prodigious: she receives him again and again, and, although Jaakob and Lea do not count their acts of intercourse, the shepherds report that they made love nine times (*JSB* 224). Perhaps the love for Rahel was more detached from "the lower part of the body."

117. A conception to which Nietzsche seems tempted in the essay on Schopenhauer as *Erzieher*. See n. 18 and the corresponding text. I have argued at length against biological determinist accounts of "human nature": see *Vaulting Ambition* (Cambridge, Mass.: MIT Press, 1985) and several essays in *In Mendel's Mirror* (New York: Oxford University Press, 2003).

118. *TB* (1949–1950) 294 (November 24, 1950).

119. The following paragraphs are indebted to comments by Mark Anderson and Fred Neuhouser.

120. I am grateful to Mark Anderson for posing this sharp question.

121. This would be appropriate for the conception of the artist-educator Aschenbach assigns himself.

122. *Notizbuch* 7, 129; "*Amor est titillatio concomitante idea re exterioris*" (Spinoza, *Tractatus de intellectus emendatione Ethica*, part 4).

123. According to the judgment of his brother Heinrich, Thomas Mann lacked the capacity fully to apprehend a different life and was dominated by raging passion for himself. The assessment was made at the time of the public dispute between the brothers and appears in a draft of a letter, never sent, written on January 5, 1918; see *THBW* 178 (Reich-Ranicki quotes the pertinent passage and attributes it to p. 141 of this volume). Heinrich's charge is substantiated by the overall tone of the *TB*; see section 8.

124. *GKFA* 8.1:588–589; *LP* 72–73, *L* 260–261, *K* 60–61, *H* 136–137.

125. See section 4 of chapter 1.

126. *GKFA* 8.1; *L* 14. It is not only significant that the event occurs at a musical performance, at an opera, at a work by Wagner, but that it is *Lohengrin*. *Lohengrin* was very likely the first opera the young Thomas Mann attended (*HarpM* 1:43), and the *Tagebücher* reveal clearly how he continued to be moved by it throughout his life. See, for example, *TB* (1937–1939) 516; *TB* (1953–1955) 250 (July 20, 1954).

127. *Perhaps* Aschenbach dies from cholera, and, if so, *perhaps* the obsession with Tadzio plays a causal role in keeping him in Venice and in leading him to eat something that transmits the infection to him. As the next chapter will suggest, we should beware of being too confident on these issues.

128. Compare GKFA 8.1:112 and 589; L 22, 261.

129. Genesis 39:7–20 provides the source for JSB 729–926.

130. This is how she is introduced in the second sentence of the part (*Hauptstück*) of *Joseph* that deals with the first half of the story of Joseph and Potiphar's wife (the first sentence echoes Genesis).

131. See JSB 891–899.

132. GKFA 8.1:531, 541. LP 26, 34; L 217, 224–225; K 22, 29; H 46–47, 62. Mann sometimes associates problematic teeth with premature death, as in the cases of Tom and Hanno Buddenbrook. As the TB reveal, he was plagued by frequent—and hard-to-solve—dental problems.

133. JSB 45–49.

134. JSB 387 (He "burned" to "show himself to the wider world"), 387–400, 404–410.

135. JSB 908.

136. JSB 925–926.

137. This is described in one of the funniest—also most touching and disturbing—chapters Mann ever wrote, a scene in which Potiphar's decrepit parents reminisce in front of Joseph, whom they take for a mute servant (*stumme Diener*); JSB 622–640 (*Huij und Tuij*). Their apparently indiscreet conversation is prompted by worries about what will happen to them after their (imminent) deaths.

138. Joyce recognizes a similar problem and a similar solution in the "Lotus Eaters" chapter of *Ulysses*, where Bloom observes the gelded carriage-horses and reflects on this as a possibility (63; 5:217–219).

139. *Briefe Grauthoff/Boy-Ed* 68.

140. Joyce takes this route and thus invites the charge leveled by the moralizing narrator. His answer is to "see life foully," to expose and probe again and again—and to come to forgiveness out of the deepest knowledge of what is to be forgiven.

141. Mann sides with Tonio Kröger against Nietzsche on this. Schopenhauer serves as his mentor (*Erzieher*) here.

142. *Von Josephs Keuschheit* ("Of Joseph's Chastity"), JSB 823–832.

143. JSB 831–832.

144. As Bence Nanay pointed out to me, the link between beauty and the erotic is essential to the quasi-Platonic argument reconstructed here. He also suggests that the coda to the novella reveals Mann's exploration of a different conception of the aesthetic, one that rejects erotic arousal in favor of calm contemplation. Perhaps that aesthetic attitude is attained in Aschenbach's final moments—see section 7 of chapter 3.

145. See John Bridcut, *Britten's Children* (London: Faber, 2006) for a discussion of Britten's relationships with young boys.

146. Humphrey Carpenter, *Benjamin Britten* (New York: Scribners, 1992), 550.

147. For a very thoughtful discussion of the film, its relations to Mann, and the reactions of critics who have compared film and novella, see Hans Vaget, "Film and Literature. The Case of "Death in Venice": Luchino Visconti and Thomas Mann," *German Quarterly* 53 (1980): 159–175. See also Philip Reed, "Aschenbach Becomes Mahler: Thomas Mann as Film," in *Benjamin Britten: Death in Venice*, ed. Donald Mitchell (Cambridge: Cambridge University Press, 1987), 178–183. Chapter 3 will take up some of the issues raised by these two excellent essays.

148. As in several of the contributions to Mitchell's *Benjamin Britten: Death in Venice*. See, for example, the essays by Colin Graham and T. J. Reed. Patrick Carnegy acknowledges a critical consensus on the point (168) but then develops a more complex view of the relations between Britten and Mann. See also Peter Evans, *The Music of Benjamin Britten* (Oxford: Oxford University Press, 1996), 523.

149. The letter is quoted by Carnegy; Mitchell, *Benjamin Britten: Death in Venice*, 168.

150. Although the marriage was one of convenience, Auden occasionally visited his nominal father-in-law. According to Edward Mendelson (in conversation), Erika had originally approached Christopher Isherwood in her search for a British passport, only to be turned down; Auden, by contrast, was willing, and apparently reprimanded his friend, allegedly asking rhetorically, "What are buggers *for*?"

151. On March 9, 1948, Mann recorded in his diary that he had played the records of Britten's "Serenade" and commented "to hear again" (*TB* [1946–1948], 234). In a letter to Ida Herz of January 16, 1948, he had written that he knew the composer's name but not his music (*TB* [1946–1948] 720).

152. *TB* (1946–1948) 243; entry of April 1. The third song of the serenade is a setting of Blake's "O Rose, thou art sick."

153. Mitchell, *Benjamin Britten: Death in Venice*, 168.

154. A diary entry, admittedly written at a time when Mann was vexed by Schoenberg's angry response to *Doktor Faustus*—the real composer resented the fact that his musical ideas had been assigned to his fictional counterpart without attribution—compares the song of the Rhinemaidens at the end of Rheingold (which had moved Mann to tears) with the efforts of Wagner's successors: "I would trade the entire works of Schoenberg, Berg, Krenek, and Leverkühn for this one piece alone" (*TB* [1946–1948] 227). The sequence of *Tagebücher* records the music Mann listened to over many years and reinforces the idea that his tastes were relatively conservative. Although Wagner features a lot in his listening,

it would be wrong to conclude, from the overwhelming attention given to Wagner in his writings, that he was only secondarily interested in others. His musical tastes center on the romantic period, with little interest in music before Beethoven (Mozart and Haydn being more popular than Bach, and earlier composers almost unrepresented; for a disdainful remark about the "clichéd" and "mechanical" character of eighteenth-century music, see *TB* [1951–1952] 26 [February 21, 1951]) and some liking for Debussy, Ravel, and Prokofiev. There is a period in the latter months of 1935 during which he listened to a lot of Tchaikovsky. Berlioz, especially *Harold in Italy*, was another favorite; Beethoven and Schubert are always much admired. For an excellent discussion of Mann and music, see Hans Vaget, *Seelenzauber* (Frankfurt: Fischer, 2006).

155. The film, directed by Franz Seitz, appeared in 1982. It is available in a (German) DVD edition from Arthaus.

156. Mann continued to listen to Britten. On January 29, 1949, he heard a radio broadcast of "an opera by Britten, tender and parodistic" (*TB* [1949–1950] 14). Almost certainly the opera was *Albert Herring*—which, unlike *Peter Grimes*, Britten's previous opera, deserves the adjectives Mann chose.

157. The "Serenissima" theme is heard as Aschenbach approaches Venice, at a moment in the novella at which Mann alludes to Platen (*GKFA* 8.1:521)—the unnamed poet who saw "the cupola and the bell-tower rising out of the water" (*PL* 92). Whether Britten intended his sensuous and ambiguous motif to capture the allusion to Platen—or whether either he or Piper knew of Platen—is a matter for speculation.

158. See Rosamund Strode's "Chronicle," in Mitchell, *Benjamin Britten: Death in Venice*, 41–44.

159. For an illuminating discussion of issues of balance between the two acts, see Peter Evans, *The Music of Benjamin Britten* (Oxford: Oxford University Press, 1996), chap. 21 (on *Death in Venice*), esp. 547.

160. For reasons given in section 3 of chapter 1, highlighting the Apollo-Dionysius opposition in this way oversimplifies the problems explored in the novella and, again, points toward the caricature of "Eminent Repressed Writer Undone by Forbidden Passion."

161. As I see and hear the opera, there are echoes of Marlowe's *Dr. Faustus* and of the two angels who compete for Faustus's soul.

162. The prominence of the hotel manager suggests thinking of him as the dispenser of pleasures to the denizens of a bourgeois order, one that is now ending, who, in his role as Dionysius is all-powerful in setting and exacting the costs of pleasure, specifically death.

163. The link between *Death in Venice* and *Billy Budd* is also explored by Colin Palmer in "Toward a Genealogy of *Death in Venice*," in *On Mahler and*

*Britten: Essays in Honor of Donald Mitchell,* ed. Philip Reed (London: Faber, 1995).

164. Characteristically, Britten is faithful in setting Melville's story. The references to Billy as "Beauty" are already there in the original (although with less of the homoerotic overtones they take on in Britten). The opera amends Billy's final words by introducing the dramatic touch of having the boy use Vere's nickname ("Starry Vere"). The Christian allusions, already present in Melville, are heightened in Britten's version. In particular, instead of following the original, where Vere dies in action early in the Napoleonic wars, Britten has the captain live on, and he is thus able to reflect in his closing monologue on the "redemption" Billy has brought him. Interestingly, Melville's story is rich in classical references—Billy is compared to Apollo, for example—a fact that invites connections to *Death in Venice.*

165. There is also a lesser kinship with the opening declamation (repeated later with variation), *"J'ai seul la clef de cette parade, de cette parade sauvage,"* of *Les illuminations.* Perhaps we should also connect all three operatic figures with Britten's Rimbaud-persona.

166. As already noted, the next chapter will scrutinize this idea.

167. For the passage in the novella where Aschenbach observes Tadzio's teeth and records his inchoate feeling of satisfaction, see *GKFA* 8.1:541; *LP* 34, *L* 224–225, *K* 29, *H* 62. Britten does not set either this or the earlier recognition of the boy's pallor (*GKFA* 8.1:531; *LP* 26, *L* 217, *K* 22, *H* 46–47), but the display of pride and scorn toward the Russian family serves the same end. In Piper's libretto, Aschenbach comments: "There is a dark side even to perfection. I like that."

168. Once again, Britten introduces a sexual focus where the novella is more open and ambiguous. After Aschenbach has heard about the cholera epidemic and considered warning the "lady with the pearls," Mann portrays him as appalled by the vision of a return to Munich: he immediately conjures up an image of the mortuary chapel, the scene that prompted his journey south, and he commits himself to remaining silent. There follows one of Mann's sinuously ambivalent sentences: "The image of the plague-afflicted and dilapidated city, hovering desolate before his consciousness, aroused in him intangible hopes, that overrode all considerations of reason and were of monstrous sweetness" (*GKFA* 8.1:581; *LP* 66, *L* 255, *K* 56, *H* 125). Piper's "What if all were dead, and only we two left alive?" is far more definite—and, to those of a certain generation, unfortunately reminiscent of the song "If you were the only girl in the world, and I were the only boy . . ."

169. Although Britten was evidently much moved by religious texts and set them with great sensitivity and subtlety—from the beautiful "Hymn to the Virgin," composed while he was still a schoolboy, to the *War Requiem* and

## 2. BEAUTY 229

beyond—he was no orthodox Christian. His religious and spiritual attitudes evolved throughout his life, always shaped by his moral commitments and ideals. Thus he could see Billy's action as redemptive without subscribing to any of the various standard versions of Christian doctrine about Jesus as Redeemer. For discussion of Britten's religious sensibility, see Graham Elliott, *Benjamin Britten: The Spiritual Dimension* (New York: Oxford University Press, 2006).

170. Mann considers this possibility and, in one of his deftly ironic pieces of "historical commentary," laments the fact that the "folk traditions" have developed it as an "oversweetened fiction." The "truth," the commentator claims, is that there were no further meetings between Joseph and either Mut or Potiphar (*JSB* 1085–1088).

171. The obsession with Tadzio might truncate his life. For reasons I shall give in the next chapter, one should be cautious in drawing firm conclusions on this issue.

172. The post-Enlightenment modification is developed in different ways by Kant, Wilhelm Humboldt, and Mill.

173. In July 1948, Mann learned of a report that the secretary of the Swedish Academy had proposed awarding him a second Nobel Prize in literature. He heard a similar rumor in March 1949 and was led to reflect on the "great success" in Sweden of *Lotte in Weimar* and *Doktor Faustus*. Apparently, in both instances, the prize committee did consider the possibility and decided not to give any individual a second prize within the same field (*TB* [1946–1948] 290; *TB* [1949–1950] 33).

174. The diaries record in some detail the number of hours Mann slept, his difficulties in falling asleep, the medicines he took to induce sleep, and the procedures he followed when he had most trouble—moving to a chair, or going to Katia's room.

175. See, for a small selection of examples from the diaries, the entries of December 24, 1919 (*TB* [1918–1921] 349); November 20, 1933 (*TB* [1933–1934] 251); December 24, 1936 (*TB* [1935–1936] 412); November 4, 1938 (*TB* [1937–1939] 316); August 10, 1948 (*TB* [1946–1948] 293).

176. For Katia's ministrations to Heinrich, see, for example, *TB* (1949–1950) 37–39. Interestingly, despite the length of her acquaintance with Heinrich and despite the many services she rendered to him, her reports of exchanges between them record them as always addressing one another formally—using *Sie* instead of *Du*: see *KMM* 155 for an example from very late in Heinrich's life.

177. Mann's attitudes toward Jews were complex. Despite his opposition to Nazism, as well as the fact that he had married into a prominent Jewish family, he was sometimes inclined to make anti-Semitic remarks and jokes and to introduce stereotypical figures into his works (a prime example is the impresario

Saul Fitelberg, who is presumably to be a source of comic relief in chapter 37 of *Doktor Faustus*). Attempting to fathom this aspect of Mann's psychology and its impact on Katia and her family would introduce a range of materials that would lead me far from my central topics.

178. *TB* (1946–1948) 264. The attraction is acknowledged and steered away — "normalized" — by supplying a family context and a gentle reminder that women, too, can be beautiful.

179. *TB* (1944–1946) 160–161. See also the entry for February 11, 1940, when Mann was reminded by a congratulatory telegram (*TB* [1940–1943] 24).

180. *TB* (1937–1939) 438, 439. See also *TB* (1933–1934) 482; *TB* (1935–1936) 148–149.

181. *TB* (1937–1939) 168.

182. *TB* (1940–1942) 389.

183. *GKFA* 11.1:526.

184. *KMM* 175.

185. Strictly speaking, one might leave open the possibility that Michael's death was an accident, that he simply misjudged the combination of alcohol and pills he ingested. Yet his friends reported earlier efforts at suicide, and the poetry written shortly before his death suggests that suicide was on his mind. For an accessible account, see Marianne Krull, *Im Netz der Zauberer* (Frankfurt: Fischer, 2002).

186. *TB* (1946–1948) 285; entry of July 12, 1948.

187. *TB* (1946–1948) 285; entry of July 13, 1948.

188. *Die Entstehung des* Doktor Faustus. Thomas Mann, *Doktor Faustus/Die Entstehung des* Doktor Faustus (Frankfurt: Fischer), 679–829. *TB* (1946–1948) 286–288.

189. *TB* (1946–1948) 295; entry of August 14, 1948.

190. Krull suggests that the elder Manns developed a fatalism about Klaus (*Im Netz der Zauberer*, 16).

191. "My deepest sympathy with the maternal heart and with E." "K.'s sighs, Eri's pain, pierces my heart beyond words. I kiss them." "Eri very sad and suffering. K. self-possessed." "Erika often in tears." *TB* (1949–1950) 57–59. Krull makes much of the fact that Mann's "paternal heart" was not touched (*Im Netz der Zauberer*, 15), and that is surely one interpretation of his words. It is, however, possible to ask if his conception of his own role as "head of the family" — and of masculinity — convinced him of the primary importance of comforting the living.

192. Reich-Ranicki, *Thomas Mann und die Seinen*, 326.

193. *Briefe* 3:91.

194. *TB* (1918–1921) 18; entry of September 28, 1918.

195. *TB* 1918–21 378; entry of February 13 1920.
196. Krull, *Im Netz der Zauberer*, 441.
197. Later references in the diaries suggest that Bibi continued to be viewed as a problematic presence. In April 1936, the then teenager experimented with some of his father's prescription drugs, and a physician had to be called—"a harmless incident, but something of a disturbance to the household" (*TB* [1935–1936] 291). A year and a half later, Michael suffered from extreme sensitivity to light, and the doctors prescribed careful treatment: "a serious business, that will make it impossible for K. to go to stay in Arosa" (*TB* [1937–1939] 146). Michael recovered his sight and six months later was back at his musical education. After he had played for the family, Mann commented, "Bibi's playing shows hard work, but to my mind nothing of the violinist's spark [*Impuls*]" (*TB* [1937–1939] 259). Did Michael's father convey that judgment to him? The negative view of his youngest child persisted until late in Mann's life. In 1951, Michael quarreled violently with Yalta Menuhin (with whom he sometimes performed) and apparently hit her above the eye. On the following day, Mann commented: "I must confess that I shall be happy when he has left. I don't really care for who he is [*sein Wesen*], including his laugh. But I talked nicely with him during the meal, and told him that he didn't really need the connection with Yalta." (*TB* [1951–1952] 130, 131; entries of November 4 and November 5, 1951).
198. *TB* [1933–1934] 57, 82, 90.
199. See Erika Mann, *Mein Vater, Der Zauberer*, 2nd ed. (Hamburg: Roholt, 2005), 91–93. For the further sequence of letters—in which both parents participated—see 93–108. The earlier disagreement is expressed in a letter of September 28, 1933 (84). Mann's reflections on these disputes are recorded in *TB* (1933–1934) 197–199 (note the praise for Erika's "organizational and intellectual work" at 199) and in *TB* (1935–1936) 245–249.
200. See, for one among many examples, *TB* (1946–1948) 115.
201. See, for one among many examples, *TB* (1946–1948) 182.
202. *TB* (1949–1950) 56. Despite Mann's appreciation of Erika's valuable service, his diaries often reveal concern about the strain she caused for Katia: see, for example, *TB* (1951–1952) 43 (April 3, 1951), and *TB* (1953–1955) 192–193 (March 7, 1954).
203. The couple married on November 23, 1939 (for Mann's feelings, see *TB* [1937–1939] 503). On subsequent visits with Medi and her husband, there are tearful partings (*TB* [1940–1943] 238), increasing irritation with Borghese's pomposity (*TB* [1944–1946] 134, 135), growing perception of Medi's marital predicament (*TB* [1944–1946] 221), and a sense of her unhappiness (*TB* [1946–1948] 156).
204. Fridolin was the eldest son of Michael and his wife, Gret. The diaries are full of Mann's delight in playing with and reading to this newfound

favorite—who served as the model for Nepomuk ("Echo") in *Doktor Faustus*, the adored child who dies from an agonizing meningitis. Krull reports that Fridolin found the identification—and perhaps the attention of his besotted grandfather—oppressive (*Im Netz der Zauberer*, 443).

205. *TB* (1918–1921) 114.

206. *TB* (1918–1921) 444, 529. Interestingly, as the next pages reveal, Monika fell seriously ill a few days later.

207. *TB* (1933–1934) 526.

208. *TB* (1935–1936) 345, 382, 412; *TB* (1937–1939) 3.

209. *TB* (1940–1943) 273, 419. See also *TB* (1953–1955) 101 (August 20, 1953).

210. *TB* (1949–1950) 25, 26.

211. Golo receives little individual mention in the early *Tagebücher* (1918–1921), but his appearance in the pre-Christmas play (1919) represents the impression he makes: "Golo as a lady in mourning uncannily funny in the highest degree" (*TB* [1918–1921], 348).

212. Golo's historical study *Wallenstein* is rightly regarded as a classic. That status could not, I think, be awarded to any of the writings of his siblings.

213. Perhaps that is why Mann preferred the material of *Death in Venice*: recall his determination to prove himself serious after *Königliche Hoheit* (see chapter 1 n. 93 and text thereto).

214. *Zur Genealogie der Moral* 1 §13; NW 5:279.

215. I draw the metaphor from Emily Fox Gordon's novel *It Will Come to Me*, in which the wife of a professor writes a draft novel with the title *Whole Lives Devoured*, about the sacrifices demanded in the name of academic culture.

216. *TB* (1949–1950) 67 (June 12, 1949).

## 3. SHADOWS

1. *THBW* 160; the letter is dated April 27.

2. The surviving diaries make it plain how frustrating he found it to go back and make substantial changes to what had already been written. The entry for June 10, 1919, expresses his annoyance at having to reorganize the early chapters of *Zauberberg* (*TB* [1918–1921] 262). Almost three decades later, his difficulties in finding the right beginning for *Der Erwählte* lead him to consider abandoning the project, although perseverance finally overcomes the obstacles (see, for example, *TB* [1946–1948] 227, 232, 236, 240, 241, 246, 249).

3. *THBW* 159, letter of April 2, 1912. Mann expresses his hope that the novella will be finished before he goes to Davos (at the beginning of May).

4. See section 7.

5. *GKFA* 8.1:523–524; *LP* 21, *L* 212, *K* 17–18, *H* 36–37.

6. Britten gives prominence to the eating of the strawberry by reintroducing a minor character, the strawberry seller, who originally appeared on the beach in act 1, scene 5, and who recurs in "The last visit to Venice" (act 2, scene 16), singing the same simple lyrical theme. The opera thus suggests the popular view that Aschenbach dies of cholera as the result of eating infected fruit.

7. The assumption that Aschenbach dies of cholera is so widespread among writers who discuss Mann's story that it is almost unfair to single out a particular discussion. Yet precisely because of the exceptional depth of T. J. Reed's treatment of the novella—and his emphasis on its ambivalence—he can serve as an exemplar of the standard diagnosis. It is made *en passant*: " . . . the cholera epidemic, which in Naturalistic terms is what kills Aschenbach, . . . " (Reed 172). As Reed explicitly notes, cholera was "an ideal accomplice in the creation of a symbolic pattern." The neatness of the thematic connections thus pushes toward indictment, and Reed, characteristically a subtle explorer of Mann's ambiguities, needs no further evidence.

8. GKFA 8.1:590; LP 73, L 261–262, K 61, H 138.

9. GKFA 8.1:541–542; LP 35, L 225, K 29, H 63.

10. GKFA 8.1:509; LP 9, L 201, K 8, H 14.

11. No reader of *Buddenbrooks* should expect its author to slight the medical details, for the account of the typhus infection that brings Hanno's death corresponds to turn-of-the-century orthodoxy. Similarly, in *Doktor Faustus*, Mann does his homework on the meningitis that causes the death of Nepomuk ("Echo").

12. GKFA 8.2:486–492; translated by Koelb (K 83–87).

13. If Aschenbach were suffering from dry cholera transmitted via the strawberry, the interval between initial infection and death would be quite short. "A few days later" ("*Einige Tage später*") would thus be misleading.

14. GKFA 8.2:488; K 84.

15. Mann's source for the transmission of cholera emphasized the role infected sellers of fresh produce might play. Aschenbach buys the strawberry from a small greengrocer's shop (*einem kleinen Gemüseladen*; GKFA 8.1:587); the notes refer to "an infected greengrocer" ("*Gemüsehändler*") as a potential spreader of disease. The vocabulary is simply taken over, even though what Aschenbach buys is fruit (easily obtainable from a street-seller—Britten's reintroduction of the seller who originally appeared at the lido is thus a minor deviation).

16. Contrast the essays by Patrick Carnegy and Philip Reed in Donald Mitchell, ed., *Benjamin Britten: Death in Venice* (Cambridge: Cambridge University Press, 1987). Mitchell himself criticizes Visconti's use of Mahler in the film (in MC 308–313, esp. 310). Since the music of the film will be central to discussions in later sections, we shall return to Mitchell's characteristically penetrating concerns.

17. There are, of course, many appreciative studies of Visconti's film in its own right, studies that praise its cinematic technique and its evocation of pre–World War I European society. In her *Luchino Viscontis Tod in Venedig— Übersetzung oder Neuschöpfung?* (Aachen: Shaker, 1994), Béatrice Delassalle attempts a more sympathetic appreciation of the relationship between Visconti's film and Mann's novella.

18. It is a tribute to the impact of Visconti's film that insightful writers on Mahler can attribute the identification Visconti makes to the original novella. Thus Stuart Feder writes: "Mann transformed what he perceived in Mahler into the fictional composer [sic] Gustav Aschenbach the following year, when he wrote *Death in Venice*" (*FGM* 249).

19. As recent biographies of Mahler have emphasized, he was not, in fact, frail. A lifelong devotee of exercise in the open air—especially swimming and mountain climbing—he was devastated by the medical advice he received in 1907 to abandon these activities. See *HLM* 3:693–695; *FGM* 137–139; Jonathan Carr, *Mahler* (Woodstock, N.Y.: Overlook, 1999), 152–154.

20. See section 6 of chapter 2.

21. One relatively weak ground for identifying Alfred with Schoenberg is the obvious prominence of Schoenberg as the young Viennese rebel of the generation immediately succeeding Mahler. Stronger, and more interesting, is Visconti's interest in connecting *Death in Venice* with Mann's later masterpiece *Doctor Faustus*, in which the central figure is the composer Adrian Leverkühn. As already noted in chapter 2, Leverkühn's musical innovations are closely modeled on Schoenberg's development of the tone row. I suspect that Visconti could not resist the gesture of pitting a Schoenberg figure against the Mahler-Mann figure, thereby recapitulating the conflict that arose between Mann and Schoenberg in the wake of the publication of *Doktor Faustus*: Schoenberg was irate that his principal compositional-theoretic ideas had been attributed to a fictional character, and Mann eventually responded by adding an explanatory note as a pendant to subsequent editions. For Mann's reactions to Schoenberg's protests, see *TB* (1946–1948) 225–229, and for the eventual "resolution," 314, 316.

22. See *HLM* 3:710–711; *AMML* 64.

23. These characterizations are offered by Mahler's authoritative biographer, Henry Louis de La Grange; see *HLM* 4:453.

24. For outstanding examples, see Donald Mitchell, *Gustav Mahler: The Wunderhorn Years* (Berkeley: University of California Press, 1995); and *Gustav Mahler: Songs and Symphonies of Life and Death* (Woodbridge, Suffolk: Boydell, 2005); the analytic appendices to *HLM* vols. 2, 3, and 4; Constantin Floros, *Gustav Mahler: The Symphonies* (Pompton Plains, N.J.: Amadeus); and the contributions to *MC*.

3. SHADOWS 235

25. She is named after a species of butterfly shown to the young Adrian by his father, an amateur naturalist and collector: *Hetaera esmeralda* is distinguished by her clever camouflage, her "transparent nakedness" (*durchsichtige Nacktheit*); *DF* 21. I owe to Bence Nanay the insightful suggestion that a more sympathetic treatment of the relations between Mann and Visconti might be forthcoming if the film were viewed not as a setting of the novella but as an attempt at a synthetic treatment of *Death in Venice* and *Doctor Faustus*.

26. *DF* 187–194. Leverkühn, realizing that he has entered a brothel, sees the piano, goes to it, and plays three chords (from the prayer in the Finale of Weber's *Freischütz*); as he stands at the piano, "Esmeralda" brushes his cheek with her arm; his response is to stumble out. Only later does he seek her out. Because of her infection she has left the brothel, and, knowing of her syphilitic state, Leverkühn overrides her concerned warnings and has intercourse with her (*DF* 205–208).

27. The story about Nietzsche descends from his friend Paul Deussen. Deussen reports that Nietzsche told him that in 1865, on his arrival in Cologne, he was shown around the city by the driver of a carriage, who eventually left him at a brothel. On discovering the character of the establishment, Nietzsche is also supposed to have gone to the brothel piano and played chords on it. Like Leverkühn, he is not supposed to have had any sexual contact on that occasion, but, two years later, he consulted doctors, apparently for syphilitic infection. *Doktor Faustus* thus follows the lines of the story about Nietzsche quite closely. In the late essay on Nietzsche, Mann recounts the essentials of the anecdote and cites Deussen as the source; *GKFA* 19.1:189–190; *Essays* 6:59–61.

28. See the last paragraph of the "Biography" chapter: *GKFA* 8.1:515–516; *LP* 14–15, *L* 206; *K* 12, *H* 22–23.

29. *GKFA* 8.2:490; interestingly, the photograph lies within the summary description of cholera.

30. *KMM* 80–81.

31. For a detailed account of Mahler's last days, see *HLM* 4:1226–1277.

32. For a concise but informative account of Mahler's family and his early life, see *FGM*, chap. 2. More detail can be found in *HLM* 1, chaps. 1–3.

33. Particularly to the elder, Maria ("Putzi"): see *HLM* 3:690.

34. *GKFA* 8.1:509; *LP* 9–10, *L* 201, *K* 8, *H* 14.

35. *WWV* 1 §56; 2:388. Britten's motif, "My mind beats on," brilliantly captures the anguish of Aschenbach's striving.

36. Milton, sonnet VII ("How soon hath Time, the subtle Thief of Youth")—see also "On his Blindness"; Keats "When I have fears that I may cease to be." For Milton, the problem is posed not in terms of his own individual strivings but in relation to the task assigned him by the Creator, in whose providence he

can ultimately trust. Keats is closer to Aschenbach, in yearning to express the contents of his "teeming brain," but the poignancy of his sonnet derives from the thought that, given a normal lifespan, he might be able to do that (and our knowledge of his early death).

37. As already argued in chapter 2. It is worth noting that Mann's Aschenbach follows an approach Schopenhauer recognizes as the closest we can come to overcoming the problem of our finitude (the artistic apprehension of the Ideas) — WWV 3. Approximations, however, are not solutions. In the end, the only satisfactory (Schopenhauerian) response is the abnegation of the will.

38. See *FGM* 14–15. The association between Isidor and Gustav may explain the parental reaction to Mahler's practice of climbing out on the roof to read (he was beaten, and the garret window walled up). Feder supposes that the deaths of his siblings had profound effects on Mahler (see 60–61). See also Mitchell, *Gustav Mahler: The Early Years*, 10–13.

39. See *FGM* 33, 65–66; *HLM* 2:334–335; La Grange is more skeptical about the enduring effects of Mahler's fears.

40. *AMML* 110.

41. Both Feder and La Grange are very clear on this point: *FGM* 271–273, *HLM* 3:692–696. Feder, however, inclines to a psychosomatic explanation of Mahler's ultimate death, a diagnosis I view as unnecessarily speculative.

42. Feder suggests that she might have heard the murmur when lying by her husband's side; *FGM* 138.

43. La Grange (*HLM* 4:217) recognizes the symphonic character of what began as a cycle of songs with orchestra; he also gives a clear account of Mahler's decision to use a different name (*HLM* 4:219–220).

44. *HLM* 4:836–852; *FGM* 179–187.

45. The long letter of December 1901, in which Mahler formulates the terms of their union, is printed in full in *HLM* 2:448–452; see also *FGM* 103–106.

46. The affinity underscores the possibility, raised in n. 25, that the novella can be fruitfully considered in relation to *Doktor Faustus* — and thus that Visconti's film might be viewed as a synthetic treatment freed from obligations of fidelity to either work.

47. *DF* 600. Although this is not a connection Visconti explicitly makes among Aschenbach, Mahler, and Leverkühn, it can vindicate, from a different angle, his allusions to Mann's late novel.

48. Mitchell's title for his third volume on Mahler, which I borrow here, is profoundly insightful.

49. Thus Natalie Bauer-Lechner reported Mahler's "explanation" of his second symphony, which included the remark "The Scherzo ends with the appalling

shriek of this tortured soul." (From Bauer-Lechner's *Recollections*; quoted in Edward Reilly "*Todtenfeier* and the Second Symphony," appendix 2, in *MC* 123.)

50. An idea that surfaces in a much quoted letter to Max Marschalk of March 26, 1896 (*GMB* 171–173), where Mahler begins by rejecting the idea of "program music" only to acknowledge later that "at the early stages" of a work's reception, listeners should have some pointers about how to approach it.

51. For insightful discussions of Mahler's "programs" and his attitudes toward them, see Reilly "*Todtenfeier* and the Second Symphony," 92–95; Mitchell, "Mahler's Fifth Symphony" (*MC* 236–325, esp. 282–285); Mitchell, *Gustav Mahler: The Wunderhorn Years*, 187–194; Hermann Danuser, *Gustav Mahler und seine Zeit* (Laaber-Verlag, 1996), 134–146; Floros, *Gustav Mahler: The Symphonies*, 83ff.; and *HLM* 2:757–758. I hasten to note that this is a very small sample of the large number of pages devoted to the issue of Mahler's "programs."

52. Although I shall offer a relatively abstract philosophical reading of *Das Lied von der Erde*; see section 6.

53. Letter to Marschalk, *GMB* 172–173.

54. In the case of the Sixth, that affirmation never comes.

55. Possibly considerably longer: see Mitchell, *Gustav Mahler: The Wunderhorn Years*, 161–163.

56. Mitchell, *Wunderhorn Years*, 165–169; Floros, *Symphonies*, 52–53; Carr, *Mahler*, 64–67.

57. The service was for the conductor and composer Hans von Bülow, and there are two sources for the impact of the setting of Klopstock's ode (from *Messias*): Mahler's friend, J. B. Foerster, to whom he had confided his problems about the finale of the symphony, also attended the funeral and visited Mahler afterward, as the composer was drafting his first thoughts and sketches; Mahler also wrote about the role of the service in his composition (*GMB* 223). See Mitchell, *Wunderhorn Years*, 168–169, 172–173.

58. Deryck Cooke, *Gustav Mahler: An Introduction to His Music* (Cambridge: Cambridge University Press, 1997), 57.

59. Mahler's father was active in the Jewish community in Iglau, playing a role in the construction of the synagogue; see *FGM* 21–22.

60. During his time as director of the Budapest Opera, he was often viewed as an outsider, a "German Jew," and anti-Semitism may have played a role in the critical reception of his First Symphony (*FGM* 35, 38; Carr, *Mahler*, 55–56).

61. See Carr, *Mahler*, 81, 83–85. Carr bluntly describes the claim of an earlier conversion as "a lie" (83).

62. See *FGM* 64; Norman Lebrecht, *Why Mahler?* (New York: Pantheon, 2010), 84.

63. For a brilliant analysis of the cycle which emphasizes the "frame," see Mitchell, "Mahler's *'Kammermusikton'*" (*MC* 217–235, esp. 218–221); and Mitchell, *Gustav Mahler: Songs and Symphonies of Life and Death*, 75–108.

64. Here I diverge from Mitchell, in hearing the opening song as bleak throughout and the close, hailing the "light of joy of the world" (*Freudenlicht der Welt*), as bitter, ironic protest. That the real light of joy has been quenched is evident from the huge cry of anguish in the closing phrase of both strophes of the third song—the second of which closes on *"erlosch'ner Freudenschein."*

65. See Mitchell, *Songs and Symphonies of Life and Death*, 122.

66. I write as a singer who has studied these songs extensively and performed them in vocal classes (although never in a public concert): I have found it impossible to conclude the first song by sincerely hailing the sun.

67. In philosophical terms, this might be understood as the vindication of "healthy-mindedness" (to use William James's terminology—see section 4 of chapter 1). La Grange supposes that the symphony "breathes happiness, joie de vivre, and serenity"—but notes that it aroused criticism because hearers sensed a lack of authenticity (*HLM* 2:755). Floros (*Symphonies*, 115) quotes a comment of Bruno Walter's, which he relates to Schopenhauer's dictum that the achievement of overcoming the will produces a condition of complete cheerfulness. In my own view, the symphony should be heard as ironic commentary on the problem Schopenhauer posed, commentary that can produce an attitude akin to the resignation recommended in the fourth book of *WWV*. The early hearers mentioned by La Grange recognized that the *joie de vivre* cannot be taken straight but failed to relate the new work to Mahler's previous struggles—with the consequence that they missed the ironic dissolution of his central problem.

68. Except, perhaps, the Sixth Symphony—although here one might take resolution to consist in clear-eyed and courageous recognition that the problem posed is insoluble.

69. Many discussions of the Adagietto lament what they view as its overpopularity, alleging that Visconti's use of it has distorted the role this short movement plays in the Fifth Symphony—it is properly seen as linked to the Finale, given the *attacca* marking in the score after the chord for violin, cello, and double bass dies away—and the film has encouraged slow, and sentimental, performances. See, for example, *HLM* 3:817–819 and Mitchell, "Mahler's Fifth Symphony (*MC* 308–319, esp. 310). It seems to me to be possible to recognize Visconti's brilliance in choosing and using this music while also recognizing the need to hear the Adagietto in its context and to free it from the oozing sentimentality of some performances and recordings.

70. The orchestration for considerably reduced orchestral forces—strings and harp—also makes the movement appropriate for the atmosphere Visconti

creates around his central protagonist. As Mitchell notes, the movement is a "song without words" (MC 312).

71. Quoted in Floros, *Symphonies*, 154. Mengelberg wrote this in annotating his copy of the score and even added a short love poem. La Grange (*HLM* 2:816–817) and Mitchell (MC 315–317) both express doubts about this story, based on musicological considerations (affinities between the Adagietto and other of Mahler's works—akin to those shortly to be discussed in the text), although Mitchell finds "it difficult to believe that Mengelberg made the whole thing up." Mitchell attributes the poem to Mengelberg, describing it as a "horrible, mawkish fabrication," casting doubt on the conductor's taste but not necessarily on his reliability.

72. The connection with the *Rückert* Lied is very common: see, for example, *HLM* 2:817; Carr, *Mahler*, 131. Mitchell (MC 317–318) maintains that there is a closer connection to the second of the *Kindertotenlieder*; for the reasons given in the text, I take him to be right about this.

73. The relation between theory and independent judgment is thus analogous to the "reflective equilibrium" Rawls seeks between ethical generalizations and individual ethical judgments. See his *Theory of Justice* (Cambridge, Mass.: Harvard University Press, 1971), §9. For further discussion, see section 8.

74. A confession is in order: over a period of four decades, I have often sung the *Rückert-Lied* and the second of the *Kindertotenlieder*, and my study of these songs predated my first hearing of the Fifth Symphony. As the movement began, I was overcome by an intense experience of familiarity.

75. Of course, in the context of the whole Fifth Symphony this is eminently comprehensible, since the Adagietto is a prelude intended to flow seamlessly into the Finale that follows it. Hence Mitchell's emphasis on not viewing the Adagietto as a standalone work (MC 308–311).

76. The idea is vigorously pursued in Wilfrid Mellers, *Caliban Reborn* (London: Gollancz, 1968).

77. Floros (*Symphonies*, 155) adduces Mahler's paraphrase as evidence for the reliability of Mengelberg's story, claiming that "Alma was a good musician and talented composer; she was bound to understand." As I suggest in the text, I think any "message" in the score was double edged.

78. There is considerable debate about Mahler's success in balancing the challenge of the opening funeral march. Adorno (*Mahler: A Musical Physiognomy* [Chicago: University of Chicago Press, 1992], 136–137) finds it "too lightweight." Mitchell defends the movement (MC 319–325), noting wryly that Adorno may have been deaf to Mahler's humor and suggesting that the movement triumphs in the possibility of the human creation of joy. I hope I do not share Adorno's supposed deafness, but, to my ears, the challenge has been

shrugged off rather than faced and met. As the next section will suggest, Mahler was more successful later.

79. According to Alma, Mahler started work in the summer of 1907 on "long, lonely walks" (AMML). Because Bethge's book was only published in October 1907, after the Mahlers had left the mountains, some commentators have concluded that Alma's report must be inaccurate. La Grange, however, offers an account of how Mahler might have received an advance copy (HLM 4:215). In any event, Mahler's letters to his close friend Bruno Walter suggest that his exercise was greatly limited: "An ordinary moderate march gives me such quickening of pulse and anxiety that I never achieve the goal of walking: to forget one's body" (GMB 368).

80. The earliest manuscripts (of the second movement) date from July 1908; HLM 4:1908. GMB 365–366, 367–368.

81. GMB 371.

82. Cited by La Grange: HLM 4:1317, from Bruno Walter, *Gustav Mahler: Ein Porträt* (Frankfurt: Fischer, 1957); English translation: *Gustav Mahler* (New York: Da Capo, 1970), 123–124.

83. Mahler toyed with the idea of using this as the title of the entire work. For reasons that will become apparent, I think he was right to reject it in favor of the actual title.

84. The challenge posed to the singer in this movement, to ring above a large orchestra playing at high volume, is frequently too great—even tenors with "large" voices often only succeed in making isolated words audible.

85. See HDL and Eveline Nikkels, *"O Mensch! Gib' Acht!": Friedrich Nietzsches Bedeutung für Gustav Mahler* (Amsterdam: Rodopi, 1989). Hefling's scholarly work on *Das Lied* is so informative and illuminating that I hesitate to criticize his invocation of philosophical influence, but he is another unfortunate victim of the view that Nietzsche's *Birth of Tragedy* is a crucial text for understanding early twentieth-century works of literature or music. To view the opening movement of *Das Lied* as pervaded by "Dionysian abandon" ("*Das Lied von der Erde*" in MC 441) is, I suggest, not only to offer a shallow and inaccurate reading of Nietzsche but also to undercut the shattering power of the movement. As the setting of "O Mensch! Gib' Acht!" in the Third Symphony makes apparent, Mahler had long been familiar with the works of Nietzsche's maturity, and it is surely these that lie behind the first movement of *Das Lied*. As I propose in the text, the singer attempts a Nietzschean affirmation of life, one that decisively fails. The palm goes to Schopenhauer, who seems to offer the only solution, the resignation of the final version of the refrain. Yet that cannot be sustained either, as the *subito ff* makes clear.

## 3. SHADOWS 241

86. Thus I attribute to Mahler, as I did to Mann in chapter 1, the third grade of philosophical involvement. All the attempts I know of that treat Mahler philosophically seem to me to be handicapped by the thought that he could only be a derivative philosopher, one who endorsed the ideas of some antecedent thinker, or moved their categories around, like counters on a board ("an eruption of the Dionysian" in the first movement, for example). Mahler felt, and thought, more deeply than that.

87. Mahler changed the title of the poem from *Die chinesische Flöte*, switching the gender from feminine (*die Einsame*) to masculine (*der Einsame*). Given that most of the manuscripts of the score specify a female voice ("*Alt*") for the even-numbered movements, the amendment is strange and may be taken to reflect a license to substitute a baritone for the mezzo-soprano/contralto. Mahler's intentions on this issue are matters of controversy: it seems to me, however, that the performances and recordings featuring a female voice are both more suited to the even-numbered songs and more powerful.

88. HDL 96; the comparison to a mirage (which Hefling quotes) is from Adorno (*Mahler*, 152).

89. TB (1946–1948) 73–74. In December 1946, when this was written, Mann was much preoccupied with the conflict between the superpowers—the entry concludes by recalling that he felt wretched (*elend*). He had heard *Das Lied*, perhaps for the first time, nearly six years earlier, at a performance in New York, conducted by Bruno Walter, a friend he shared with Mahler, and had reported its great effect on the audience (*TB* [1940–1943] 214–215; January 23, 1941). A year and a half later, in June 1942, he received a recording of *Das Lied* for his sixty-seventh birthday and listened to it the next day. From 1942 onward, the work figures from time to time in his evening listening at home, and, even after the negative judgment of December 1946, Mann went back to it (for example, on November 2, 1947; *TB* [1946–1948] 179). Interestingly, a few years later he referred to *Das Lied* as Mahler's "happiest work" ("*Mahlers glücklichstes Werk*"—the words support the connotation that this is Mahler's most "fortunate," that is, best, composition). Mann's negative assessment of the fifth movement misquotes the text: the bird is located in a tree, not simply in the wood ("*Ein Vogel singt im Baum*").

90. At the premiere of *Das Lied*, Webern was deeply impressed by the moment at which the singer listens to the bird, describing it as "the most enigmatic thing ever." See HDL 102.

91. The sun "departs"—"*Die Sonne scheidet*."

92. As already noted, these words are Mahler's own. They replace the reproachful exhortation that ends the Mong-Kao-Jen poem, "*O kämst du, kämst du, ungetreuer Freund!*" ("O that you would come, that you would come,

unfaithful friend!"). Plainly, the resonances are very different—as are those indicated by Mahler's earlier modifications of the verses he found in Bethge.

93. Again, Mahler amends Bethge's gloss on Wang-Wei, replacing the idea of a voluntary departure with a necessary one: *"warum er reisen wollte"* becomes *"warum es müsste sein."*

94. At this point there is an awkwardness in Mahler's text. The reply should come from the vocal persona, but Mahler needs to indicate that he is moving from the Friend to the original singer. Consistency would require him to replace Bethge's third person with a first-person pronoun—*"Er sprach"* should become *"Ich sprach."* But that will not do, since the voice is not commenting on a previous declaration but making the declaration. So Mahler leaves the original words: "He spoke; his voice was muffled." It is better, I suggest, to view these as the persona's comment on the act of questioning just performed by the friend—although that would require a change of punctuation (a period instead of a colon) that is not noted in the score. Perhaps the fermata that follows *"umflort"* ("muffled") is intended to serve this function?

95. Again, Mahler moves the Bethge text in the direction of acceptance and consolation. Instead of *"Müd ist mein Fuss, und müd ist meine Seele"* (literally: "My foot is tired, and my soul is tired"), he gives us *"Still ist mein Herz und harret seine Stunde"* ("My heart is still, and awaits its [final] hour").

96. *"Ewig"* is set to a descending whole tone. The first three occasions are paired: the singer sings two *Ewigs*—e-d, d-c. For the last, only the first half of the paired phrase is given: *"Ewig,"* e-d. Perhaps the voice has been interrupted by the anticipated death; the marking that follows in the score is "completely dying away" (*"Gänzlich ersterbend"*).

97. Quoted in *HDL* 116.

98. Thomas Nagel, "Secular Philosophy and the Religious Temperament," in *Secular Philosophy and the Religious Temperament* (New York: Oxford University Press, 2010), 3–17.

99. Ibid., 8. Nagel is effectively renewing the investigation pioneered by Schopenhauer and Nietzsche in the nineteenth century, and his essay offers a cogent defense of that project against the efforts of Anglophone ("analytic") philosophers to dismiss it.

100. My reasons for maintaining this are given in the last chapter of *Living with Darwin* (New York: Oxford University Press, 2007).

101. The considerations that arise here are similar to those raised long ago by Plato in the *Euthyphro*.

102. Thus La Grange supposes that "Mahler's favorite philosopher" lies behind the Seventh Symphony; *HLM* 3:851.

103. See *FGM* 150, and for more extensive discussion *HDL* 116–117; Hefling, "Das Lied von der Erde" (*MC* 438–467), 442–443.
104. See section 4.
105. "*Der Einsame*" ("the lonely one") has been a phrase frequently used to designate Aschenbach. The *Herbstlichkeit* ("autumnal quality") of the beach is marked by the absence of color, the discolored sand, and the cold breeze—counterparts to the faded flowers, the frost, and the wind described by Mahler's singer. Mann's characterization of the scene is unusually visual and specific, and the introduction of the unattended camera suggests a condition of detached observation. Perhaps we should conclude that Aschenbach has attained a new and purified aesthetic stance, that he has transcended the connection of beauty with the erotic, escaped the lure of beauty. The coda would thus consist in a repudiation of the Platonic argument that has preceded it (see section 5 of chapter 2).
106. *GKFA* 8.1:523–524; *LP* 21, *L* 212, *K* 17–18, *H* 36.
107. *GKFA* 8.1:536; *LP* 31, *L* 221, *K* 26, *H* 55.
108. Ibid. In apprehending the eternal, the permanent, the enduring, Aschenbach has already moved toward the vocabulary of his Socratic reflections.
109. Compare Vere's final reflections in Britten's *Billy Budd*. We might think of both Vere and Aschenbach as "lost on the infinite sea" and as discovering a right conclusion for their lives through the beauty manifested in a young boy.
110. *Essays* 1:108. The echoes of Schopenhauer are evident both in the sympathy for Indian thought and in the dislike of individuation (division and measurement). Those echoes permeate the following discussion of the moral perspective.
111. *Essays* 1:109.
112. *Essays* 4:283.
113. Many writers have commented on the various allusions to and presentations of Hermes in Mann's fiction. The confidence trickster, Felix Krull, is a Hermes figure, and an Egyptian version of Hermes is woven into the Joseph novel. *Death in Venice* is framed by characters who take up characteristic poses of Hermes—Mann alludes to famous statues of the deity—the challenging presence in the cemetery chapel portico and Tadzio's stance on the sandbar. The two appearances correspond to the principal forms in which Hermes is depicted: as a mature man and as a "beardless youth."
114. *WWV* 1, book 4 §54; 2:349.
115. See below.
116. Thus, although I have read *Death in Venice* against the grain of many common assessments of it, my intention has not been to insist that the

interpretation I have woven around my three thematic clusters—Discipline, Beauty, Shadows—is the unique best approach to the novella. Rather I have aimed to uncover possibilities, lines of thought often overlooked or dismissed by eminent commentators and critics, who press on to the motifs they favor, with unprobed assumptions about issues they do not perceive as open—as with the hasty diagnosis of Aschenbach's death. Surely, too, I have been similarly hasty at some junctures and have overlooked important further possibilities.

117. *DF* 602.

118. *DF* 648.

119. Of course, Mann might have asked one of the composers he knew to write a piece to his specifications, or he might have selected an existing work and revealed its identity. Zeitblom's exhortation makes excellent sense even in the absence of these potential extensions of the novel.

120. To fill in the outline completely would require a psychological account and a synthesis of psychology with philosophy that we do not yet have. Nevertheless, existing psychology and philosophical psychology might make some progress with the spare sketch I shall give. I aim only to offer what is needed for my principal purposes.

121. Bentham notoriously draws this conclusion, prompting Mill to enter the lists on behalf of higher pleasures. As I suggest in "Mill's Consequentialism," in *The Routledge Companion to Nineteenth-Century Thought*, ed. Dean Moyar (London: Routledge, 2010), Mill's attempt to "rank" pleasures is neither successful nor his considered position: he subscribes to the view defended in the text, to wit that works of art rightly make a lasting difference.

122. Because previous sections have been focused on literature and music, I shall confine my attention to these art forms. The fact that painting and sculpture, architecture and dance, are not included should not be taken to imply that the approach I outline could not be extended to them.

123. Very occasionally, of course, we identify particular musical sounds with scenes in nature or with human activities: we hear the motion of Gretchen's spinning wheel even before she begins to sing, we hear birdsong in Messaien's orchestral works, and so forth. By far the more common experience, however, is the less definite attribution of mood or emotion.

124. My formulation here is inclusive, in recognition of the fact that an emotion may be attributed without being felt: one can judge the music to be sad without feeling sad (and without any conclusion about the sadness of composer or performers). For subtle exploration of these and kindred issues, see Christopher Peacocke, "The Perception of Music: Sources of Significance," *British Journal of Aesthetics* 49 (2009): 257–275. I have learned much from Peacocke's writings about music and from discussions with him.

125. See *Bleak House*, chaps. 25, 46, 47.

126. John Dewey, *Experience and Nature*, vol. 1 of *John Dewey: The Later Works* (Carbondale, Ill.: University of Southern Illinois Press, 1985), 306. The passage is quoted at the end of section 2 of chapter 1, text to n. 92.

127. For insights into the focusing of musically expressed emotion through the setting of poetry, see Peacocke, "The Perception of Music," 263–264; as Peacocke rightly observes, the text can enable the expressed emotion to be specified more exactly, and the musical setting can allow for an expression that the words alone could not have achieved. Hence the possibility of philosophical content, and novel philosophical content. Recognition of the content then enables the listener to hear similar themes, and novel developments of them, where there are no words—thus the "bridge" referred to in the text. I do not suppose, however, that this is the only way in which philosophical issues and perspectives can be discerned in instrumental and orchestral music. The question of alternative routes can be left open.

128. Here I draw on a familiar philosophical distinction: investigators can think up new hypotheses in all sorts of ways, but responsible investigation then requires the gathering of evidence.

129. If someone does not share the contemporary scientific understanding of inorganic and organic things, her panpsychical inclinations may be forgiven—the leap she makes is diminished, since the place in which she lands is already prepared by her antecedent attitudes. Of course, if she lives among us, she should be diagnosed as urgently in need of education.

130. My suggestion here is a version of the ideal of reflective equilibrium, originally introduced by Nelson Goodman in connection with inductive judgments and transferred by John Rawls to the moral-political sphere. See Nelson Goodman, *Fact, Fiction, and Forecast* (Indianapolis, Ind.: Bobbs-Merrill, 1956); John Rawls, *A Theory of Justice* (Cambridge, Mass.:: Harvard University Press, 1971).

131. I develop an approach of this sort in *The Ethical Project* (Cambridge, Mass.: Harvard University Press, 2011); another version is articulated by T. M. Scanlon in *What We Owe to Each Other* (Cambridge, Mass.: Harvard University Press, 1998).

132. The first of these points is proposed and defended in *The Ethical Project*, chaps. 8, 9; the second in *Science in a Democratic Society* (Amherst, N.Y.: Prometheus, 2011).

133. See TB (1953–1955) 81 (July 6, 1953). Similar judgments are made less explicitly at other places in the same volume: 104–105, 234, 241 (August 28, 30, 1953; June 4, 1954; June 19, 1954). Expressions of discontent at his failing powers permeate the years during which he was struggling to write *Felix Krull* (TB [1951–1952]).

134. For presentation of this approach to the Ninth and critical discussion of it, see *HLM* 4:1394–1400; Floros is more sympathetic (*Gustav Mahler: The Symphonies*, 272–275). Feder supposes that "tragic autobiography," specifically Mahler's awareness of the Gropius affair, is "encoded in the Tenth Symphony" (*FGM* 197).

135. *TB* (1937–1939) 179–180.

136. See *Essays* 1:49, cited in section 1 of chapter 1 (text to n. 12).

137. As noted above, the attitude of partial affirmation and partial resignation is difficult to sustain, and the difficulty is exacerbated for those whose endeavors center on critical probing.

138. Someone inspired by the closing measures of *Das Lied* might extend this by allowing value to accrue from contributions to the maintenance of nonhuman life, to the preservation of the earth and its beauties. Contributions of this sort are rarely, if ever, detached from promotion of other human lives, so I shall explore what I take to be a far more typical pattern.

139. My formulation incorporates an addition derived from Humboldt and Mill (and seconded by Nietzsche in some of his guises), to wit that the mode in which the connections are made should be a matter of the agent's choice.

140. Analogous in some respects to the world Wotan contemplated long before the opening of the *Ring*, a world of innocent joy personified by the Rhinemaidens.

141. Mann follows Nietzsche in thinking of self-probing as constitutive of serious art (see chapter 1, text to nn. 13 and 14). I allow for the possibility of other modes and other themes that suffice for artistic contribution at the highest level.

142. The phrase is Mill's. See the closing paragraphs of *A System of Logic*, vol. 8 of *Works of John Stuart Mill* (Indianapolis, Ind.: Liberty Fund), 952.

# INDEX

Adler, Jeremy, 200n54
Adorno, Theodor, 239n78, 241n88
Alcibiades, 72, 94, 99
Alfred (character in *Morte a Venezia*), 28, 130, 131, 132, 152, 189, 234n21
Anderson, Mark, 194n5, 224n119, 224n120
anti-Semitism, Thomas Mann and, 116, 229n177
Apollonian, 26–28, 189, 205n95, 205n97, 206n104, 206n108, 207n109, 227n160
Aristotle, 11, 18, 21, 22, 25, 199n50
artist, role of, 64, 67, 68, 69, 70–71, 72, 82, 94, 95, 96, 99, 101, 102, 107, 121, 122, 187. *See also Erzieher; Künstler*
asceticism, 49, 50, 53, 60, 211n147. *See also* Nietzsche, ascetic ideal
Aschenbach, Gustav von, 2, 3, 7, 55; childhood of, 84, 127, 135, 208n120; daily routine of, 37, 83, 104, 134; death of, 29, 30, 60, 97, 106, 110, 112, 125–29, 133, 171–76, 225n144, 243n105, 243n109; dedication to beauty, 28, 70–71, 73, 76, 79, 83, 99, 101, 104, 110, 122, 152, 176, 218n29, 225n144; ill-health of, 38, 127, 130, 133, 135, 136, 152, 172; marriage of, 87, 135; moral degeneration of, 26, 38–46, 58–59, 72, 99, 101, 113, 114, 122; represented as composer, 28, 130–31, 133–34, 135, 136, 152, 172, 175; respectability of, 7, 61, 63, 64, 65, 67, 68, 107, 111, 114, 197n32; sexual orientation of, 62, 63, 64, 65, 73, 83, 84, 89, 92, 93, 94, 104, 105, 106, 114, 135, 196n21, 220n44; social isolation of, 37, 83, 113, 188; Socratic reflections of, 29, 38, 72, 73, 83, 95, 99, 101, 102, 105, 112, 130, 136, 153, 225n144, 243n108; status as writer, 26–30, 57, 59, 60, 68, 107, 111, 114, 122, 123, 129, 176, 188, 189, 206n108; as

Aschenbach, Gustav von (*continued*)
victim, 62; works of, 41, 74, 134, 140, 146, 176, 188, 193n2, 206n108, 220n44
Auden, W. H., 103, 226n150
autonomy, 18, 66, 113–14, 229n172. *See also* Kant, Immanuel; Mill, John Stuart

Bauer-Lechner, Natalie, 236n49
beauty, 28, 32, 63, 64, 68, 69, 76, 79, 80, 82, 83, 93, 94, 96, 99, 104, 107, 109, 110, 111, 112, 152, 172, 218n28, 218n29; lure of, 96–99, 101, 102, 107, 113, 114, 122, 136, 225n144, 243n105. *See also* "higher" beauty
Beethoven, Ludwig van, 62; *Für Elise*, 132, 150
Benedig, Katrin, 223n100
Bennett, Jonathan, 200n58
Bentham, Jeremy, 244n121
Bertram, Ernst, 193n1
Bethge, Hans, 138, 153, 155, 160, 162, 163, 167, 240n79, 241n87, 241–2n92, 242n93, 242n94, 242n95
"Bilse" novels, 3, 19, 195n11
Bloom, Harold, 204n86
Bogarde, Dirk, 129
Bridcut, John, 225n145
Britten, Benjamin, 10, 120, 122, 163, 169, 190, 191, 225n145; *Albert Herring*, 227n156; *Billy Budd*, 107–12, 113, 227n163, 228n164, 228n169; *Death in Venice*, 102–7, 109–12, 114, 126, 129, 130, 179, 190, 212n162, 214n185, 226n147, 226n148, 227n147, 227n163, 228n167, 228n168, 233n6, 233n15; *Hymn to the Virgin*, 228n169; *Les Illuminations*, 228n165; *Peter Grimes*, 107; *Serenade for Tenor, Horn, and Strings*, 103, 226n151; *War Requiem*, 104, 228n169
Broch, Hermann, 12–13, 200n54

Buddenbrook, Bethsy (Frau Konsulin), 54–55, 56, 58
Buddenbrook, Christian, 5, 55, 107
Buddenbrook, Gerda, 5, 6
Buddenbrook, Hanno, 4, 5, 6, 225n132
Buddenbrook, Thomas, 5, 6, 8, 18, 34, 174, 196n23, 198n38, 198n41, 225n132
*Bürger* (citizen), Mann's conception of, 5, 6, 7, 24, 30, 43, 50, 61, 64, 68, 85, 94, 95, 102, 107, 113, 195n20, 196n21, 216n11

Carnegy, Patrick, 226n148, 233n16
Carpenter, Humphrey, 226n146
Carr, Jonathan, 234n19, 237n56, 237n60, 237n61, 239n72
Carroll, Lewis, 200n58
Cartwright, Nancy, 23, 25, 149
Castorp, Hans, 2, 58, 194n7
Cavell, Stanley, 204n91
Chekhov, Anton, 218n29
cholera, 2, 30, 38, 76, 110, 113; as cause of Aschenbach's death, 126–29, 133, 224n127, 233n6, 233n7, 233n13, 233n15
Christianity, 17, 111, 112, 142, 143–44, 145, 170, 228n164, 228–29n169
Claggart, John, 107, 108, 109, 110, 112, 172
coda to *Death in Venice*, 29–30, 59, 106, 112, 125, 126, 153, 172–75, 186, 208n117, 243n105
Cohn, Dorrit, 205n103
Cooke, Deryck, 142–43, 170, 237n58

Damasio, Antonio, 201n60, 201n61
Dante, 11, 199n50, 200n58
Danuser, Hermann, 237n51
death, premonitions of, 125, 126, 133–34, 135, 136, 138, 139–40, 146; quality of, 53–54, 112, 123, 126
de La Grange, Henry Louis, 234n23, 236n41, 236n43, 238n67, 239n71, 240n79, 240n82, 242n102

INDEX 249

Delassalle, Béatrice, 234n17
de Mendelssohn, Peter, 2, 222n100
Detering, Heinrich, 193n1
Deussen, Paul, 235n27
Dewey, John, 25, 65, 182, 201n64, 217n12, 245n126
*Dichter*, 2, 3, 4, 6, 10, 19, 67, 86, 194n5, 195n18
Dickens, Charles, 11, 17, 190; *Bleak House*, 17, 181, 183, 184, 245n125; *Hard Times*, 11, 17
Dierks, Manfried, 198n42, 199n49, 205n97
Dionysian, 26–28, 57, 106, 110, 207n109, 207n112, 227n160, 240n85, 241n86
Diotima, 32, 72, 77, 188, 189
discipline, 37, 52, 53, 58, 60, 64, 69, 87, 94, 95, 96, 99, 102, 104, 115, 121, 122, 136; breakdown of, 38–46, 83, 97

education, 65–66, 72, 101, 208n124, 217n12
Ehrenberg, Paul, 67
Eliot, George, 11, 12
Elliott, Graham, 229n169
*Erzieher* (educator), 66, 67, 69, 70–71, 72, 85, 94, 96, 99, 100, 121, 172, 187, 217n119. *See also* education
"Esmeralda" (*Doctor Faustus*), 132, 235n25, 235n26
ethical judgment, 17, 121–23, 185, 186
Evans, Peter, 226n148, 227n159

Fechner, Gustav Theodor, 170, 171, 183, 242n102. *See also* panpsychism
Feder, Stuart, 234n18, 236n38, 236n41, 246n134
Floros, Constantin, 234n24, 237n51, 237n56, 238n67, 239n71, 239n77, 246n134
foundationalism, epistemological, 16–17
Friedemann, Johannes, 5, 56, 64, 96–97, 98, 107

Gatens, Moira, 201n64
Goethe, Johann Wolfgang, 13, 38, 65, 67, 84, 194n5, 197n33, 209n135, 211n151, 211n158, 217n26; as character in *Lotte in Weimar*, 84, 85, 90, 92, 121, 197n33, 217n26, 222n87
Goodman, Nelson, 245n130
Gordon, Emily Fox, 232n215
grades of philosophical involvement, 11–12, 17, 47, 52, 241n86
Graham, Colin, 226n148
Grauthoff, Otto, 35, 99, 210n146
"Greek idyll," 45, 70, 104, 106, 126, 206n103
Gropius, Walter, 139, 246n134

Hampshire, Stuart, 23
heart failure, as cause of Aschenbach's death, 129, 133
Hefling, Stephen, 240n85, 241n88
Heine, Heinrich, 76
Hermes, 126, 175, 177, 213n169, 218n30, 243n113
Heuser, Klaus, 89–90, 223n109
"higher" beauty, 68, 69, 70, 71, 82, 100; erotic responses to, 71, 72, 82, 85, 96, 101, 218n28, 225n144; young men as embodiment of, 71, 72, 100, 107, 109, 218n30
Hoffmann, Martina, 198n42, 205n97
Hofmann, Paolo, 5
Homer, 22, 27–28
homosexuality, 39, 62, 63, 64, 65, 67–68, 71, 73, 74, 75–82, 83, 87–91, 102–3, 104, 115, 118, 120, 135, 136, 216n11, 219n36; incomplete sexual expression, 80–82, 83, 84, 89–91, 92, 93, 94, 95, 96; vision and, 80, 83, 89, 93, 95, 96, 101, 223n106
Humboldt, Wilhelm, 229n172, 246n139

Ibsen, Henrik, 61
Isherwood, Christopher, 226n150

imagination, role of in reading, 17, 24, 201n64
irony, 10, 27, 39, 60, 129, 194n7, 215n204, 229n170
Iwanowna, Lisaweta, 6, 7, 64

James, Henry, 11, 12
James, William, 31, 51
Jaschu, 29, 59, 69, 106, 110, 130, 172, 216n215, 222n88
Joseph, 97–98, 100–101, 113
Joyce, James, 13, 21, 24, 25, 194n5; *Dubliners*, 22, 36, 189; *Finnegans Wake*, 13, 22, 23, 122, 189, 202n68, 204n85, 225n140; *Portrait of the Artist as a Young Man*, 21, 22, 189; *Ulysses*, 13, 21, 22, 23, 189, 196n23, 202n68, 203n78, 204n80, 225n138; anti-elitism, 22–23, 189

Kant, Immanuel, 18, 33, 34, 47, 48, 66, 68, 171, 208n129, 209n131, 209n135, 229n172
Kassner, Rudolf, 214n183
Keats, John, 136, 235n36
Klaus Heinrich, 86–87, 92. *See also* Mann, Thomas, *Royal Highness*
Kröger, Tonio, 6, 7, 24, 30, 50, 52, 62, 63, 64, 100, 102, 107, 187
Krull, Marianne, 230n185, 230n190, 230n191, 231n196, 232n204
*Künstler* (artist), Mann's conception of, 5, 6, 7, 24, 30, 62, 64, 68, 85, 187, 196n21, 216n11
Kurzke, Hermann, 198n42

Lebrecht, Norman, 237n62
Leverkühn, Adrian, 54, 55–56, 103, 104, 132, 140, 177, 178, 187, 215n202, 215n203, 215n204, 234n21, 235n25, 235n26, 235n27
Lion, Ferdinand, 8
life, value of. *See* philosophy, oldest question of

literature, as medium for philosophy, 11–19, 21–26, 179–87

Mahler, Alma (née Schindler), 130, 137, 138, 139, 147, 152, 187, 236n42, 239n77, 240n79
Mahler, Anna ("Gucki"), 130, 139
Mahler, Gustav, 13, 130, 131, 132, 136, 140, 171, 185, 188, 189, 190, 191, 236n38, 236n39, 241n86; Adagietto (Fifth Symphony), 132, 147–50, 152, 238n68 239n72, 239n71, 239n75, 239n77; *Das Lied von der Erde*, 138–39, 153–71, 172, 173, 174, 175, 178, 179, 182, 183, 186, 187, 236n43, 240n79, 240n83, 240n84, 240n85, 241n86, 241n87, 241n89, 242n93, 242n94, 242n95, 242n96, 243n105; *Kindertotenlieder*, 130–31, 144–45, 148–51, 182, 238n63, 238n64, *Rückertlieder*, 148–50, 239n72; Symphony No. 2 ("Resurrection"), 141–43, 170, 183, 236n49, 237n57; Symphony No. 3, 132, 133, 143, 240n85; Symphony No. 4, 146, 238n67; Symphony No. 5, 146, 147, 153, 239n75, 239n78; Symphony No. 6, 237n54, 238n68; Symphony No. 7, 242n102; Symphony No. 8, 134, 143; Symphony No. 9, 139, 187, 246n134; Symphony No. 10, 139, 187, 246n134; death of, 134, 138, 139, 236n41; ill-health of, 137, 138, 152, 153, 234n19, 236n42, 240n79; Jewish ancestry of, 135, 143, 237n59, 237n60; 239n72; marriage of, 135, 139, 236n45, 239n77, 246n134; symphonic programs, 140–42, 237n50, 237n51;
Mahler, Maria ("Putzi"), 130; death of, 130, 137, 138, 139, 152, 153
Mann, Elizabeth ("Medi"), 114, 118, 119, 194n5, 231n203
Mann, Erika, 103, 114, 117, 118, 119, 120, 122–23, 226n150, 230n191, 231n199, 231n202

Mann, Fridolin, 119, 231n204
Mann, Golo, 103, 114, 120, 212n164, 222n96, 232n211, 232n212
Mann, Heinrich, 2, 115, 125, 126, 134, 153, 195n16, 224n123, 229n176
Mann, Katia ("Katja," née Pringsheim), 1, 2, 37, 86, 87, 88, 90, 91, 92, 114, 115, 116, 117, 118, 119, 121, 122, 134, 187, 211n149, 213n164, 219n40, 220n55, 222n89, 222n100, 223n102, 223n115, 223–4n116, 229n174, 229n176, 230n177, 230n191, 231n202
Mann, Klaus, 88, 90, 91, 114, 117, 118, 119, 120, 122, 223n113, 230n190
Mann, Michael ("Bibi"), 114, 117, 118, 230n185, 231n197, 231n204
Mann, Monika, 114, 119–20, 232n206
Mann, Thomas: *Buddenbrooks*, 1, 2, 4, 5, 6, 194n6, 195n16, 196n23, 198n38; *Confessions of an Unpolitical Man*, 7, 207n114; *Death in Venice*, 2, 3, 4, 5, 7, 9, 10, 15, 17, 19, 26, 63, 114, 122, 125, 134, 195n16; *Das Gesetz*, 204n89; *Der Erwählte*, 204n89, 232n2; *Der kleine Herr Friedemann*, 56–57, 63–64, 96–97, 98, 210n146, 224n126; *Der Wille zum Glück*, 5; *Doctor Faustus*, 9, 40, 54, 55–56, 103–4, 114, 117, 132, 140, 177, 194n6, 199n43, 210n145, 213n169, 215n202, 215n203, 215n204, 226n154, 229n173, 230n177, 232n204, 234n21, 235n25, 235n26, 235n27, 236n46, 244n119; *Felix Krull*, 2, 193n3, 196n27, 196n30, 243n113, 245n133; *Fiorenza*, 1; *Gesang vom Kindchen*, 194n5; *Joseph and His Brothers*, 92, 97–98, 100–101, 113, 114, 194n6, 204n89, 206n103, 223–4n116, 225n130, 225n137, 229n170, 243n113; *Lotte in Weimar*, 84, 85, 90, 92, 116, 121, 197n33, 213n169, 217n26, 222n85, 229n173; *Magic Mountain*, 9, 58, 114, 117, 194n6, 210n145, 232n2; *Royal Highness*, 1, 3, 4, 67, 86–87, 115, 193n1, 194n6, 195n16, 204n93, 220n55232n213; *Schwere Stunde*, 5, 197n33; *Tonio Kröger*, 1, 2, 5, 6, 63–64, 65, 100, 187, 195n16, 196n27, 196n30; *Wälsungenblut*, 203n76; annotations of philosophical texts, 29, 33, 47; as philosopher, 10, 11, 13, 15, 17, 19, 24, 47–48, 51, 52, 60, 179–91, 202n67, 210n140, 214n186, 246n141; daily routine of, 37, 40, 41, 213n168; diaries of, 40, 59, 63, 73, 84, 87, 88, 90, 92, 115, 118, 119, 194n15, 197n35, 212n164, 219n40, 222n96, 222n100, 226n154, 229n174; marriage of, 1, 87–88, 114, 115, 211n149, 213n164, 220n55, 222n89, 222n100, 223n102, 223n115, 223–4n116, 224n123, 229n174, 230n179; medical knowledge, 128–29, 233n111; pessimism and, 37, 115, 122; philosophical allusions in *Death in Venice*, 7, 11, 18, 19, 26, 29, 30, 31, 32, 35–36, 37, 47, 48, 51, 60, 66, 67, 71, 73, 74, 103, 130, 171, 207n114, 207n115, 214n183, 216n111; presentations of death, 54–59; projected works, 2, 3, 4, 41, 211n158, 217n26, 220n44; reactions to Mahler, 134, 139, 158, 241n89; relations to his children, 116–21, 123, 194n15, 230n191, 231n197, 231–2n204; sexual orientation of, 63, 67, 73, 84, 87–93, 94, 115, 116, 219n41, 219n42, 219–20n43, 220n44, 222n96, 222n100, 223n102, 223n103, 223n106, 223n109; style, development of, 1, 7, 129, 194n6; visit to Venice, 1, 2, 3, 125, 134, 139. See also Aschenbach, Gustav von; coda to *Death in Venice*; discipline; "higher" beauty; "Greek idyll"; Kröger, Tonio; "obituary" chapter; Tadzio
Mellers, Wilfrid, 239n76
Mendelson, Edward, 226n150

Mengelberg, Willem, 147, 239n71, 239n77
Menuhin, Yalta, 231n197
Mercier, Pascal, 200n58
Mill, John Stuart, 18, 202n66, 217n12, 229n172, 244n121, 246n139, 246n141
Milton, John, 136, 200n58, 235n36
Mindernickel, Tobias, 5
Mitchell, Donald, 233n16, 234n24, 236n38, 236n48, 237n51, 237n55, 237n56, 237n57, 238n63, 238n64, 238n65, 238n69, 239n70, 239n71, 239n72, 239n75, 239n78
Moes, Wladyslaw, 216n215
*Morte a Venezia*, 28, 129–35, 171, 238n69. *See also* Visconti, Luchino
Murdoch, Iris, 200n58
music, as highest art, 6, 34; as medium for philosophy, 19–21, 156, 169, 179–87, 245n127
Musil, Robert, 12
Mut-em-enet, 97–98, 100, 101, 107, 113, 114, 122, 225n130

Nagel, Thomas, 170, 242n98, 242n99
Nanay, Bence, 200n54, 225n144, 235n25
narrative voices, 27, 100, 205–6n103; in *Death in Venice*, 27, 39, 52, 56, 59, 60, 62, 65, 102, 206n103, 215n205
Nazism, 114, 118; Thomas Mann's resistance to, 114, 207n114, 212n164, 215n204, 222n96, 229n177
Nehamas, Alexander, 194n7, 210n142
Neuhouser, Frederick, 224n119
Neurath, Otto, 201n63
Nietzsche, Friedrich, 3, 4, 5, 7, 8, 9, 10, 13, 18, 19, 24, 25, 29, 30, 31, 35, 56, 62, 74, 132, 156, 167, 171, 177, 189, 194n5, 197n35, 199n43, 208n128, 208n129, 211n150, 235n27, 242n99, 246n139, 246n141; ascetic ideal, 47, 50, 51, 60, 215n197; *Birth of Tragedy*, 26–29, 64, 114, 122, 198n42, 199n43, 199n45,

206n104, 206n107, 206n108, 206n109, 207n110, 207n111, 207n112, 210n141, 240n85; *Genealogy of Morality*, 36, 37, 121, 199n44, 215n197; *Schopenhauer as Educator*, 66, 67, 82, 210n140, 217n19, 217n26, 224n117; on the worth of human lives, 18, 19, 21, 25, 32, 36–37, 52, 60, 185
Nikkels, Eveline, 240n85
Nobel Prize for Literature, 37, 114, 229n173

"obituary" chapter, 39–40, 41, 53, 56, 69, 135, 212n163, 215n205

Palmer, Colin, 227n163
panpsychism, 170, 184, 245n129. *See also* Fechner, Gustav Theodor
Peacocke, Christopher, 244n124, 245n127
pessimism, 18, 19, 21, 34–35, 37, 78, 136, 242n99. *See also* Schopenhauer, Arthur
philosophy: and argument, 12, 13–14, 15–16, 23–24, 190–91; character of, 12, 13, 14, 25, 36–37, 149, 245n127; oldest question of, 17, 18, 19, 22, 23, 30, 35, 47, 64, 114, 141, 146, 170, 177, 179, 185–89, 190–91, 242n99. *See also* saying and showing
Piepsam, Lobgott, 5
Piper, Myfanwy, 103, 105, 130, 227n157, 228n167, 228n168
Platen, August von, 75–82, 83, 87, 90, 220n53, 220n55, 221n73, 223n111; Mann's reaction to, 75–76, 80, 82, 92, 194n5, 221n68, 227n157
Plato, 15, 25, 30, 31–33, 50, 51, 64, 65, 69, 70, 92, 100, 112, 189, 208n129, 211n147, 216n11, 217n12, 242n101; *Meno*, 70; *Phaedrus*, 32, 45, 70, 71, 76, 80, 94, 197n34, 214n183, 218n28; *Republic*, 31–32, 66, 208n124; *Symposium*, 63, 70, 72, 76, 94197n34

Plutarch, 71; *Dialogue on Love*, 71, 76, 77, 216n11, 219n36, 220n53
Potiphar, 97–98, 100, 102, 113
Proust, Marcel, 13

Rachel, death of, 92. *See also* Mann, Thomas, *Joseph and His Brothers*
Rawls, John, 239n73, 245n130
Reich-Ranicki, Marcel, 219n41, 223n115, 224n123, 230n192
Reed, Philip, 226n147, 233n16
Reed, T. J., 198n42, 199nn48–49, 205nn97–99, 205n102, 211n147, 211n151, 212n161, 212n163, 213n170, 216n11, 226n148, 233n7
Reginster, Bernard, 210n142
Reilly, Edward, 237n49, 237n51
Richardson, John, 210n142
Rousseau, Jean-Jacques, 217n12

Sartre, Jean-Paul, 12, 200n55
saying and showing, 12, 13, 23, 25–26, 37, 52, 149, 185–88
Scanlon, T. M., 245n131
Schacht, Richard, 210n142
Schiller, Friedrich, 5, 62. *See also* Mann, Thomas, *Schwere Stunde*
Schoenberg, Arnold, 103–4, 130, 131, 226n154, 234n21
Schopenhauer, Arthur, 6, 7, 8, 9, 10, 13, 18, 19, 21, 24, 25, 28, 30, 31, 32–36, 47, 48, 50, 60, 66, 67, 72, 74, 78, 136, 156, 167, 171, 174, 176, 177, 185, 189, 197n35, 198n38, 198n39, 198n41, 208n128, 208n129, 209n131, 209n134, 209n135, 211n150, 236n37, 238n67, 242n99, 243n110; reality as Will, 33, 34, 35, 47, 48, 49, 50, 51, 52, 96, 112, 140, 209n130, 214n186, 214n187; theory of art, 34, 35, 206n107, 209n135. *See also* pessimism
*Schriftsteller*, 2, 4, 194n15
Schweigestill, Max, 177, 178, 187–88

Scruton, Roger, 202n70
self-control, 32, 69
Seitz, Franz, 227n155
sexual urge, 35; as burden, 35, 78, 102, 210n146, 225n138; as manifestation of Will, 35, 49, 50, 72, 78, 96, 102
Shakespeare, William, 13, 194n5; *King Lear*, 20
Socrates, 7, 14, 15, 31, 32, 45, 51, 69, 70, 71, 72, 80, 94, 99
Spinell, Detlef, 5
Spoelmann, Imma, 86–87, 92, 115, 220n55
Strode, Rosamond, 227n158
synthetic complexes, 148–49, 181–87, 204n90; reflective stability of, 184–86, 190

Tadzio, 2, 26, 29, 38, 42, 43–46, 49, 57, 59, 63, 68, 69, 70, 72, 74, 83, 85, 93, 94, 95, 97, 98, 104, 105, 106, 110, 112, 122, 127, 130, 132, 150, 152, 172, 173, 174, 175, 176, 216n215, 218n30
Tear, Robert, 103, 106
Twain, Mark, 200n58

Vaget, Hans, 226n147, 227n154
Vere, Edward Fairfax, 107–12, 113, 114, 122, 172, 243n109
Visconti, Luchino, 10, 28, 103, 110, 129, 130–33, 135, 136, 138, 147, 150, 171, 177, 189, 233n16, 234n17, 234n18, 234n21, 235n25, 236n46, 236n47, 238n69, 238n70. *See also Morte a Venezia*
von Growicka, André, 205n97
von Levetzov, Ulrike, 38, 65, 211n151, 211n158

Wagner, Richard, 8–9, 19, 23, 31, 36, 171; *Lohengrin*, 96, 224n126; *Ring of the Niebelung*, 13, 19–21, 203n76, 226n154, 246n140; *Tristan und Isolde*, 9, 19, 150, 152, 202n70, 203n76,

Wagner, Richard (*continued*)
　221n68; Nietzsche and, 9, 10, 203n75;
　Schopenhauer and, 10, 19–20, 34,
　202n70, 203n72, 209n131
Walter, Bruno, 117, 153–54, 238n67,
　240n79, 240n82, 241n89
Webern, Anton, 241n90
Westermaier, Franz, 220n43, 223n103
Wilde, Oscar, 39, 212n159

Williams, Bernard, 202n65
Witkop, Philipp, 39, 63
Wittgenstein, Ludwig, 200n53

Xenophon, 69, 70

Zeitblom, Serenus, 56, 140, 177, 178, 179,
　215n204, 244n119
Ziemssen, Joachim, 58, 59